How to Win

in a Winner-Take-All World

Also by Neil Irwin

The Alchemists

How to Win

in a Winner-Take-All World

THE DEFINITIVE GUIDE TO
ADAPTING AND SUCCEEDING IN
HIGH-PERFORMANCE CAREERS

NEIL IRWIN

St. Martin's Press New York

www.stmartins.com

Designed by Maura Fadden Rosenthal

Library of Congress Cataloging-in-Publication Data

Names: Irwin, Neil, author.
Title: How to win in a winner-take-all world : the definitive guide to
    adapting and succeeding in high-performance careers / Neil Irwin.
Description: First edition. | New York : St. Martin's Press, [2019] |
    Includes bibliographical references and index.
Identifiers: LCCN 2019001792| ISBN 9781250176271 (hardcover) |
    ISBN 9781250176288 (ebook)
Subjects: LCSH: Career development. | Success in business.
Classification: LCC HF5381 .I65 2019 | DDC 650.1—dc23
LC record available at https://lccn.loc.gov/2019001792

Our books may be purchased in bulk for promotional, educational, or business use. Please contact your local bookseller or the Macmillan Corporate and Premium Sales Department at 1-800-221-7945, extension 5442, or by email at MacmillanSpecialMarkets@macmillan.com.

First Edition: June 2019

10 9 8 7 6 5 4 3 2 1

To the marvelous Sarah Halzack

Contents

How to Win

in a Winner-Take-All World

Introduction

The Wind and the Current

═══════

THE NEW ECONOMICS OF
CAREER MANAGEMENT

I was twenty-two years old and fresh out of college when I started my first job at *The Washington Post*. My job description in those days was to report and write about local companies. But it's more accurate to say that I was simply a worker at one end of a long assembly line.

After I finished writing an article—say, four hundred words with a boring headline like "CyberCash to Unload Assets for $20 Million"— it would be launched on a step-by-step process that was repeated hundreds of times each day. First my editor would revise my draft to try to make it better. Then it would go to the copy desk, where another editor would make sure it complied with the paper's Byzantine style rules; God forbid I ever mention a company without spelling out its full legal name and noting the town in which its headquarters was located. Then a couple more editors would give it yet another look, before passing it along to the prepress department, whose role in the process I never totally understood. After that, it was printed and the resultant paper folded, bound into tiny packages, moved to trucks, and finally dropped off with individual delivery drivers who would deposit it on hundreds of thousands of doorsteps in the Washington metropolitan area.

Careers in those days were equally linear. If a writer did a good job, he or she might be promoted to become an editor overseeing a few people, and then an editor overseeing a lot of people. Many of my colleagues had done the exact same job for years, even decades. Those who were ambitious knew exactly how to channel that ambition.

Even if you weren't able to snag a job at *The Washington Post* or my current employer, *The New York Times,* it wasn't a big deal, because dozens of newspapers in other big cities offered career opportunities and compensation that were nearly as good. The technology of print newspapers created local monopolies that allowed at least one big paper in each city of any size to be highly profitable and offer many good jobs. In career terms, there just wasn't that big a gap between, say, *The Philadelphia Inquirer* or *The Baltimore Sun* and the *Times* or the *Post.*

What I didn't know at the time was that the economics of our industry were about to change, with radical implications for people like me trying to make a career in it. If you visit the *Post* or the *Times* today, you will find not a single giant assembly line in which reporters feed articles into the newspaper, but rather teams of people with a myriad of skills creating not just newspapers but a range of products—addictive podcasts, apps optimized for mobile devices, and immersive virtual reality experiences, to name only a few.

As you'd imagine, this has upended what it takes to have a successful career in the media industry. When the underpinnings of a business are in flux, and the best work is done by teams of people with dramatically different skills—a team might include software engineers, graphic artists, data scientists, and video editors, along with writers—it is no longer so obvious what people should do to ensure they will remain employed, let alone get ahead.

The gap between the top handful of publications and the next tier has widened, both in terms of the number of jobs available and how well they pay. In digital media, the handful of organizations with the very best products and technology reach readers around the planet, while the old local print monopolies are no more. Consequently, if you want to sustain an upper-middle-class life as an investigative reporter or foreign correspondent, opportunities are fantastic at places such as the *Times* or *Post* or *Wall Street Journal*—the top handful of organizations with global reach—and brutal if you are in a second-tier organization.

And long gone is the old pattern in which people who got hired at a leading media outlet could expect to remain employed there for decades doing mostly the same job. Those who do stay with an employer for a long time tend to do so by adjusting to changing strategies and ways of working; those who fail to adjust are likely to find themselves laid off.

I've had to pay close attention to these changes in my industry for existential reasons. But the more I've spoken with people in other industries, the more I've been struck that people who seek a well-paying, professional-track career in nearly every sector are grappling with the same challenges: reinvention of business models due to digital technology; the rise of a handful of successful "superstar" firms; and rapidly changing understandings around loyalty and the level of mutual commitment to the employee-employer relationship.

In manufacturing and retail, banking and law, health care and education, and certainly all corners of the software business and the rest of the tech universe, what it means to do a job well and have a successful career is changing faster than most people's understanding of how to navigate it. This has made the workplace seem scarier, particularly to midcareer people who suddenly find that their parents' advice (show up early, work hard, learn your craft) is no longer enough.

But, as importantly, it has conferred an advantage—a significant advantage—on those strategic enough to shift their approach.

THE SURVIVOR'S CODE

Most of the people I worked with when I joined the *Post* are long gone from the industry, many having fallen victim to waves of buyouts and layoffs that took place as the internet upended the economics of our business.

But some have had tremendously successful careers beyond the imagination of the average reporter only a couple of decades ago. You may have heard of a few of them. Mike Allen and Jim VandeHei were White House correspondents, attending press conferences and speeches and dutifully reporting what they heard, when I was a young business writer. But in 2007 they surprised all of us by starting *Politico* and then a decade later *Axios*; both ventures have been leaders in reinventing the media industry for the digital age. Michael Barbaro, a young fellow writer on the *Post* business desk back when I was starting out, is now managing editor and host of *The Daily*, a wildly popular podcast from *The New York Times*; he has helped pioneer a new form of storytelling that has helped millions of people understand the world better. Kara Swisher had left the department a couple of years before I arrived; she would go on to be not just the leading tech journalist of our time, at *The Wall Street Journal* and then as founder of *Recode*, but an innovator in building a media business model reliant on live events.

Beyond those notable names are hundreds of people behind the scenes whose careers have thrived in the digital era, doing jobs that would be unrecognizable to their younger selves. Copy editors used to do comparatively rote work fixing typos and applying style rules; they had a reputation for being crusty introverts. Those who have thriving careers now are, in effect, digital strategists. They try to figure out how to package each article in ways that will maximize its chance of finding an audience. They select visuals, predict what web address is most likely to appeal to algorithmic search engines, craft social media copy, and collaborate with writers, graphic artists, and others to come up with the most engaging possible headline.

Indeed, for those who have successfully made the transition these are in many ways the best of times. Working in fluid, creative, entrepreneurial teams is a lot more fun than being on an assembly line.

I wrote this book because my career has given me a unique window into the skills that have allowed people to thrive in the current economy. My goal, my mission, is to distill for you the skills and habits and attitudes common to people who are likely to enjoy rewarding, high-performance careers in virtually any major industry in this era.

━━━━━

If you had asked me in the early 2000s to predict which of my colleagues would lead the pack two years later, I probably would have pointed to those known as brilliant writers or editors, along with others whose work ethic was off the charts. A more cynical person might have mentioned people best known for their ability to ingratiate themselves with bosses.

Those three answers weren't wrong, exactly. Of course, being really talented, really hardworking, or really good at office politics helps in having a durable career! But by far the most significant factor dividing winners and losers in my industry was a willingness to embrace the rapid change and inherent fluidity of digital-age business as an opportunity rather than recoil from it as a threat. Winners detected that our industry was shifting beneath us and spent time thinking about how to drive that change; losers sought to run out the clock. Winners studied the shifting economics of our industry; losers hoped they would eventually shift back.

I might not have predicted that Mike Allen and Jim VandeHei

would become successful entrepreneurs—but I did know how much Mike chafed at the way the physical constraints of print newspapers prevented him from sharing everything he had learned with readers quickly, and sought ways to overcome them. I couldn't have imagined that Michael Barbaro would become a voice that so many people wake up to every morning, but I knew how much he hungered for fresh ways to tell every story even in an era when this type of creativity was sometimes discouraged. Kara Swisher was a competitor who constantly scooped us on tech stories; what I didn't know at the time was that she was already figuring out how to turn that franchise into a revenue generator for her organization.

None of these people were particularly senior when they began the shift. Once upon a time, only the most senior executives in a company needed to worry about the high-level shifts in the economy that this book will spell out. What we've seen over the last decade is that low- to midlevel employees also need to cultivate an ability to understand the shifting economics of their industry and the business world more generally.

Fortunately, it turns out that this ability to see around the corner— to understand how the economics of an industry are changing and position yourself well to capitalize on them—isn't something you have to be born with. It can be learned, *if* you are open to learning.

HOW TO MAKE YOURSELF INDISPENSABLE

This book is aimed at anyone seeking to have a rewarding career in a high-end profession, whether in traditional companies, tech giants, or cutting-edge startups, and whether in early, mid-, or late career. In writing it, I drew on the work of hundreds of academics, consultants, and others who have mined all manner of data sources to understand these trends, and much of this work is reflected in the pages to come. Perhaps even more fruitfully, I sought out leaders from a range of companies and sought answers to the following questions:

1. What does an ambitious person need to do to have a successful career at your company in the modern age?

2. Can I meet some of the people there who have exemplified that success?

My reporting took me to some of the best-known companies on earth, including Microsoft, Goldman Sachs, General Electric, and Walmart. I also visited smaller enterprises that offered particularly important lessons, learning from people who make *Planet of the Apes* movies, Shake Shack cheeseburgers, driverless Volvo cars, and Jim Beam bourbon. I traveled around the world, literally, to meet the people whose stories are contained in these pages, which reveal their answers.

There are furious debates over how people can best prepare themselves for a modern career. Depending on who you ask, the answer is to major in a STEM field in college, or go to boot camps to become a first-rate coder, or get a liberal arts education that gives you wide exposure to all sorts of fields. But what I found over and over was the importance of training yourself in the art of *adaptability,* the skill of how to learn something new and hard. What separates those who have durable careers in this fluid economic landscape from those who don't is an ability to adapt when the prevailing coding language changes or the old approach to marketing stops working. But how do you get this superpower?

The first three chapters explain how to become the type of professional who is most desired—and rewarded—by modern employers. Among the things I heard again and again: it's a big mistake to get locked into an overly narrow role as a skilled specialist responsible for a single function. For one thing, what's important today may not be important tomorrow, so you'll need the adaptability and resilience that result from exposing yourself to new things. And today's ultracomplex organizations demand people who have exceptional skills, yes, but who also understand how the different parts of the business fit together. They need people who can work in teams with other people who may have very different technical abilities, in groups that can create products much greater than the sum of their different parts.

The best way to become one of those people, I found, is to actively seek exposure to different specialties, across departmental boundaries, from the earliest days in your career. I will introduce you to people who have done this effectively and flourished as a result.

We then turn in chapters 4 and 5 to lessons from cutting-edge work on big data and management economics. In effect, the largest employers' newfound ability to crunch terabytes of data about how people go about their work—undertaken for the benefit of the company—also offers a surprising road map for data-driven changes in how to be a successful employee, if you know how to use it. And if you understand the latest evidence about what management approaches are most effective, you have greater potential to find better managers to help you learn and grow, and eventually become one yourself.

Chapters 6 through 9 provide the context for understanding the four profound economic shifts that are shaping the modern workplace: the rise of winner-take-all effects; the growing importance of information relative to physical capital; the end of loyalty between employers and their workers; and the more widespread use of contract and other nontraditional employment relationships.

Armed with this information, you can *dramatically* increase your odds of having a long and fulfilling career (or, more accurately, series of careers). You will be empowered to embrace and drive change rather than fear and deny it.

Of course, the goal of life is not simply to have a fulfilling career but to have a fulfilling *life*. Fortunately, as we'll see, the same skills that produce the one also lead to the other.

SETTING SAIL

If you take a sailboat out for a cruise, there are some things you can control, like how you position the sails and guide the rudder. There are others that you cannot, like the winds and the currents. Still, to get where you're looking to go, it's essential to understand those winds and currents. Successful sailors adapt the things under their control to react intelligently to the winds and currents that are not.

In our careers, we can control the jobs we apply for, the training and education we seek out, the assignments for which we raise our hands. But our fortunes are shaped significantly by huge economic and technological shifts that are remaking nearly every industry. This book is a guide to understanding those winds and currents.

None of us should entertain any delusions that we can tame them, but we can attain the confidence to understand them and make them work for us. After all, for a sailor, high winds and rough seas may be scary, but they can also be the most fun.

1

Rise of the Glue People

===

The forces shaping the new world of work and careers—information economics, winner-take-all effects, globalization, the shift toward unconventional employment arrangements, and more—are crashing together with particular violence in the business of making movies. Meanwhile, far from the glamour of Hollywood premieres and awards ceremonies, vast armies of people with all kinds of complicated technical skills toil. As such, the film industry is a microcosm for many of the broader trends in the business world. Which means we all have something to learn from the people who have carved out a successful career within it, which in turn is why I flew 9,000 miles to Wellington, New Zealand, to meet a few of them.

I got the most compelling answers from a thin, wiry Italian named Marco Revelant. You may know him as the man who groomed King Kong.

On the Wednesday morning I met him, Revelant was wearing rimless glasses, a gray hoodie, and stubble that suggested he had gone two or three days without shaving. We met in a conference room in a low-slung building around the corner from a spot where tourists unloaded from buses to gawk at props from the *Lord of the Rings* trilogy.

A native of Padua, in northeast Italy, Revelant studied law in the 1990s, but he loved video games and, as a hobby, dabbled in using computers to create three-dimensional images. He got a job with an architecture firm, helping the architects move from traditional blueprints to computer-assisted design software, while in his spare time teaching himself to create digital images for video with computers, using software he had bought with his own savings. He soon found a way to make his hobby his profession, taking a job with a company in Milan that made graphics for TV commercials. It wasn't particularly glamorous, but working in a small company doing small-budget projects, he got a taste for how all the different pieces of making a commercial that involved 3D effects came together—not only the digital images but also the script, the actors, the live-action shots, the audio. He was, by necessity, focused not just on generating images using his artistic touch and the power of computers but on understanding how those different moving pieces fit together. "It was a small firm," he told me, "so you were doing a little bit of everything, a generalist."

When he received an offer to apply these skills to a big-budget movie, he was thrilled, even if it meant moving to the other end of the planet. He signed a nine-month contract with a firm called Weta Digital to work on the third *Lord of the Rings* movie; he was still there fifteen years later, which is how I ended up sitting across from him that morning as various assistants buzzed around offering anyone in sight a bottled water or espresso. What enabled him to have staying power in an industry in which the technology and economics were shifting beneath his feet?

THE ERA OF COMPLEXITY AND THE
QUEST FOR PERFECT FUR

In 1933, Radio Pictures released the original *King Kong,* a technological marvel of a movie that enraptured audiences with its stunning portrayal of a giant ape rampaging through Manhattan before plummeting from the recently completed Empire State Building. Kong was portrayed by a stop-motion puppet with an aluminum skeleton beneath a rabbit-fur coat.[1] The crew for the film numbered 113 people—from cameramen and makeup artists to the 21 men who worked on visual effects.[2]

In 1976, director Dino De Laurentiis updated the film for that era. The newly built World Trade Center replaced the Empire State Building as the site of Kong's demise. Kong was now a twenty-five-year-old technician in an ape suit in some shots, and a forty-foot-tall puppet-robot controlled by hydraulics and covered in horsehair in others. Even as the production expense and sophistication of the effects had increased, the crew was the same size as in the earlier movie—113 people.

In 2005, it was Peter Jackson's turn. He chose to return to the 1930s, with the climactic scene back atop the Empire State Building. His Kong was performed by a British-born actor named Andy Serkis, who wore not an ape suit but motion-capture equipment that brought his remarkably expressive face and mannerisms to a creature who was rendered digitally in server farms located in Miramar, a suburb of Wellington.

Jackson's *King Kong* lists a crew of no fewer than 1,659 people, including plenty of jobs that would be familiar to those who worked on the earlier versions of the movie, like costume designers and carpenters, and even more that would be completely foreign: "data wrangler" and "stereoscopic compositing lead," for example.

This fifteenfold increase in the number of people it takes to make an immersive, visually stunning movie full of fantastical creatures is more than just a trivia fact. It is one piece of evidence for a fundamental shift in how the global economy works, with profound implications for how ambitious people should manage their careers.

First, when the 1933 version of *King Kong* came out, the market for movies was relatively small; only a sliver of humanity, in the United States and a few other countries, could see a motion picture at all, and only by going to a theater. Now, billions of people in nearly every country on earth can do so. The ranks of the global middle class—the people who can afford an occasional splurge—have exploded, and if they prefer not to go to a theater, they can watch a movie on television at home or even on the phone in their pocket. The potential worldwide market of movie watchers is exponentially larger.

Second, for all the hundreds of movies made each year, only a few hit big. Of 289 films that were released in US theaters in 2017, just 5 accounted for 19 percent of their cumulative global box office revenue, and the top 50 were responsible for 81 percent. The bottom 200 were responsible for 6 percent of the total.[3] It costs a great deal of money up front to make a film, but then a trivial amount of money to distribute it. Those economics mean that it is worth spending every dime—and bringing on every additional data wrangler or stereoscopic compositing lead—it takes to increase the chances of a film becoming one of those select few that achieve global dominance; the payoff is massive.[4]

Third, digital technology has made possible ways of working that were unknown just a few years ago. The makers of the 1976 *King Kong* had to put a technician in an ape costume and build a forty-foot-tall hydraulic puppet because that was the only way they could think of to make a plausible-looking giant ape; the computing power that goes into making a three-second shot of a digitally rendered scene in a modern movie wouldn't have been available at any price in the not-too-distant past. Moreover, technologies like email, cloud storage, and videoconferencing make it easy for teams to collaborate across continents in a way that would have been unimaginable not that long ago.

Sometimes, these seem like the best of times for the independent entrepreneur, the lone wolf. There is, after all, something inherently exciting about the idea of the startup, a couple of ambitious young people starting a company in a garage and bootstrapping to become the next Apple or Google—or, to extend the movie metaphor, a group of film students with a digital camera and ambitions to become the next Steven Spielberg or Peter Jackson. But the data doesn't lie. This is an age in which the largest, best-managed, most technologically advanced companies are winning in the marketplace more than ever. For all the talk about how digital technology has leveled the playing field—enabling those entrepreneurs in the garage or moviemakers with a digital camera to make their mark—in important ways it cuts in the other direction.

And the kinds of movies that achieve global reach and box office returns in the hundreds of millions of dollars almost always rely on the kind of sophisticated digital effects that they make at Weta Digital, which, in addition to working on the *Lord of the Rings* films and the 2005 version of *Kong*, contributed to the memorable (and wildly successful) *Avatar* and the *Planet of the Apes* trilogy that concluded in 2017. To understand how this impacted Revelant's career, it's important to understand how the digital effects that are fundamental to most of the biggest-budget films in the modern era are created.

It may be tempting to watch a scene in an effects-heavy movie like *Avatar* or *War for the Planet of the Apes* and assume that their creation works something like a painter drawing a scene. In fact, what the creators of these movies do is build a complete on-screen universe that is modeled in excruciatingly precise three-dimensional detail, to emulate the real world as closely as technology will allow. So, for example, in the 2005 *King Kong*, the sweeping vistas of 1930s Manhattan were created not by having someone draw portraits of the city from the necessary angles but by building an entire three-dimensional model of the city down to each individual building. First, the artists at Weta Digital manually created 3D models of the buildings that are particularly noticeable on the skyline, which they call "hero buildings," from old photographs. Then they developed a custom piece of software called CityBot that allowed them to fill in less memorable buildings of the appropriate height and style on each block of the city, with the software designing each individual structure. The result was that Peter Jackson could take shots from any angle and ensure that the backdrop looked realistic. By building the city block by block, they gave Jackson a virtual time machine.

One of the great insights of the last thirty years of advancement in visual effects is that the key to viewers' losing themselves in the movie (the worst insult you can give one of these artists is to say that a shot took you out of the moment or looked fake) is to sweat the details. Designers employ real-world physics, biology, and anatomy in building the environment and the characters. So, for example, the forests shown in *War for the Planet of the Apes* were created by simulating a hundred years of growth in a virtual forest, with plants of different types growing, competing for light, dying, and decaying. That simulation generates a forest with greater verisimilitude than a virtual forest created by a human artist scattering trees and bushes around. In a climactic battle scene in 2014's *The Hobbit: The Battle of the Five Armies,* thousands of simulated soldiers are controlled individually by artificial intelligence governing their own behavior and reactions to the things happening around them. As a viewer, you don't notice exactly what any one "soldier" is doing, but it makes for a more realistic-looking chaos of warfare than simply having thousands of soldiers moving in lockstep. The warrens of cubicles at Weta Digital are filled with people who have spent years studying the anatomy of apes, the physics of a falling raindrop, the chemistry of a gas explosion.

Getting those fundamental details right is doubly important for living creatures created in a computer. Graphics artist Joe Letteri was part of a huge inflection point in moviemaking in the early 1990s when Steven Spielberg decided that *Jurassic Park* would be the first major film to create dinosaurs using 3D digital renderings, at least in long shots (physical models were used for close-ups). Even when creating digital dinosaurs, though, the technology works by building the beasts from the skeletons out. The level of detail that goes into animal anatomy in more recent films is vastly more complex. Letteri would go on to lead Weta Digital. In the *Planet of the Apes* trilogy, Letteri said, "we never want you to think that this is a guy in an ape suit. So we're trying to solve everything about how to make an ape look realistic. What makes a hair fiber a hair fiber? How does it move? How does it attach to the body? How does light reflect off of it or shine through it? How do the teeth and the lips and the gums all articulate?"

When Revelant arrived at Weta to work on the last film in the *Lord of the Rings* trilogy, he was tasked with adding detail to the Witch-king of Angmar, a terrifying villain, before being put on feather duty— more specifically, designing the feathers on the giant eagles that provide deliverance for our heroes. The starting point was, in effect, a completely naked bird, with only bone, muscle, and skin. ("It looked like the chicken you get on Sunday for lunch," Revelant said.) He was on a team that had to ensure that the eagles had the right number of feathers, in the right places, groomed correctly so they would look realistic in each of dozens of shots. (A shot, typically lasting two or three seconds, is the atomic unit of visual effects work; there can be a couple of thousand of them in an effects-heavy film.) When that was done, Revelant was assigned an even bigger challenge on Weta Digital's next big film, *King Kong*. He received, as it were, a promotion from feathers to fur; his job was to ensure that the lead character of a movie that cost more than $200 million to make looked like you would expect a giant mythical gorilla to look.

Part of the reason it took 1,659 crew members to make that version of *King Kong* is that creating convincing 3D visual effects requires a continuum of skills. At one end are the pure artists—people who imagine scenes and visuals, some still drawing them by hand. At the other end are the more purely technical staff members—people who code software and deploy advanced mathematics to turn those artistic ideas into an actual movie. In the middle is a group that includes modelers like Revelant, who straddle that divide, with a mix of artistic vision and technical background. A two-second shot can involve dozens of people at different points on that continuum putting their skills to work. Modelers who spend all day every day working on lighting or sets or anatomical structure, or fur, must work together to make the shot, and ultimately the movie, as good as it can be.

One thing that made Revelant good at his job—the reason he was entrusted with King Kong's fur—is that he understood both the artistic vision and the technical needs, and he also understood how to integrate them, better than most. Making Kong's fur—10 million individual hairs, modeled on yak fur—look right was both an artistic challenge *and* a programming challenge, and Revelant was in the rare position of being able to guide people with different types of talent toward that goal. He had very little software coding experience himself, but he was able to recognize problems in the way many of the other modelers interacted with the programmers who created their software. They were too focused on asking for changes that seemed like things that would make the job easier but in practice would require either too much processing power or too much time and too many programming resources.

"It was interesting trying to understand the coders' perspective, because you start thinking differently about the problem you want to solve," Revelant said. "What I found is a lot of users will be able to tell the coder, 'I want to be able to move this slide and do this.' But that's not actually what they want. They try to give the solution but don't abstract the problem to understand the bigger picture."

He worked with software developers to create a program—which they called, naturally, Fur—that let the modeler manipulate the direction of one "guide hair" that would control the behavior of thousands of hairs around it. That allowed them to apply directions to each patch of fur: make a clump of mud here, make this patch more scraggly, that type of thing. It was labor-intensive work that lasted about a year; each patch of fur had to be manually adjusted in each of the hundreds of shots that included Kong. Revelant's daughter was born during production, and he took only a single day off. When it was done, Weta's people were proud of their work but saw they had a problem. There would surely be more movies in the future that involved furry creatures. Their software was simply too clunky and labor-intensive to use if, for example, they were to make a movie that had many digitally rendered characters instead of just one.

"I was talking to one of the coders and said, 'Do you think it's possible to touch the hair? To manipulate the curve of each hair? Could you manipulate millions of hairs directly?'" That is, instead of having to manipulate a smaller number of guide hairs, could a program be written that would allow artists, using tools on a computer screen, to comb, tease, trim, muss, or otherwise manipulate a virtual character's fur just the way a real hairstylist can go to work on an actor's hair? Part of the challenge was thinking beyond making the old software a little better and imagining how, starting fresh, the process of creating realistic, digitally rendered fur could become more efficient. The Weta team set to work creating a better system for making digital fur, which they called, appropriately, Barbershop. Revelant was the go-between for two different types of highly skilled professionals who frequently didn't know how to communicate with each other—at a moment when successful collaboration was the only way to get an important task done. "The thing is a lot of the coders don't know how to groom. They rely on someone to tell them what the software needs to do. But sometimes it's difficult for the person who is skilled at grooming to tell them in a language they understand," Revelant said. When groomers and others with a modeling background try to talk to the coders, they tend to focus on narrow features rather than really engage on how to solve the underlying problem. "People tend to think, 'I want to do this, ergo I will tell the coder what to build.' They don't tell the coder, 'I want to achieve this,' and work together to figure out the best way to achieve it."

Revelant can speak the language of moviemakers and artists but can also read technical papers on new modeling techniques. "He doesn't actually look at the code," explained Paolo Selva, the head of software engineering at Weta Digital. "But he understands how something like the elastic rod dynamics on hair work. He'll understand the logic behind it even if he may not know how to implement it himself. It's not a skill many artists have. If all of the artists were able to do that, it would be much easier to talk to them."

When they started, they were hoping to use Barbershop to handle the fur on Snowy, the dog in *The Adventures of Tintin*. They had no idea how urgent, and important, the software would become. As work was under way, Weta Digital landed the visual effects work for *Rise of the Planet of the Apes*. This was meant to be the first installment in a major film franchise in which most of the principal characters were virtual creations, all covered with fur: Maurice, a wise old orangutan; Koba, a tortured, violent bonobo; and most of all Caesar, the chimpanzee who leads the apes. With Barbershop, the artists could manipulate each of Maurice's flowing orange hairs as effortlessly as if they were retouching an image in Photoshop—but unlike in Photoshop, they were manipulating not just a two-dimensional image but the entire three-dimensional map of how millions of individual hairs were positioned. This enabled Weta Digital to turn around a movie with dozens of apes—not just one, like Kong—in under a year. The company went to work with half-finished software, yet created a movie that would be nominated for an Oscar for best visual effects, started a trilogy that grossed $1.7 billion globally, and in Caesar created one of the most memorable characters in modern film, fur and all.[5] The Barbershop software itself won Revelant and his collaborators Alasdair Coull and Shane Cooper a technical achievement Academy Award. All that came out of an uncanny ability to communicate with and channel the efforts of people with very disparate skills toward a common purpose.

WHY THE WORLD NEEDS GLUE PEOPLE

In the old days of moviemaking, when even a blockbuster might have only a hundred crew members, directors and producers could survey their domain and see, and more or less understand, everything that was going on. Of course, there were plenty of technicians on the set who had highly specialized skills. But their work was all within physical view of the director, who probably knew most of their names and understood what they did all day, even if he was unable to do it himself.

The massive scale and technological complexity of modern effects-heavy movies have changed all that. Rupert Wyatt, the director of *Rise of the Planet of the Apes,* didn't know the names of the programmers on the other side of the planet in New Zealand who were writing software that would enable Revelant's team to deliver apes with realistic fur on time; he certainly had no idea how to do their jobs.

That complexity has created extraordinary opportunity for people like Revelant, who can bridge the communication divide between people with different types of deep expertise. The more people and the more technical skills that are involved, the more in demand are the skills of someone like Revelant who can ensure that the connections and handoffs between those different artists and technicians are successful. Kathy Gruzas, the chief information officer at Weta Digital, has a term for them: glue people.

"I think the only way you can make something so big and complex work is to have a lot of people spending a lot of time talking about stuff and discussing and getting it right," Gruzas told me. "It's the people who speak both the artistic and technical languages well who can translate between them, who can keep everything running and translating the vision and overseeing quality." What makes someone successful at Weta Digital is the ability to offer not merely technical skill but also an ability to put that technical skill to use as an element of something that is bigger than the sum of its parts. "You'll find the most useful people in the organizations are the ones who have moved around, who know about the process and how the pieces interconnect. You can't just know your bit," Gruzas said.

In visits to dozens of companies over the course of reporting this book, I heard variation upon variation on this theme. Because of the scale and complexity of the companies that increasingly dominate the global economy, there is more value than ever in being a glue person, one of the people who make these wildly different parts of an organization work effectively together.

Yves Morieux, a partner at the Boston Consulting Group, has seen this rising complexity as he travels to visit clients, typically big companies trying to improve their organizational structure. A few years ago, Morieux started noticing a disturbing trend. He heard, over and over again, stories of unwieldy bureaucracy making life impossible. A global manufacturer's director of sales in Germany, for example, reported to both the president of the German division and the global head of sales. He worked all week on a presentation requested by the first boss, only to have the other reject it out of hand and demand that it be redone over the weekend. Morieux also recalled interviewing a midlevel official at a US bank who broke down in tears—this in a businesslike meeting in a conference room—as she explained the cumbersome mix of approvals she needed to carry out the most basic of tasks.

These stories will seem familiar to anyone who has worked in a large, complex organization. But less obvious is why things are this way, how to mitigate the problem, and how to be the kind of person who can thrive despite the bureaucratic obstacles that big organizations tend to throw in one's way.

As more of these conversations piled up, Morieux realized that at the root of employees' dissatisfaction was the inherent complexity of modern business—or rather, companies' use of processes and organizational charts and management matrices and all kinds of other formal methods of grappling with that complexity. Once upon a time, that German sales manager could have answered simply to the German division president, and his only job would have been to sell more products in Germany. That became more complicated in a world where product supply chains and customers are multinational, and an effort to sell in Germany really means selling to a company that also has facilities in Poland and China and Brazil. And, in a bank with thousands of branches and hundreds of billions of dollars in assets, you can't have a branch manager simply decide whether to extend a loan based on her judgment of the borrower's creditworthiness. Rather, that work involves advanced analytics based on troves of data, risk management and regulatory compliance judgments, and high-level corporate strategy.

Not that long ago, even fairly large companies could operate with different units each doing straightforward jobs to the best of their ability—more like making *King Kong* in 1976. The product engineers develop products. The operations staff makes and distributes them. The salespeople sell. The finance people balance the books. Of course, these departments had to interact, but in effect each had a clear goal and could work in a silo with a hierarchy of its own; you could have a great career hitching yourself to any of those functional specialties at a large company and working hard to rise from entry-level worker bee to executive vice president or beyond.

But in today's company, these functions—and many more—are intertwined. To be a good product engineer means gaining a deep understanding of customers' needs, not simply trusting sales and marketing staff to figure that out. Finance is more deeply interwoven with operations; successful management of inventory levels and supply chains can determine whether a company thrives or fails. Add whatever function you want—marketing, information technology, human resources, legal affairs, government relations, communications: each, in a modern organization, is effective only so long as its practitioners can collaborate effectively with the other parts.

Morieux compares it to a relay race. What might seem like a simple contest of speed is in fact a contest of speed and *coordination*. In the

2016 Summer Olympics in Rio de Janeiro, the gap between the gold-medal Jamaican men's relay team and the second-place Japanese was a third of a second; only 0.04 seconds separated the Japanese from the third-place Canadians. In a contest with such narrow margins of error, what separates winners from losers is skill at passing the baton. Yes, you can measure the time each of the four runners takes to run his leg—but that time alone isn't telling you what you really need to know about whether a given runner helped or hurt his team's chances. For that, you need a harder-to-measure, subjective insight into how well the runners worked with their teammates to have the most efficient possible handoff.

"In a company, we can measure individual productivity and the things you've achieved at the end of the year," Morieux said. "But this silos productivity. It's like measuring the speed of each runner in their leg. At the world-class level, what makes the difference is the way we pass the baton, not who is individually fastest."

It's important to excel in your area, but the real value in a modern organization comes in making the handoffs work more seamlessly. A person who can successfully manage the intersection between different types of expertise will have much greater value than an area expert who keeps blinders on to focus on that area.

Deep expertise is essential, but so is the ability to work with those who have different expertise. No sprinter can *just* be good at handing off the baton and expect to make an Olympic team, but conversely, a really fast runner who routinely bungles the handoff isn't going to be very useful, either.

Morieux argues that management approaches that emphasize accountability, measurement of results, and the like create a vicious cycle in this world of complexity, "an exponential spiral of more matrices, more scorecards, more rules, more process, more job descriptions that hinder agility, speed, and satisfaction at work."[6] Anybody can put a bunch of people with different skills and backgrounds in the same conference room with a whiteboard. Great ideas and products and solutions to hard problems emerge when those people can talk to and understand each other and can apply their different backgrounds and technical abilities toward the same cause.

HOW GLUE PEOPLE MAKE AN AIRPLANE FLY

When I heard Kathy Gruzas talk about how glue people make modern moviemaking possible, and Morieux's metaphor of the relay race as the way things happen (or don't) at modern, complex organizations, it struck me that this was the exact lesson, using slightly different language, that I learned at an icon of business history: General Electric.

GE was experiencing hard times when I visited in 2017. Some poorly placed bets on the power industry had gone sour, costing CEO Jeff Immelt his job; fourteen months later, Immelt's successor, John Flannery, would be fired as well. The company was reviewing which units to sell off in order to become a leaner organization. As it reinvented itself, what I found most telling was the types of skills and abilities demanded of the people who would have a future at the twenty-first-century General Electric.

As Susan Peters, who was senior vice president of human resources when I visited in 2017, described it, what it takes to be successful at GE is radically different from what it took a few years ago. "Designers don't just sit at a [computer-aided design] program and do their work. They design in groups. Engineering and supply chains, everything connects in whole new ways," she said. "You can't design something without understanding how to build it. Then, what are the properties that your marketing and product people will emphasize? And how do you sell that? How do you cost and price it, and how do you service it? I think we used to do all that in very siloed ways, but the world is moving too fast for that."

Essentially, wherever people are in an organization, they need to understand how their specialty fits into the business as a whole. Line-level workers need to able to understand interconnections that at one time only fairly senior managers worried about. "Some people are more naturally comfortable with the stage presence aspect of leadership, but even an engineer who is shy and doesn't want to do anything but design can learn to interface and talk about their product. And that's more important than ever, because work is not done by one person anymore," Peters said. "Nothing is done in isolation." She didn't use the words, but she was essentially extolling the virtue of glue people, the people who enable the different parts of the organization to stick together.

To see it in practice, I went to a GE division that is among its most innovative and financially successful, at a cavernous building twenty minutes north of Cincinnati. GE has been building jet engines almost since jet engines were invented in the 1940s. By the time Josh Mook arrived at GE Aviation in 2005, the company was supplying the engines that power most Boeing airliners and many from Airbus; if you took a flight on a wide-body aircraft anytime in the last couple of decades, there's a good chance that a GE engine got you where you were going.

In his early years at the company, Mook became immersed in the details of the parts that make the engines work. "I've pretty much touched almost all the parts of a jet engine, really focused on deep mechanical design," he said. "Turbine airfoils"—the blades that propel the plane—"was a place I spent a lot of time." Then, in 2011, Mook received a big promotion: to lead the team in charge of designing fuel nozzles. That may not sound like a promotion, but the nozzles, even though they're not much bigger than a walnut, are a very important part of a jet engine. Making even small improvements in how efficiently the fuel is injected can save millions of dollars in fuel over the engine's life. Conversely, if the fuel injector clogs or otherwise causes the engine to fail, the results could be catastrophic.

Around this time, Mook and other engineers were starting to use a new technology to test out new designs for parts. It was a form of three-dimensional printing called "additive" manufacturing; instead of shaping existing metal pieces, machines use powdered metals to build the part by adding one precise layer after another. In 2011, the machines were so expensive and slow that it made sense to use them only in a research capacity: engineers could design a new part, make one using additive manufacturing, and then test the sample to see how it performed under different conditions of heat, pressure, and so on. The actual parts would then be manufactured by traditional methods.

Mook and his colleagues realized that additive manufacturing could be useful for more than just testing. Much of the way jet engine parts were made was premised on the limits of production technology; it was manufacturing techniques that limited, for example, how narrow the tubes jet fuel flows through could be, and that determined how many parts would be involved in a single fuel injector. But if fuel injectors were manufactured with additive machines, those constraints would no longer exist. Fuel injection tubes could be made in whatever shape the physics determined was optimal. In effect, moving the production of the part entirely to additive machines might make it possible to make a part that used jet fuel more efficiently while simultaneously being lighter and more reliable.

In the jet engine business, changes like that aren't made lightly. Mook had to persuade not just his boss but also an entire panel of unconvinced engineers that this approach would work to create parts that were up to the extraordinary safety and reliability standard demanded of jet engines. So one Saturday morning in 2011, he and a couple of members of the team arrived at a vice president's conference room promptly at 8:00 A.M., along with a 500-plus-page document explaining all the technical justifications for why it would work, to undergo a brutal process known as design review. No breakfast pastries were served, only extremely hard questions.

"It was a battle, quite frankly," Mook said. "It was met with extreme resistance. All people could think of were the reasons why it wouldn't work and why it violated our design rules and how the technology was immature. And all of those things were correct—it was immature, it did violate our rules for how we design combustion systems and fuel injectors. And those design rules are the basis for institutional learning. I'm basically standing on this book of institutional learning and saying I don't want to use it, all this information that's documented and passed down generation to generation. When you fly on an airplane, you love to know that you're standing on a hundred years of experience in how to build an engine. So we had a higher climb than anybody because we couldn't just ignore [the rules]. We had to prove why they didn't apply."

After about eight hours, leaving the room, Mook knew that a ton of technical issues would need to be solved, but he was also confident that the challenges raised would all have solutions. When we spoke in the fall of 2017, in the next room over, a technician wearing a ventilator was pouring titanium powder into a machine to make a part that would eventually end up on an aircraft. Improved design software and three-dimensional printing have sped up the ability to experiment with new designs. Only a decade ago, it might take two years to go from an idea for a new design to a testable part; now that can be turned around in days or weeks. With a fuel nozzle, GE engineers can tweak a design, print a sample, and then go to a testing facility down the road to get real data about whether the tweak worked as intended. "It used to be you were lucky if you got two iterations before you committed it to a product," Mook said. "Now we might have 250 iterations. Think about all the refinement I can do over 250 iterations."

What does this have to do with being a glue person? Not that long ago, an engineer like Mook could spend years—even an entire career—focused on a single bolt. He wouldn't have needed to interact much with the manufacturing operations staff who would ultimately build the product, and even less with the marketers and business strategists who would figure out how the product fit into GE's overall strategy. He certainly wouldn't deal with customers; that was the job of sales. Yet it was *because* Mook understood not just product engineering but also the manufacturing operations and business strategy questions that his team was able to realize the potential in using additive technology for this purpose.

"In the traditional models, engineers were specialists," Mook said. "They went very deep in their domain, so they would be experts in heat transfer, or aerodynamics, or stress and life. And then we had people who were responsible generally for systems designs. Those were the architects, the people who thought about the whole system. Now what you have is engineers who need to be able to do all of those things. The skill set has changed from people who were extremely deep in one thing to people who can have a systems-thinking approach. They really empathize with the customer and understand how the products are going to be used, how they're going to be maintained, things like that. . . . Every engineer on our team has built a full business plan for everything they're working on. What can we sell it for? What's it cost? What's the timing, and how do we market? How do we capture market share and revenue?"

No one expects an aerospace engineer working on turbine blades or fuel injectors all day long to be as skilled at product strategy or marketing or sales as someone who does that work all day long. And, of course, GE still has plenty of product managers and marketing executives and salespeople. But engineers need to understand those business realities, just as modelers or coders at Weta Digital need to understand how their work fits in with the creative ambitions of the movie.

Whether it's aircraft engineers in the American Midwest or moviemakers in New Zealand, in other words, the pathway to success in the complex, technologically innovative companies that dominate the modern economy consists of acting as the glue that can bind fast-changing teams and people with lots of different skills together.

Or so it seemed to me, until I plugged the term "glue people" into the Google search engine and learned that it was viewed as a pejorative at one of the most successful of these complex, technologically innovative companies that dominate the modern economy: Google itself.

THE RISKS OF BEING A GLUE PERSON
(AND HOW TO AVOID THEM)

Eric Schmidt joined Google in 2001, when the company was a venture-capital-funded rising star but not yet the global colossus it would become. He was the "professional" CEO—a veteran of Novell and Sun Microsystems—who served as the adult in the room to help founders Larry Page and Sergey Brin build the company beyond its startup roots.

"When I was at Novell, I noticed there were all of these 'glue people,'" Schmidt said in 2015 while speaking to a class at Stanford.[7] "These glue people are nice people that sit between different groups who assist in activities. They are very loyal and people love them, but the reality is you don't need them—they just slow things down." When he started to see Google hiring too many of these glue people, Schmidt said, he and Page and Brin began reviewing every prospective new hire. "Everyone that looked like glue people," he said, didn't get hired.

That didn't line up with what I was hearing at innovative companies around the world, so I asked Laszlo Bock, who was Google's senior vice president of people operations during that era, to try to make sense of it.

"The idea was basically that there are people who do in-between jobs that you may not actually need if everyone else is doing their job," Bock said. "A canonical example would be somebody who was in something like a chief of staff role." In effect, the Google leaders were concerned that anyone whose job was managing process was gumming up the work of innovation and creating products. "One of the fears in the early days was that this stuff is pernicious. Once you start creating these kinds of jobs that exist solely to make up for the deficiencies of the people around them, they will self-replicate across the organization."

Interestingly, speaking to Bock, I got the impression that "glue people" wasn't even quite the right term for what Google senior managers were so intent on avoiding. Rather, they were looking to eliminate "glue jobs"—managing process and bureaucracy rather than actually building things or selling things or otherwise driving the business forward. The issue wasn't so much anything particular in the job candidates' background or skills. It was the structure of the job into which they were being inserted.

So what distinguishes the good type of glue people I saw at Weta Digital and GE from the bad type of glue people—those stuck in process-oriented, bureaucratic jobs whom Eric Schmidt was trying so hard not to hire into Google? I pushed Kathy Gruzas at Weta on this question.

"I think it's the 'without skills' and 'without much productive ability of their own' bit that is the problem," she wrote in an email. "The problem is glue that gums things up rather than holds things together and going in the same direction. I have had that problem—hired someone that I thought was closer to 'smart creative' glue person, and found them more a Novell 'glue person,' lacking initiative and drive and adding little value in the end. You have to move those people on, they slow things down. . . . It sounds like Novell's problem was 'dead wood' hiding in large structures. These aren't the glue people I'm talking about . . . they're the people you recognise immediately and are like gold, not the people you wonder how they have a job."

Her answer speaks to one of the fundamental risks of managing a career in a world where some of the greatest success lies at the intersection of different forms of expertise. What is the difference between a successful glue person and someone who embodies the old saying "jack of all trades, master of none"?

The answer can be found in the work of a famous Italian economist and in a line attributed to the great *New Yorker* writer A. J. Liebling: "I can write faster than anyone who can write better, and I can write better than anyone who can write faster."

BEING A PARETO-OPTIMAL EMPLOYEE

The good type of glue person—the type highly valued in the organ-izations that dominate the modern economy—can become so through multiple pathways. There are extreme technical specialists who develop the communication and business strategy skills, and so can work well with others who don't share those skills. There are others who sit at the nexus of two or more areas of technical specialties, whose entire job is to push teams toward achieving a goal.

Think of the range of possibilities as a continuum, using a line that will look familiar to anyone who has studied economics.

In managing a twenty-first-century career, it helps to take a page from the Italian economist, philosopher, and sociologist Vilfredo Pareto. Pareto, who died in 1923, was often stubborn and caustic with those he thought beneath him intellectually, which seemed to be just about everyone. But for all of his faults, he left us with a series of insights so important that they have outlived him by nearly a century. One of them was an idea that came to be called "Pareto optimality," which is a state in which you cannot improve things on one frontier

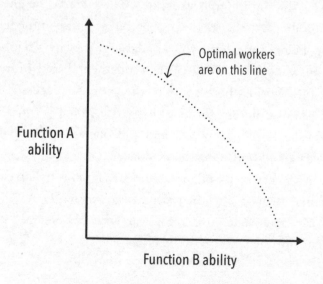

without making them worse on another frontier. This was initially used to think about how scarce goods were allocated in a society. An economy is Pareto optimal when one person cannot receive more stuff without someone else receiving less. If one person in society makes more at the cost of someone else making less, that society is moving from one location on the Pareto curve to another. But if a society increases its productive potential so that one person can earn more while others earn the same as before or more, it is a Pareto improvement— the entire curve shifting, rather than just an individual moving to another point on the curve. That's what you want to see.

Meanwhile, a society functioning beneath the curve of Pareto optimality is failing in some way—essentially leaving gains on the table that could be picked up to improve someone's well-being. You don't want to be there.

The same applies in terms of what types of employees are most valuable at the superstar firms of the modern economy. There is room for deep specialists, but they had better be extraordinary at their work. The lesson of Weta Digital and GE is that more and more opportunity in modern organizations is found toward the middle of that curve, where the glue people reside. The good kinds of glue people are highly valuable at connecting the work of people with different specialties— but only if they are at that Pareto-optimal frontier, with substantial expertise themselves.

So, for example, imagine an organization that makes and sells software, and hence requires both coders and software developers to create the product and business-minded marketers to sell it. Four people in this organization might fit on our curve as seen on the next page.

Darla is a rock-star coder; that's her main contribution to the team. She can communicate fine with the marketers, but only enough to know what features she should be building into the software. Deborah, meanwhile, is an ace marketer. She can't write a line of code but can at least communicate with Darla well enough to explain what customers are asking for. Damien is the product manager. He has some

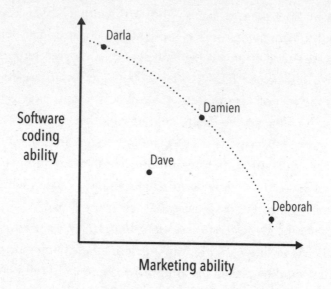

software development experience, not at Darla's level, but enough to understand what is technically possible, what is hard, and what is easy. He has an MBA and can make sure that the product is delivered on time in ways that fulfill the customers' needs.

The three of them have very different backgrounds and skills, but each is a Pareto-optimal employee—in the same way that Liebling combined writing ability and speed, each of these three knows more coding than anybody who knows more marketing, and more marketing than anyone who knows more coding. All are valuable parts of the team and should be rewarded with plenty of opportunity in the future. Damien, as a classic glue person, embodies an archetype that is especially valuable in the way successful organizations are evolving (to put it in more mathematical terms, the shape of the curve has shifted to favor the middle part of it).

Then there's Dave. Dave doesn't have the technical proficiency to make the company more successful either through better marketing, software development, or product management. Dave probably spends a lot of his time writing agendas for meetings, playing office politics, and trying to make up for his lack of ability to contribute by adding lots of process and bureaucracy instead of good ideas and execution. Dave is the type of glue person Eric Schmidt tried mightily not to hire at Google. You don't want to be Dave.

One popular type of employee that fits nicely into this Pareto-optimality concept is the "T-shaped" worker. The term "T-shaped worker" has been used by the consultants at McKinsey for years and has been popularized by IDEO, the influential global design firm. The idea is that the vertical part of the T symbolizes depth of skill in one particular area, while the horizontal part symbolizes the ability to collaborate across disciplines. "T-shaped people have both depth and breadth in their skills," Tim Brown, the chief executive of IDEO, once explained in a magazine interview,[8] in contrast to "I-shaped people," those who go deep in one area but cannot collaborate well with people from other fields and those who can collaborate well but lack sufficient depth in any area to make a meaningful contribution.

In effect, the T-shaped worker occupies one particular spot on the Pareto-optimality line and is one type of glue person. It looks like this:

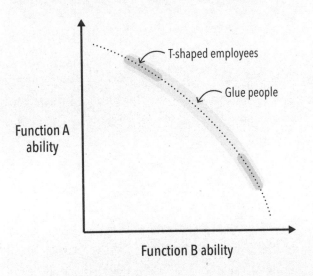

In managing a career in the modern economy, we should all aim to be Pareto-optimal workers. While there is still room for narrow technical specialists—people at the far ends of the Pareto curve—in the modern economy they need to be truly extraordinary to have good prospects. The types of organizations that dominate the modern economy tend to require more glue people, those who function well at the intersection of different technical specialties.

That leaves a big question: How do you mold yourself into one of those people? That is what the chapters ahead are dedicated to answering.

2

Becoming Pareto Optimal

———

HOW TO BE THE PERSON SUPERSTAR FIRMS NEED THE MOST

It's well and good to set out to become a Pareto-optimal employee—to try to be the person who understands how different parts of a modern organization intersect, to make teams work better, to acquire different types of technical expertise and thus speak the languages of multiple tribes within your company. But describing that framework doesn't answer two crucial questions that are essential for actually becoming the kind of employee that the types of organizations that dominate the twenty-first-century economy most desperately seek and most lucratively reward.

First, what combination of functional expertise is most uniquely valuable in your industry? And second, how do you manage your career choices to ensure you acquire it?

FIGURING OUT WHICH SKILL MIXES MATTER

In the late 1990s, Matt Sigelman, a young consultant barely removed from college, took a job at an American bank that had ambitions to expand into India, and particularly to bring a more methodical, quantitative approach to consumer lending. At the time, Indian banks tended to lend money in a highly subjective fashion. Loan officers would visit would-be borrowers' homes and make lending decisions based on such things as the quality of their rugs, the size of their house, and the number of servants they employed. And they weren't above allowing personal biases to affect their decisions. "I spent a bunch of time interviewing underwriters, and they totally spitballed it," Sigelman said. "Like, 'That guy is an attorney, so I will never lend to him because he'll sue me.'"

Not much came of the effort, and Sigelman ended up leaving the bank to go to business school. But the experience of trying to turn messy, unstructured information into something that could be computed, crunched, and analyzed stuck with him.

A few years later, Sigelman and a partner would acquire Burning Glass Technologies, which aimed to help companies use technology to make better hiring decisions. As he began to dig into hiring managers' recruitment and hiring processes—even those at big, professionally run companies—he was struck by how similar they seemed to the way Indian banks had given out loans. Some of the criteria seemed legitimate: what school candidates attended, where they'd worked previously, and so forth. But sometimes people would be hired over better candidates simply because they had some connection to the hiring manager, or not hired because that manager didn't connect with them.

Burning Glass's primary offering to its clients at that time was software designed to help them sort and analyze incoming job applications. But, Sigelman wondered, why not turn that on its head and try to analyze more rigorously what jobs employers were struggling to fill, and therefore what job-seekers, colleges, and others involved in education and training can do to produce the workforce the modern economy needs? What data existed about jobs and compensation tended to be very broad-brush—average pay levels, total number of job openings, and so on. He saw an opportunity to go deeper.

So, starting in 2007, from an office overlooking Boston Harbor, Burning Glass has been scraping every job listing it can find—combing through popular for-profit job boards, individual employers' online job listings, trade group publications, and so on. By 2017, the company's computers were scraping 50,000 sites a day, encompassing millions of job openings, and converting their plain English (or corporatese, depending on the listing) into structured data, such as the specific skills and experience the posting required and any salary information included. It also tracked how long a posting remained up, providing a decent proxy for whether the company had an easy time or a hard time filling the position. Over time, Burning Glass accumulated a data set of hundreds of millions of job listings in a form that could be searched and organized. The result of all this work is an extraordinarily detailed, granular map of the US job market over the past decade and counting. Sigelman bet that by looking at what skills employers were seeking, and what they were finding or not finding, his company could develop insights into the job market that were available nowhere else.

In 2014, though, Sigelman noticed a curious pattern with a surprising category of jobs. Many schools and camps in the United States are associated with a church or other religious institution and employ a "director of religious life" to guide the spiritual experience of their enrollees. Usually, these jobs are pretty easy to fill; countless graduates of divinity schools, or just devout people who have the right personality, tend to apply. But according to Burning Glass's data, suddenly those jobs were starting to take much longer to fill on average, for no obvious reason.

"I remember first looking at the numbers and saying, 'Guys, we are clearly doing something wrong in our data, because there is no shortage of religious talent in the United States of America,'" Sigelman said. When they dove deeper, what they found was not so much a general shortage of people looking to work in religious life. Rather, camps were increasingly looking for a new skill set among their directors of religious life. "Most of these jobs were clearing very fast, and there was no holdup," Sigelman said. "But there was this corner of them where they were looking for religious life directors who had social media skills and database marketing skills—people who could really market to young folks. But there weren't too many people with that combination of skills, and that was driving the overall average to make it look like there was a shortage." The problem, in other words, wasn't that there was a shortage of people interested in religious life but that there was a shortage of those people *who also knew how to do database marketing.*

"I still remember that because it was eye-opening for me in realizing that overall numbers aren't sufficiently enlightening. Saying 'Hey, directors of religious life jobs are hard to fill' isn't actually that helpful if you're not training people with the skills that are actually the ones that make that job hard to fill."

Sigelman realized that across the modern labor market it has become increasingly important not just to look at what job titles companies are posting but also to parse the details of what mix of skills they seek. As with the religious life directors, many of the jobs that were most in demand—as revealed by positions that were both posted in the highest numbers and went unfilled for the longest periods of time—were those that featured a mix of skills that, as Sigelman put it, don't really go together in nature. Often, when companies are posting a job, they emphasize the qualifications that they are most struggling to find. For example, a pharmaceutical company hiring an in-house lawyer might not bother specifying some of the skills and qualifications that an experienced lawyer is assumed to have, like a law degree. Instead, it might emphasize knowledge of medical science—

an expertise that is relatively rare in lawyers but would be a particularly useful qualification for a lawyer in the pharmaceutical industry.

Moreover, as Economics 101 might predict, the imbalance between supply and demand for these people with hybrid skills pushed their wages up. In Burning Glass's data, for example, the average advertised salary for an engineering manager was $95,000 a year—but that increased to $120,000 when the posting was for an engineering manager who also had strategic planning experience. A $70,000 supply chain and logistics manager job received a bump to $83,000 when he also had forecasting experience. A $58,000-a-year facilities manager became a $72,000-a-year facilities manager when she also had contract management experience. Many of the jobs for which demand has soared the most in the decade the data covers are prime examples of this hybridization. To be a data scientist, a job title that barely existed at the start of the twenty-first century but now can be found in virtually every major company,[1] one generally needs a combination of computer programming skills, statistics expertise, a sound understanding of business strategy, and communication skills good enough to explain findings to generalist colleagues. Mobile app developers are another example. "We've found that compared to web developers or software developer jobs, mobile app developers are more likely to need not just coding skills but also skill in design, business, marketing, an ability to develop e-commerce applications," Sigelman said. "It's a much more hodgepodge role than the title would lead you to believe."

In other words, the jobs in the greatest demand in the modern economy require people like our Pareto-optimal friends Darla, Damien, and Deborah.

That still doesn't answer the question, though, of, How do you know what particular mix of hybrid skills is most likely to pay off, and therefore which to try to develop? The examples from the Burning Glass data above are from 2017, and by the time you read this, the market may easily have shifted again. And while scraping 50,000 job sites a day and employing a bunch of data scientists to glean lessons from the results might be appealing, it is not terribly practical for an individual.[2] But Sigelman offers a shortcut that is both awfully useful and relatively simple to apply.

In every sector, there are some companies that are known for being on the cutting edge of where the industry and its talent needs are going, and others that are slower to adjust. Even if you work at one of the laggard companies, it is beneficial to monitor job postings by the cutting-edge companies. The skills they seek are likely to offer a window into the future of the job in question. Your own employer may not realize it needs X skill yet, but if its highly innovative competitor is trying to hire a lot of people with X skill, seek out every opportunity to learn more about X. For example, Burning Glass examined job listings for mechanical engineers at Tesla and General Motors—ostensibly similar jobs at a bleeding-edge automaker versus a legacy one. There were plenty of similarities; at both companies, large numbers of postings sought skills in validation and simulation. But while 54 percent of Tesla postings sought experience with the CATIA three-dimensional design software, and 19 percent sought experience with 3D modeling and design more generally, those requirements were less prevalent in GM listings. The implication: if you're a mechanical engineer in the auto industry and think the future of automobiles looks more like Tesla than like GM—*whether Tesla itself succeeds or fails*—it would be awfully useful to gain experience with 3D modeling techniques and particularly CATIA.

More than anything else, becoming a Pareto-optimal employee who is qualified for the hybrid jobs that, according to Sigelman's data, present the greatest opportunities takes active thought. "Precisely because the job market is increasingly dynamic because different sorts of skills are showing up in different types of jobs, the expectation that through a standard career path you are going to wind up acquiring the skills you need is more and more tenuous," he said. In an age when work is fluid, team based, and less hierarchical, it is the Pareto-optimal employee who is most up for the challenge of getting the next project done.

In other words, your career can't be a passive effort to log more and more years in a cubicle doing good work and getting the occasional bonus or promotion; instead, you should look around the corner— whether by scanning cutting-edge competitors' job listings or asking the most visionary people in your field for advice—and actively prepare for the future.

That's a nice idea, but I wanted to see more about how that can look in practical terms. The automobile industry, as Sigelman's example of Tesla and General Motors shows, makes for a fascinating case study. That's how I ended up in Gothenburg, Sweden, on a dark winter day, hoping to see how to turn this broad instruction into concrete advice for becoming a Pareto-optimal employee with just the right mix of skills for your industry.

PARETO OPTIMALITY IN THE CHANGING AUTO BUSINESS

It is an indicator of how massive the global auto industry is that Volvo is considered tiny despite having sold nearly 600,000 cars in 2017, booking $25 billion in revenue, and employing 38,000 people (the biggest global automakers, Volkswagen and Toyota, are around fifteen times as big). But its relatively modest scale makes it a fascinating place to see what an era of technological transformation in autos means for a career in the industry. Cars were once just one of many products made by the Swedish industrial conglomerate Volvo Group, before its automaking unit was sold to the American giant Ford in 1999. It spent years as something of a neglected misfit, until Ford sold the company to Zhejiang Geely Holding Group, the Chinese automaker founded by Li Shufu, in 2010.

While the cultural differences between China and Sweden might make this seem like an odd match, it has to date worked surprisingly well. Geely has provided a sense of global ambition and access to the

Chinese market, while leaving Volvo's mostly Swedish leadership to innovate and expand the company. "They have supported us by trusting in the brand and supporting it, including helping us enter into China," the chief executive, Håkan Samuelsson, told me. "We were a Swedish exporting company, earlier. Now we are a truly global company." The company is adding manufacturing capacity in both China and the United States, with a plant near Charleston, South Carolina.

The auto industry, meanwhile, is in an era of tumult, on all fronts. The underlying technology is changing, with gasoline-powered internal combustion engines starting to give way to hybrids and battery-powered electric motors. The ways that people interact with cars is also on the verge of massive change, as driverless cars have gone from pipe dream to reality in just a few years. Both of those shifts portend a revolution in automakers' business model, as they imply that fewer people will own a car in the years ahead, with more cars being part of a fleet, summoned by app, rather than spending most of their time parked in their owner's driveway. A multifaceted competition is on the way, in which legacy automakers like Volvo and its larger rivals face off against Tesla and other startups, and Silicon Valley powerhouses like Uber and Alphabet seek to create software to power driverless cars. In this moment of flux, if you're an automaker it's hard to know if, say, Uber is a competitor or a customer. On the one hand, it is developing its own autonomous car technology, and on the other, it signed a nonbinding deal with Volvo just before I visited to buy 24,000 cars once driverless capability was sufficiently advanced to allow them to operate as a fleet.[3] In the summer of 2017, Samuelsson made a splashy announcement that all new cars introduced from 2019 forward will be either electric or hybrid.

It is a business environment in which Volvo desperately needs leaders who are Pareto-optimal automakers—able to understand how hardware, software, and the underlying business model intersect. Henrik Green is one of them. Green's title in late 2017 was senior vice president for research and development, but his history at the company shows how he was uniquely positioned to help it compete in this era when the entire industry is in flux.

Green grew up in Trollhättan, a city an hour's drive north of Gothenburg, in a car family. Both of his parents worked at Saab, which was the other Swedish automaker before it shuttered in 2012. In his university studies in the early 1990s, Green was torn: he loved computers and studied computer science, but he also loved the mechanical world and the excitement of tinkering with car engines. At the time, these areas seemed hopelessly disconnected. When he took a job in Volvo's engine division in 1996, he started to understand how interlinked they were becoming. During this era, the mechanics of cars were being computerized. The steering wheel, instead of being connected to a gear that turns the front wheels, communicated that you wanted to go left or right to a computer, which relayed this information to a motor that controlled steering. The gas pedal no longer opened a valve that allowed more gasoline into the engine, causing acceleration, but instead conveyed information to a computer that in turn controlled the throttle. Green was in the rare position of being able to understand both the lines of software code governing those processes and the mechanics of how they worked, and he rose rapidly. Nevertheless, he recalls that as a time of fundamental simplicity. "It was still very much just about applying new technology to the basic concept of the existing car," he said. "The car was still four wheels and a steering wheel and a combustion engine in the front for propulsion, and we used electronics and software and advanced materials to make that experience the same, but a little better."

Green's mix of software and engineering expertise allowed him to rise through the ranks when those were the two important pieces of auto engineering. He worked on power-train engineering, leading efforts to figure out how software could make engines more reliable and fuel-efficient. While Ford owned Volvo, he spent lots of time in Detroit, learning how things worked at the bigger organization, and then, after the Geely acquisition, he spent three years in China to help

lead Volvo's expansion there. So by the time he came back to
headquarters in Sweden in 2013, he had a distinctive perspective that
pulled together many of the threads essential to this global business:
he knew something about both mechanical engineering and software
development, the intersection of technological and business strategy
concerns, and how business works in the United States, China, and
Europe. He had the Liebling-esque version of a Pareto-optimal career:
he knew software better than anyone who knew hardware better,
hardware better than anyone who knew software better, engineering
better than anyone who knew business strategy better, and so on.

Even with that varied experience, his current task makes those
earlier jobs seem downright simple. "I think in the '90s, almost
everything came down to execution," he said. "It was whoever exe-
cutes the best level of performance will have the best product. Now
it's much more about change and flexibility—who is fastest in understanding the potential of a new technology and what level of consumer experience you can actually achieve by doing things differently.
To comprehend that and to have teams that are receptive to this
change is what makes a difference."

As important as Green's Pareto optimality was to his own rise
in the company, it is becoming all the more essential in this era of
major change—not merely helpful for an ambitious person looking to be promoted but necessary for the company's survival. In fact,
the very way that Volvo and other auto companies have traditionally built cars—the processes that have made modern automobiles
extraordinarily reliable—now stands in the way of the changes
that will make an automaker competitive. As recently as a few years
ago, Volvo set up an electric car team, which operated parallel to
its combustion team, each working on its own to make its type of
propulsion system the best it could be. But this structure created the
wrong incentives, executives realized. For one, the people working on
combustion engines became overly invested in trying to prolong the
lifespan of those engines, because their jobs depended on it. Essentially,

employees' own near-term career survival instinct put them at cross-purposes with what needed to happen to ensure that the company had a viable future over the longer run.

In response, Green decided that the key was reorganizing teams so they focused on the fundamental engineering and business goal, rather than on preserving a particular technology. "We've basically merged those teams, saying, 'You lead the power propulsion of the vehicle, regardless of whether this is a combustion engine or electrical motor propulsion.' This means that there is no structure that would see the change as a threat to their existence," Green said. It also, of course, means that engineers need to become proficient with both types of engines. This structure makes a particular type of Pareto optimality essential for anyone looking to have a future at Volvo.

The same principle applies on every part of the car. Companies like Volvo have had one group in charge of gearshifts and another responsible for heating and cooling systems and another dealing with seats and the controls that adjust their position. It was one thing for each to act in isolation when the basic form of the car and the business model of the industry were stable. Each of those teams could work in isolation trying to make its feature work as well as possible; the team worrying about the temperature-control knob worried only about that. But with the direction the auto business is going, more and more features will be controlled by flat-panel displays and voice commands. It is even an open question whether fully automated cars will have steering wheels and gearshifts. That means there is no such thing as a job worrying only about the shape and location of a single knob. "We can no longer have 125 specific feature owners and each and every one of them decides that 'my feature is controlled in this way by the consumer,'" Green said. Instead, successful auto engineers have to understand exactly how their small piece of a car fits together with the whole.

"Traditionally, we are strong in specialists as an industry, but what we'll need more of in the future is broader experiences instead of very specific knowledge in one area," Green said. "The business model is changing so much that tomorrow, cars may be pooled; it could be that we ship a car with hardware and the consumer is actually subscribing and activating, piece by piece, options that up the value of that subscription. So we need people who have an understanding of what the consumer wants, how the business works, and a broad technical understanding of how you develop digital features and mechanical features."

That has big implications for people navigating a career in the auto industry (or, with minor adjustments, any similarly complex industry undergoing rapid technological change). To succeed, they need to seek experience in multiple facets of how an automobile works—not just design or just electronic systems or just power trains. And they need to understand how it all connects to their company's underlying economics. That could mean reading articles in the automotive trade press and research analyst notes to stay up to speed on the economic forces reshaping the business. It could mean a mechanical engineer taking coding classes at night to better understand what the software engineers she collaborates with do all day. It could mean asking for temporary assignments to other teams to gain a panoramic view of how a car is designed and made.

The key is that being Pareto optimal in the automobile industry means not simply burrowing into how to make one tiny piece the best it can be, but learning how to do it while understanding the broader system in which that piece works—including asking whether it is needed at all.

THE PATH TO THE EXECUTIVE SUITE

Being a Pareto-optimal worker is necessary up and down the corporate hierarchy of the organizations that dominate the modern economy. And the higher up you go, the more essential it becomes.

Almost by definition, the people on the upper rungs of an organization—in the C-suite, say, where the chief executive officer, chief operating officer, and so on reside—are going to be responsible for overseeing people doing jobs they themselves do not know how to do and can never fully understand. As the people at the top of a complex enterprise, though, they need to be thoroughly familiar with its many moving pieces and how they intersect. The technology entrepreneur and venture capitalist Marc Andreessen wrote in a 2007 blog post that the key for ambitious people setting out in the business world is to "seek to be a double/triple/quadruple threat." As he put it, "All successful CEO's are like this. They are almost never the best product visionaries, or the best salespeople, or the best marketing people, or the best finance people, or even the best managers, but they are top 25% in some set of those skills, and then all of a sudden they're qualified to actually run something important." He suggests, for example, that developing skills in communications *and* management *and* sales *and* finance *and* working in international markets—becoming reasonably accomplished in each area—is the "secret formula to becoming a CEO."[4]

A study that analyzed the résumés of 4,500 chief executives at 1,500 major companies from 1993 to 2007 set out to distinguish those with narrow firm-specific experience from those with general managerial skills.[5] Its findings? Generalist CEOs earned a premium of 19 percent in annual pay, amounting to almost $1 million a year in extra compensation, compared to specialists. The generalist pay premium was highest in firms dealing with restructurings and acquisitions, adapting to a fast-changing business environment, or more generally coping with shocks and distress. When the going gets tough in the corporate world, generalist CEOs evidently get going.

In 2016, I worked with LinkedIn to analyze its trove of data on professionals' career pathways to see if we could identify factors that led to career advancement to the highest levels. LinkedIn researchers identified 459,000 people worldwide whose profiles indicated that they had worked at any of the large management consulting firms between 1990 and 2010. They then analyzed the subset of 64,000 who went on to reach the milestone of being a vice president, partner, or C-suite executive (like chief financial officer or chief information officer) at a company with more than 200 employees.

Some of the results were fairly intuitive. Getting an MBA, particularly from a top program, increased a person's likelihood of ending up in the executive suite.[6] Certain cities—international business capitals like New York, Mumbai, and Singapore—seemed to offer higher odds of ascending to top executive ranks than others with similar size but perhaps less interconnection with global commerce, like São Paulo and Madrid. The LinkedIn data showed no meaningful relationship, positive or negative, between how often people changed employers and how likely they were to ascend to the executive ranks; lifers at one company had about the same odds as employees who moved every couple of years.

What leaped out at me was this strong relationship: the more functions people had worked in, the more likely they were to make it to the executive suite. Each additional function—finance, marketing, operations, strategy, and so on—increased their odds of ending up in a top executive job as much as three extra years of experience; working across four functions was worth the same as getting an MBA from a top-five university.

More recently, researchers at LinkedIn looked at how the acquisition of any of 50,000 different skills contributed to later success. One crucial lesson was that, especially for people in school or early in their careers, there was a bit of a high-low strategy. The most successful people had strong foundational skills—analytical and quantitative ability, communications skills—that they supplemented with narrow skills like familiarity with a specific programming language. Less successful were people who zeroed in on a particular career focus early, such as by getting a master's degree in a specialty. "The main lesson I draw is don't focus on what seems like it's hot and booming right now, because you have no idea whether by the time you finish your degree if it's still going to be trendy," said Guy Berger, LinkedIn's chief economist. "I wouldn't say specialist skills are worthless, but you should view acquiring those in a more judicious way. 'How long is it going to take me to acquire this, and will I learn something that will help me quickly adapt even if this particular thing isn't as in-demand in a few years?'"

It's still striking how many of the most successful executives at leading companies have the telltale signs of being Pareto optimal. Sundar Pichai, the chief executive of Google, combined a master's degree in materials science and engineering from Stanford with an MBA from the finance-centric Wharton School at the University of Pennsylvania, and worked at the consulting firm McKinsey before climbing the ranks as a product manager at Google. Sheryl Sandberg, the chief operating officer at Facebook and author of *Lean In,* began her career in Washington at the World Bank and US Treasury Department before joining Google in 2001 to essentially build out its advertising revenue business. It was a job at the intersection of sales, technology, finance, and even some policy issues of the type she had dealt with while in Washington (think Federal Trade Commission rules, how to handle advertising from firms of questionable legality, and the like.) She joined Facebook in 2008 to build its advertising business, and can plausibly claim to have engineered the revenue model of the era's most profitable companies.

Or consider what has happened with one senior job that every company over a certain size has: chief financial officer. When I interviewed Bill Zerella in 2017, he was the CFO of Fitbit, the maker of physical activity monitors. (By the time this book went to press, he had moved on to an autonomous-driving startup called Luminar Technologies.) One of his first jobs, in the 1980s, was in the finance department of a company at a different extreme of technological complexity: it was called Simplicity Pattern Company, and it made sewing patterns. Zerella took over financial planning and analysis from a man who was probably in his seventies but to the young man's eyes seemed at least ninety.

"He's putting together this financial plan for a New York Stock Exchange company, and he pulls out this folder and unfolds this spreadsheet that ended up being like twenty feet wide, all these pieces of paper taped together. It's got all the numbers in it written with pencil. This was the company's financial plan, and every time you changed a number, it took about a week to get a new answer." Zerella tried to persuade him to spend $10,000 (in 1984 dollars) on an IBM personal computer with Lotus 1-2-3 spreadsheet software, but the CFO was convinced it was a waste—just a bunch of computer salesmen trying to sell something that would never work.

Zerella eventually won that battle—and when his boss asked for some changes to the company's projections, he returned the results in an hour instead of a week. "The idea that you could change one thing, like headcount or pricing, and instantly know what that would mean for cash flow over the next X years was revolutionary," Zerella said. "The guy was just blown away." That CFO had spent an entire career doing more or less the same task over and over, updating his massive spreadsheet with a pencil and making sure the company's books balanced. Now it could be done with a few clicks of a mouse and milliseconds of processing time. "You took decisions that would take a week or a month to make, and you could literally make them in minutes." When Zerella became a CFO himself, in 1987, the job was almost as straightforward. "I don't remember getting involved with the strategy at all. We'd have a weekly staff meeting with the CEO, the COO, the guy who ran sales and marketing, the guy who ran engineering, and we would go around, and I'd say, 'Here's what the numbers are, here's the forecast for next quarter.' It was pretty one-dimensional."

In the years that followed, as Zerella took a series of CFO jobs, mostly in the technology industry, that started to change. The job was less about providing simple answers about the state of the company's finances and more about shaping strategy to become more profitable. At his next employer, the CEO structured the job such that the head of human resources answered to Zerella. There is some obvious logic to this. Especially in services companies, much of the financial destiny of the company is tied to staffing levels, salaries, and attrition rates, and to aligning those numbers properly with demand and pricing. To be effective, a person who had started his career in accounting and thought of himself as a financial planner had to learn, on the fly, how to run an HR department responsible for hundreds of workers, dealing with everything from labor regulations to recruitment strategies. How did he do it? "You read a lot. You do research. You ask a lot of questions. I enjoyed it because it was all new to me. There were absolutely times when I thought, 'I don't have a clue what I'm doing here,' but that's when you roll up your sleeves and try to figure it out.

"An important revelation for me was that I needed to be smart enough to know when I don't know something, because that's when you can really make bad decisions and be dangerous," he went on. "I'd rather admit I really don't know how to do this and get help than make a decision that could have really bad implications for the company."

Zerella has been the CFO at eight different companies, and at various times has also overseen information technology, legal affairs, supply chain management, and other operations. "The CFO role has expanded beyond 'the guy who knows what the numbers are,' because I think that companies have realized over the years that no matter what the business issue you're dealing with, there's a financial component that underlies it, and having [an understanding of] that discipline helps CFOs play a bigger role at the company," he said.

In other words, to make it from entry-level finance professional to CFO, it's not enough to be good at keeping the books straight. It takes a deeper understanding of how the financial functions of a company serve its broader goals and intersect with everything else it does. That becomes even more true if you aspire to the very top of the corporate hierarchy—whether the product is created with bleeding-edge technology or one that humans have been using for quite a long time.

BEAM SUNTORY AND THE PARETO-OPTIMAL CEO

Sometime in the early 1000s, monks in Scotland and Ireland, lacking the grapes that their counterparts farther south could distill to make alcoholic beverages, had the idea to use grain mash. The results were the earliest versions of what we now know as Scotch and Irish whiskey. About a thousand years later, I found myself in the Chicago headquarters of a company that is responsible for some of the best whiskeys made on three continents,[7] to meet with the chief executive of this embodiment of the modern winner-take-all economy.

Beam Suntory, formed by the 2014 acquisition of the American spirits company Beam Inc. by Suntory Holdings, based in Tokyo, is perhaps most recognizable for its Kentucky bourbon whiskeys (including namesake Jim Beam, Maker's Mark, and, my own favorite, Basil Hayden's), Irish and Scotch whiskeys (including Laphroaig), and some of the best Japanese whiskeys (Hibiki and Toki). Each of these spirits has a long history and built its reputation on a certain old-world craftsmanship. In many cases, the family that started the brand is still involved in its production; Fred Booker Noe III, the master distiller of Jim Beam, is the great-grandson of James Beauregard Beam, who ramped up production after the end of alcohol prohibition in the United States in 1933. But amid the history and storytelling, what gets these products into bars and restaurants and stores worldwide is very much a modern, corporatized enterprise. Which is where Matt Shattock comes in.

Shattock grew up the son of a police officer and served as a tank commander in the British Army during the waning days of the Cold War. After his service ended, he went to work at Unilever, the giant consumer goods company with headquarters in London and

Rotterdam. Unilever at that time offered recent college graduates an entry-level position that amounted to a crash course in how the business worked; new employees would serve a series of rotations designed to introduce them to different parts of the company. Shattock, fresh from commanding tanks, entered the program and found himself selling various sausages and meat snacks to the supermarket chain Sainsbury's. His next job was with Birds Eye Walls, a unit that made frozen foods.

Shattock was put in charge of the group that sold frozen poultry and meat, as general manager. This was his first experience being the boss, which included being accountable for profits and losses. He was in charge of a factory manager and a sales manager and dealt with trademark and regulatory issues and human resources—the full range of functions involved in getting frozen meats into European grocery stores. "It instilled a great appreciation of the things I really had no idea how to do," Shattock said. "I can count, but I'm not a finance expert, so I learned a great deal from having a really good finance partner. Having a factory manager who knew how this incredible machinery would work and how to make it most productive was a wonderful experience. I would deliberately spend time with them, put on the overalls and spend time in the plant to understand what they did so I could ask intelligent questions and try to align them with what we were trying to do."

His next stop was in the United States, where he was responsible for integrating Unilever's disparate US food businesses into one cohesive unit, for which he became chief operating officer. That experience led to a job offer from Cadbury, the giant confectioner, which hired him to manage the integration of a newly acquired unit that made Trident gum, Halls lozenges, and other products in the United States. Shattock was next approached about a job with Fortune Brands, an old-school conglomerate that made products as varied as Master Lock padlocks, Titleist golf balls, Moen faucets, and Jim Beam bourbon. Fortune was spinning its individual units off into more focused companies, with the spirits business staying behind. Would Shattock be interested in running it?

That's how he landed as chief executive of Beam Inc., charged with building a thriving global business out of liquor brands that had long histories but suffered from underinvestment. "We had a set of products that were of the highest quality in the industry but which had not been talked about and portrayed in ways that were worthy of their heritage and their quality," Shattock said. They also had a big supply of inventory aging in barrels but weren't sure there would be enough demand.

The job required Shattock to employ the same kinds of branding strategies that consumer products conglomerates are organized to execute—essentially transferring his knowledge from decades of selling sausages and gum to the spirits business. The company sought to make their products feel fresh and exciting for younger consumers, who are just forming their preferences, and to reach different demographic groups. The reconfigured Beam Inc. launched new advertising campaigns, including one featuring the actress Mila Kunis, designed to project a youthful, edgy tone, and experimented with innovations such as Jim Beam Red Stag (bourbon infused with black cherry), which women consumed at twice the rate of the regular product.[8]

The company put its scale to greater work. It already had a sales force that had relationships with liquor distributors and with hotel and restaurant chains around the world, and a basket of products that the customers wanted. They built on that market power to get new products in front of customers, like Jim Beam Devil's Cut, aged longer than the original. "A lot of this was adopting best practices," Shattock said. "Account management, revenue management, category management, these are the basic building blocks, and they've been around for decades."

Those efforts reflect a systematic shift in the spirits business that has been evident as the industry has become more concentrated and corporatized over the last couple of decades. As one of Shattock's competitors explained to me, in the not-too-distant past, a job in sales at a place like Jim Beam largely involved glad-handing and socializing with clients. Today's salespeople are "much more educated when they go in and they talk to the distributor about the status of our brand and the health and where the distribution opportunities are," said Allan Latts, the chief operating officer of Heaven Hill Distilleries in Louisville, which makes Elijah Craig bourbon. To thrive in today's marketplace in an industry that celebrates its traditions, Latts said, "you need to be analytical and know how to use data to make decisions. And you have to understand the full business, not just what you're doing but what impact your job has on the overall organization."

In 2014, five years into Shattock's tenure, Suntory approached him with a surprise offer to purchase Beam Inc. for $16 billion, aiming to create a global powerhouse. Like Beam, it had a deep and illustrious history. Shinjiro Torii, considered the father of Japanese whiskey, had founded the company in 1899; it was his grandson, Nobutada "Gary" Saji, who drove the acquisition. Beam would be its beachhead in the United States and give it a broader suite of products that would allow it to go toe-to-toe more easily with the spirits giants Diageo (based in London, with brands including Johnnie Walker and Crown Royal) and Pernod Ricard (based in Paris, with products including Absolut and Jameson). The early returns are good: among the direct benefits from the combination, sales of Jim Beam in Japan rose from 320,000 bottles premerger to around 8 million in 2018,[9] and millions of dollars were being invested in increasing the supply of Kentucky bourbon to match a forecast rise in global demand.

There was no way that a young Matt Shattock could have known what he was studying for when he put on overalls and asked a lot of questions about how a factory that makes frozen meat products works, or boned up on the finances behind selling fish sticks, or developed a turnaround strategy for a candy company. He would become CEO of a company that makes products with considerably more brand resonance, more deeply tied to their consumers' identities, and perform with great effectiveness. But he couldn't have done it without using each of those career stepping-stones to become a Pareto-optimal executive—learning how sales, marketing and branding, factory operations, product development, and finance all fit together.

The people we've seen so far—from moviemakers to aerospace engineers to people who lead a massive bourbon company—have arrived at their Pareto optimality through different career paths. Some have spent most of their working life at one place, like Henrik Green of Volvo and Josh Mook of GE. Others have hopped around frequently, like Bill Zerella. It's well and good to say that we all need to become Pareto-optimal employees in our field to succeed in the modern economy. It's a whole different thing to turn that general advice into something actionable given the unique circumstances of each industry.

There may be no truly one-size-fits-all advice. But as I dove deeper into the evidence about who succeeds in different business environments and why, things started to become more clear. Two executives from two iconic global companies—and a ten-year-old boy's soccer game—provide some answers.

3

The Power of Mindset

THE CAREER LATTICE AND MAKING
YOURSELF PARETO OPTIMAL

When Jennifer Merluzzi graduated from college in the mid-1990s, she, like so many other people, was unsure about what she wanted to do with her life. Initially she'd planned to become a lawyer—until a couple of years as a paralegal showed her that the day-to-day of a legal career bore little resemblance to a courtroom drama on television. She pivoted and instead got an MBA, then became a manager at an industrial supply company in small-town Elmhurst, Illinois, where she tried to move a warehouse and a call center into the digital age, with mixed success. She next went into consulting, advising major companies on strategy. The common thread she learned in all those jobs was that changing an organization, even in the face of existential threats, is very, very hard. She soon decided she'd make studying that challenge her life's work. She enrolled at the University of Chicago's Booth

School of Business, studying for a doctorate in a program called Organizations and Markets, essentially economic sociology.

She and a colleague, Damon Phillips, soon started talking about a paradox they had noticed among the students studying for an MBA at the school. Most students at Booth come with a few years of experience in the working world, and in surveys taken before they started classes the vast majority said they wanted to use business school to change their career direction. Yet once they arrived, many of these students seemed to double down on fields where they already had a strong background: students who had previously worked in banking focused yet more on finance; former brand managers studied marketing; former strategy consultants lapped up strategy classes. Career-advice books offered details of how to go in the weeds of one field. Would-be bankers might be told to read *The Wall Street Journal* every day, study finance texts, master financial formulas, and learn about the cultural differences between this Wall Street firm and that one. When it was time to choose classes, they would tend to take all the financial modeling courses they could, to the detriment of other areas.

The trouble was that this focus on specialization didn't really align with what recruiters on campus said they wanted. "When we spoke informally to business people who hired our students, they saw through the specialization and downgraded it," Merluzzi said. Their comments, as she paraphrased them, were along the lines of "I'd much rather hire someone who did not spend all their time on one thing in the MBA program—that's a total waste. For one, I'd rather have someone who can show accomplishment in many areas. That shows talent and adaptability. And secondly, let's face it, whatever finance expertise they learn in an MBA program—even a top one—we are going to retrain them on our way of doing things anyway." They were looking, in other words, for a track record that looked a little bit more like Merluzzi's— maybe a little wandering and unfocused at first glance, but reflecting a keen intelligence, curiosity, hard work, and adaptability.

Merluzzi and Phillips wanted to figure out which approach was more rewarded by the marketplace: the specialization students actually embraced or the varied experience recruiters said they valued. To do so, they'd need to draw from people who had demonstrated broadly similar levels of intelligence and accomplishment (prior to business school), to ensure that they weren't just picking up differences in underlying levels of talent or drive. Second, they needed people who were going into a structured corporate setting in which there were clear measures of success. This would ensure that their data would be able to distinguish which group—the generalists or the specialists—was truly being rewarded by the marketplace. The data, it turned out, was right under their noses. Graduates of an elite MBA program who go to Wall Street investment banks fit the bill on both fronts. By getting admitted to a top business school, they have cleared a high bar of ability, and in banking there are fairly uniform measures of success like number of job offers, salary, and bonus size.

Merluzzi and Phillips obtained data on graduates of the MBA classes of 2008 and 2009 at an elite business school who went into banking. They coded the young bankers based on their pre-business-school experience and internship choices, and controlled for such factors as the candidates' grades, their standardized test scores, and whether they had attended an elite undergraduate college. When they'd finished this work and crunched the numbers, the results were striking: those with no previous exposure to investment banking and finance were more than twice as likely to receive more than one job offer as those with extensive experience in the field.[1]

Moreover, the starting median bonus for those with a past focus on investment banking was $64,438—which is 26 percent less than the $87,402 median bonus among those with no exposure to the field. The anecdotes from recruiters about their desire to hire creative, adaptable generalists rather than hard-core finance specialists seemed to tell the more accurate story.

This doesn't necessarily mean it's best to be a generalist at all times and in all fields. It is easy to find evidence, and anecdotes, to support the value of deep knowledge and specialization in different circumstances. If I ever need major surgery, or am on trial for a crime, you'd better believe I will want a surgeon who's spent a lifetime practicing that exact procedure, or a lawyer with a deep specialization in criminal defense, respectively. But I do take it to be a piece of evidence that generalists—people who are Pareto optimal at multiple types of functions, who act as the good kind of glue people within their organization—are in the shortest supply and hardest for companies to find (and hence, in Merluzzi's study, were most handsomely rewarded).

So how do you actually mold yourself into such a person?

When I interviewed Merluzzi in 2017, she had joined the faculty of George Washington University's business school and was living in the suburbs of Washington, DC. Her twin son and daughter, she explained, were both good athletes for their age, her son at soccer and baseball, her daughter at swimming and gymnastics. But there was a problem, Merluzzi told me. They were under pressure from coaches to specialize in one or the other.

Her son had an offer to join a traveling baseball team, which would mean playing against top players from the region rather than just other neighborhood kids—but the coach withdrew the offer "due to his dual commitments," the email said, meaning the boy wanted to keep playing soccer as well. The long hours her daughter needed to dedicate to swimming practice to stay competitive were such that she would have to give up gymnastics. The message from these coaches was clear: success required Merluzzi's children to focus all their energies on only one sport. "It's this pressure to collect more and more specialized experiences in this sort of arms race to show how dedicated you are and keep up with the competition," Merluzzi said. "It's like the baseline keeps going up and up and that leads people into this narrower and narrower path toward continual specialization, which shuts out all other possibilities."

When Merluzzi told me about this, the twins were ten years old.

This tendency to push talented American children to specialize in a sport has much-chronicled downsides. For athletic activity involving repetitive motion, like pitching a baseball or swinging a tennis racket, year-round play means a higher likelihood of serious injury.[2] Perhaps more pernicious, an overwhelming focus on one sport can cause psychological stress, making young people tie their self-worth to their ability to kick a ball or shoot a basket. They may be more likely to quit playing the sport altogether, even if it once brought them joy. Paradoxically, the best pathway for young people to become well-adjusted, injury-free adults who enjoy athletic pursuits may be to limit the share of their time they spend playing any one sport, no matter how good they are at it.

That's true about specialization in a business career, too. At every step of the way, it looks like the sensible choice to strengthen intellectual or managerial or technical muscles that are already strong. And, of course, the world needs specialists with the knowledge to do hard things. But the lesson from the research on the surprising payoffs of being a generalist is that in the long run, it frequently pays to focus on building the muscles that are weak instead of those that are already strong.

Essentially, the pathway to becoming a Pareto-optimal worker is overcoming one of the most natural inclinations in the world—to keep doing the things that you're really good at. At the same time, if you take that advice too expansively, you won't end up being good at anything. For Merluzzi's kids, the goal is to play soccer and do gymnastics enough to fully develop whatever gifts they may have, while mixing things up enough to ensure they're trying new things and exercising new muscles, figurative and literal, all the time.

It's a tough challenge when what you're juggling is a ten-year-old's sports schedule. Figuring out the same thing in a career context can seem downright impossible. But Omer Ismail's story helped me understand what it looks like when you do it successfully.

AN ACCIDENTAL BANKER ON THE NEW WALL STREET

Ismail grew up in Karachi, Pakistan, where he attended a British-run school, before coming to a cold rural corner of New Hampshire for college. As he reached his senior year at Dartmouth, he wasn't sure what career he wanted but did know he wanted to stay in the United States. He asked the career services office which employers were willing to sponsor work visas for fresh-out-of-college young employees. There were basically two options, he was told: the big consulting firms and the big Wall Street banks. Ismail interviewed with both. He recalls one big consulting firm asking him how many cars could fit on a football field; that kind of brain-teaser was ridiculous, he thought. Things went better on Wall Street.

Ismail was a government major and hadn't taken courses in finance or done an internship in banking. But he had excellent grades, was good at math, and had even had a little business experience as president of the Dartmouth college paper, overseeing advertising sales and budgeting. That experience was enough to snag him an offer to become an entry-level analyst at Goldman Sachs, then and now the most elite of the large Wall Street investment banks.

Ismail initially felt out of his depth among the incoming analysts, most of whom had the internships and coursework that he lacked. During the six-week training program, when most of his counterparts enjoyed social activities in the evenings, he consistently put in another three hours or so to try to catch up on the financial modeling and analysis that his bosses would expect of him on Day 1. He joined the bank in the fall of 2002, assigned to a group that provided investment banking services for the telecommunications, media, and technology industries—against the backdrop of an economic downturn that was eviscerating those very industries and causing a collapse in the mergers and acquisitions that are an investment banker's reason for being. Within a few months of his start date, a layoff ended the Goldman careers of about half of the people in the group (newly hired analysts like Is-mail were spared).

In the fourteen years that followed that inauspicious beginning, Ismail rose to become a partner at Goldman Sachs; most of his analyst class is long gone. When I spoke with him, he was leading one of the firm's audacious attempts to spread into areas in which it historically had no role, part of its adaptation to the new world of finance in the aftermath of the 2008 financial crisis. He did it by becoming a Pareto-optimal executive—by combining an understanding of financial analysis, strategy, risk management, regulatory compliance, digital technology, and consumer marketing (with varying levels of expertise at each) to be an effective leader. And he did so inside an institution that dates to 1869 but has arguably changed more during Ismail's time there than in any other similar window.

The shifts at Goldman Sachs over the last generation are em-blematic of those that have transformed the business world more generally. The scale and complexity of the firm have expanded: it had 13,000 employees and a $230 billion balance sheet when it filed to go public in 1999; in 2016 those numbers were 37,000 and $917 billion.[3] It is competing in an industry that is more concentrated among a small number of winners: before the 2008 crisis, Goldman Sachs was one of five major Wall Street investment banks,[4] a number now down to two. Even as the traditional financial industry becomes consolidated within megabanks, those players face novel challenges from upstart financial technology firms. The industry has also become more global, with those Wall Street institutions clawing for business against rivals based in London, Frankfurt, Hong Kong, and beyond. And what once was a business built mainly on relationships between bankers and clients is more and more a competition for the best asset-pricing algorithms or the best platform to execute trades efficiently.

Goldman has retained hints of the genteel structure of the old Wall Street. Its internal hierarchy is rigid enough that its thousands of financial professionals have only a handful of titles: analyst, associate, vice president, managing director, partner.[5] But change is evident. Perhaps most notably, it is not just hiring polished, suit-wearing finance obsessives from Ivy League schools but also scouring more technically oriented schools for talented software engineers with backgrounds in computer science, theoretical mathematics, even physics. More superficially, both Ismail and the public relations official who sat in on our conversation at Goldman's Lower Manhattan headquarters were wearing jeans instead of a suit.[6]

In the old model of Wall Street, someone who started as a junior telecom investment banker might want nothing more than to climb through the hierarchy toward partner, becoming more and more deeply networked within the industry, a trusted adviser (and golfing buddy) to CEOs who might reward the firm with valuable commissions on megamergers. That pattern hasn't disappeared entirely, but many of the people who thrive at Goldman Sachs today find that they must take a more peripatetic career journey.

After three years in investment banking, Ismail went to business school, then returned to Goldman—not as a somewhat-more-senior investment banker but to work in one of the firm's private equity funds. Ismail hungered to try something new. "I am a little bit impatient by nature," he said. "I operate well under a healthy level of anxiety and have a constant need to prove to myself that I can do something different." He asked to focus on debt investing, looking for opportunities in acquiring big blocks of corporate debt that was misvalued by the market. "I thought it was going to be a more interesting learning experience, so that's what I did," he said. "Most people at the time really questioned my judgment around doing that."

Many of his peers, to use the metaphor of Merluzzi's young son, wanted him to keep getting better at soccer when he really wanted to try tennis.

It worked out. Ismail learned a great deal about how things worked in different industries, and debt investing became a particularly hot area during the 2008–9 financial crisis, when bonds of risky companies traded at deep discounts, and picking the right distressed debt to buy could achieve huge gains. In 2012, Ismail pivoted again; he saw intriguing opportunities in the US health care industry being created by the implementation of President Obama's Affordable Care Act and set out to identify targets for private equity investment that were likely to be winners.

To someone outside the financial industry, Ismail's various jobs might look similar; all basically involved building financial models and negotiating huge transactions. But by the standards of Wall Street, they were very different. At each step, Ismail was learning new industries and entirely new ways of thinking about business challenges—how a hospital can adapt its business model as policies on insurance reimbursement shift, for example, or how a regional sports network can rework its economics when "cord cutters" cease subscribing to cable service.

His managers recall the latter deal as particularly illustrative of Ismail's ability to stretch into new areas. Goldman held a stake in the YES Network, the venture that controlled the broadcasting rights of New York Yankees games. Ismail helped manage this investment as a young up-and-comer in the private equity unit.

"Most people at that stage of their career would have been all over hitting the numbers, renewing contracts, and making sure the operating performance was tracking the budget," said Richard Friedman, head of Goldman's merchant banking division. "He went further to understand where the business was going, where the market and technology was going, and how the market might change. Around here, we use words like 'range.' Omer was rangier. He had more of an ability to see the whole picture and how the pieces fit together." Rupert Murdoch's 21st Century Fox ultimately purchased the property in a 2014 deal that valued it at $3.9 billion.[7]

Although he navigated these career steps within a prestigious investment bank, all of his moves involved a certain amount of career risk. Instead of taking on more seniority and responsibility in a given area in which he'd proven himself, he tried something new in order to learn something different.

"The ability to take the fourth risk felt a little bit better than when I took the first risk," Ismail said. "Could somebody start as a mergers and acquisition banker and twenty years later become a really expert M&A banker? Absolutely. But I think that for me personally, the feeling of being uncomfortable has been really valuable."

His most dramatic move was yet to come, though. In the summer of 2014, Gary Cohn, then the president of Goldman Sachs, convened a group of senior executives at his weekend home in the Hamptons to plot the company's future as it tried to emerge from the long shadow of the financial crisis. In 2008, Goldman had changed its legal structure to become a "bank holding company," which gave it greater access to a government backstop. Six years later, however, it still didn't do much of what an ordinary civilian would recognize as banking—taking deposits and making loans. It remained very much a Wall Street firm engaged in the workings of high finance. But what if there were an opportunity in lending to ordinary people and smaller enterprises, Cohn and the chief executive, Lloyd Blankfein, wondered. They asked Friedman, the merchant banking chief, to assemble a team to investigate the possibility. Ismail, having impressed Friedman with his range and his ability to see the big picture, got the call.

Ismail led a small team that vetted some options, seeking out corners of the banking marketplace that the existing commercial banks served poorly yet were big enough to be worth Goldman's time. They concluded that there was indeed an opportunity to get into the business of taking consumer deposits and making consumer loans— without the costly physical bank branches of traditional banks, but with the credibility and technical know-how Goldman had at its disposal. After much debate, the company named the unit Marcus, for the German financier who founded the firm in the 1800s, Marcus Goldman. In building the team to run it, Friedman recalled, he told

Ismail he had a lucrative, safe option waiting for him back in the health care investing team if he wanted to take it.

Instead, after a career advising on mergers and acquisitions, managing a sports media investment, and choosing which distressed debt or health care companies to bet on, suddenly Ismail was becoming an operational executive of a consumer-focused bank. In his role as chief operating officer, he was part of a rapidly assembled team that, in about 18 months, built an online-only consumer bank scaled to its parent megafirm and able to meet the regulatory requirements that came along with operating as part of one of the world's biggest financial institutions. It was a tremendous adjustment from merely picking investments, as in his earlier jobs.

"In the world of investment banking or merchant banking, you oversee people whose job you know how to do," Ismail said. "If my analyst or my associate was out of pocket and I really had to dig into the model, I could figure out how to do it because I've done it before. In an operating job, you have to learn to oversee people whose jobs you don't know how to do." Ismail had never been a credit risk manager, or built a consumer-facing website or mobile app, but he was hiring and overseeing the work of people who could do all that. The key to his job, he found, was approaching each function with eagerness to help specialists focus in on the crucial questions. "Our chief technology officer will come to me with a couple of choices, and it's a deeply technical, complicated issue, what cloud provider has better load-balancing capabilities, for example. My job is to push to understand, 'OK, if I go with Option A or Option B, what are the implications for our business and our customers? And if we take a shortcut here, what implications does that have down the road?' Every day was making countless choices like that. When hiring a new deputy for the head of product, do you go with a candidate with great vision or more focused on execution and details? Do you keep all operations in one place in New York or set up teams in lower-cost locations like Dallas, or even Bangalore?"

Marcus emerged as a small but fast-growing part of Goldman Sachs; it had $208 million in loans outstanding at the end of 2016, $1.9 billion at year-end 2017, and $3.1 billion in mid-2018. And on November 9, 2016, when Goldman Sachs announced its list of new partners, those men and women who had made it to the top of the venerable firm's hierarchy, Omer Ismail's name was on it. He is gifted with a natural intelligence and worked very hard, of course. But it was his willingness to push himself into areas of discomfort that made his rise in the firm possible.

THE CAREER LATTICE, TOURS OF DUTY, AND THE GROWTH MINDSET

Is it possible to turn what came naturally to Ismail into a strategy that anyone can follow in navigating a career? There is no shortage of ideas, frameworks, and models coming from the people who think about career paths for a living.

For example, consider the old idea of a career ladder. It's a wonderfully simple if outdated idea. You emerge from your education and begin working in your chosen field in some junior role. You gain a little more experience, are trusted with more complicated projects, and then climb a rung and have a slightly more impressive title and get paid a little more. A few years later, you repeat the process. If you keep your nose clean and get better and better at doing that one thing, a fine career awaits you, culminating with a lovely retirement ceremony and a healthy pension. This works best in organizations where the hierarchy is both stable and linear.

As we have seen in several companies, that pathway is no longer available for most people: companies change too quickly; jobs disappear or become all but unrecognizable. That's where the "career lattice" comes in. I was able to find a use of the term as far back as 1966,[8] and it has received book-length treatment more recently.[9] Still, internet searches for "career ladder" are about twelve times more common than those for "career lattice," suggesting that the one-dimensional version of how to think about a career is still the most common one, realities of the modern labor market be damned.

In fact, a modern career involves not just upward moves toward greater responsibility within a single functional specialty but lateral or even downward moves across functions that enable a steeper ascent later. Here's a simple illustration of a person's hypothetical lattice compared with a conventional career ladder. (Of course, the exact job titles used, and how they correspond with years of experience, vary a lot by company and industry.)

This, in other words, is a visual illustration of the career of someone

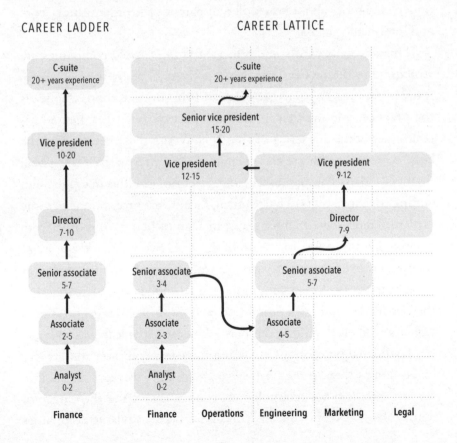

gradually becoming a Pareto-optimal executive. Sheryl Sandberg has suggested that a "career jungle gym" is a better metaphor—perhaps you could think of the third dimension as the type of firm (big established company, startup, professional services company, etc.).[10]

Whether you prefer a lattice or a jungle gym, lateral moves, or even moves slightly downward, are not merely acceptable but often *crucial* to getting to where you want to be. Think of it this way: it will be exceedingly rare for an employer to simultaneously offer you a promotion to a higher rank *and* a move into a functional specialty where you are unproven. Typically, the choice is one or the other—either a promotion to greater responsibility in a function where you have proven ability, or a lateral (or even downward) move to an area where you are unproven but where you have the opportunity to grow and understand more about how different parts of the organization work and intersect.[11]

This dovetails with some other shifts in how big companies are structured in the modern age, such as those done by the human resources group at the Gartner research firm. Brian Kropp, who leads the practice, told me that in the early part of the 2010s, he and his colleagues noticed a series of trends converging as they studied the large companies that are their clients. In the aftermath of the global financial crisis, companies cut out layers of middle management, aiming to reduce costs. That, in turn, meant that promotions became rarer and represented larger leaps: instead of being promoted from running a team of five to a team of ten after two years, a rising manager might have to wait five years but would jump from five employees straight to thirty. As a result, more people were getting frustrated as they went years without a promotion, and those who did get promoted were more likely to fail in their new job because the leap was so large.

Traditional promotions are going to be less common and involve bigger jumps than in the past *even while* younger workers are hungry for advancement *and* technological change is shifting the nature of many jobs. So Kropp and his colleagues began advising companies that in response to this reality, they can offer advancement in the form of more varied experiences that will make young workers more adaptable to a changing economy.

"As an employee," Kropp said, "you have to think about 'What do I need to get on my résumé in order to be promoted at some point in the future?' rather than 'What task do I need to achieve this quarter to get promoted now?' You can't be thinking about your job anymore as just 'How do I have a career in this company?' You have to be thinking about, and this sounds incredibly mercenary, but you have to be thinking about 'How do I get promoted at any company? And what are the skill sets that are going to help me be successful no matter where my career leads?'"

For an idea of how to do that, we can borrow a concept from the military and diplomatic worlds. When a country sends soldiers to fight in a faraway land, or diplomats to represent its interests, it's typically for a predetermined duration, after which another assignment might await. This concept of a "tour of duty" is being seen more and more in discussion of careers in the corporate world. For this, we can thank Reid Hoffman.

Hoffman, the founder of LinkedIn, is now a venture capitalist at Greylock Partners. In a series of books and articles about careers and talent management in the digital age,[12] he argues that the tour-of-duty model is often the best approach to navigating a career in the twenty-first-century corporate world. In Hoffman's view, the traditional model of what it means to have a job involves a lot of mutual lying. Employers *pretend* when they offer you a job that they expect you to stay at the company indefinitely. Employees *pretend* that they have every intention of doing so. In truth, most of us on both sides know that situations can change in unforeseeable ways on both sides of the equation. This fuels dissatisfaction. Everybody knows that the employer will lay people off if business tanks or their skills are no longer needed. Everybody knows that an employee will quit if a better offer comes along. Instead of living in this fantasy land in which both sides pretend the employment relationship is permanent, companies and their workers will both be better off with a more honest accounting of the relationship. In the best case, Hoffman believes, "the employer says, 'If you make us more valuable, we'll make *you* more valuable.' The employee says, 'If you help me grow and flourish, I'll help the company grow and flourish.'"

That is part of why, starting in the early days of LinkedIn, Hoffman worked out explicit tour-of-duty arrangements with some employees, generally two to four years. The agreement, of course, didn't preclude the person from staying at the company for many years; it simply created an understanding that the employee was coming in for X purpose, and that after a few years both sides would reevaluate the best way to help the company develop and help the employee advance. Sometimes a tour would end with the employee taking on a new project; other times, with a firm handshake and best wishes.

You can see echoes of this approach in other places. Investment banks and consulting firms hire recent college graduates for a job in a two-year analyst program—essentially creating an environment where moving on after a couple of years is expected rather than stigmatized. Big conglomerates have traditionally made management training through a series of tours a core part of their strategy; at General Electric, for example, a rising executive might spend three years with the locomotives division in India, followed by three years in the health care division in Brazil, then another two years in corporate strategy at the Boston headquarters. (In contrast to Hoffman's purer version of the tour-of-duty concept, those arrangements for promising executives tend to be premised on the idea that the person will stay with the company indefinitely, through multiple tours.)

Hoffman's analysis of the realities of the modern workplace is powerful, and his proposed solutions compelling. To have a job, at least in the twenty-first-century economy, is more akin to dating someone than to a (high-quality) marriage. It might be good, or even great. It might last a year, or many. But the expectation has to be that it will end, and the employer and the employee should be clearheaded about what they're getting out of it. For people who seek to be Pareto-optimal executives, that something is usually going to be the kind of broadening of experience that will enable them to take on the next thing.

A corollary of Hoffman's "tour of duty" is what I think of as a "three-year itch." The first year doing a job, you're just learning your way around. The second year, you're starting to make change happen and coming into your own in the new role. The third year, you're beginning to see the payoffs of that work and to get *comfortable*. At that point you have a choice—you can enjoy the comfort, and perhaps seek to continue to improve at your present job, though surely with diminishing returns. Or you can seek discomfort—pushing for new experiences, and the growth that tends to come with them.

That certainly describes Omer Ismail. At juncture after juncture, when he had a choice between sticking with a job at which he was already proven or pushing himself to try something new and uncomfortable, he chose the latter. The act of moving into unfamiliar situations over and over was its own form of training. "I think on some level I just never want to be too comfortable," Ismail said.

WHY MINDSET MATTERS

The narrow career advice that emerges from all this data and anecdote is straightforward: try to get really good at multiple things, in a combination that will be valued by the marketplace, so that you can work well on teams with all kinds of different specialists.

But the real advice is bigger and simpler than that: cultivate in yourself a sense of open-mindedness, in which you hunger to try new things. Aim to be comfortable with discomfort.

Carol Dweck, the Stanford University psychologist, wrote in her 2006 book *Mindset* of the importance of a "growth mindset," which she contrasts with a "fixed mindset." It is a concept that came up in more than a few of my interviews with senior executives more than a decade later. In effect, what I saw over and over was that this growth mindset was a necessary precondition for the people who would go on to acquire the specific mixes of skills that have enabled them to thrive in the modern corporate world. It's Dweck's growth mindset that *results* in a person having a three-year itch whenever they're getting too comfortable in a job, which *causes* them to think of their career as a series of tours of duty, which *enables* them to navigate a career lattice with a lot of lateral moves, which *turns them into* a Pareto-optimal employee.

Which raises the crucial question of whether we can mold ourselves into this type of person, and hence have this type of career. Of course, everyone is born with different natural abilities and is raised in different circumstances. But we all have to push ourselves in ways that aren't necessarily natural for us; we all study subjects in school or try experiences in the professional world that are outside our comfort zone. An athlete might spend one workout focused on developing strength in shoulders and arms, another on abdominals, a third on legs—but the modern athlete who wants to excel will likely also work on flexibility, through stretches or yoga. The key to cultivating the growth mindset that allows a person to become a Pareto-optimal worker is thinking of this kind of varied experience.

This mindset isn't a single line on a résumé. It is the itch that forces us to take stock every few years and try something new, even when no boss is forcing the issue. There are all kinds of ways to do that in phases of life when the risk isn't as great as it will be later. Every time a college English major signs up for a hard course in econometrics, or a shy computer scientist tries the debate club to work on their communication skills, or an aspiring chemist decides to write for the college newspaper, people are exercising those discomfort muscles.

In the early years of a professional career, there are often similar opportunities with low stakes, or at least low compared to what they will be when you're more senior. An executive asks for help on a special project; a committee is forming to oversee the internship program; the sales team asks if someone from engineering can come along on a client visit.

In all these examples, it's not just the literal breadth of experience you're getting by trying new things and moving horizontally on the lattice. It's the *act* of moving into unfamiliar areas that is its own form of training.

THE LILY PAD STRATEGY

In working on this book, I visited a number of accomplished people and asked them all the same question: What advice do you give to the younger executives you mentor, or to your own family members? One of those people was Steve Case, who made a billion-dollar fortune as chief executive of America Online during its heyday, and in the years since has put that fortune to work as a venture capitalist and philanthropist. In his elegant wood-paneled office overlooking the Dupont Circle neighborhood of Washington, DC, Case said a lot of things consistent with what you've read in this book so far. "The mentality in the next wave is going to be much more one of having multiple chapters in your life and multiple subplots within each chapter," he said. "My dad had one job for his career. That clearly isn't happening anymore. Knowing a little bit about a lot of things and being able to connect the dots is an increasingly important skill." He particularly believes that the next wave of great business success stories will involve merging cutting-edge digital technologies with industries that are hugely important but not at the forefront of putting those technologies to use, like health care, education, and agriculture. That, in turn, will require executives who aren't merely looking to build an easy-to-use app but who understand the moving pieces of software and computing technology, regulatory processes, and the mechanics of how doctors, teachers, and farmers actually work.[13]

As I kept pushing Case to articulate how ambitious people should put those observations to work in planning their careers, I could sense that he felt I was too fixated on trying to arrive at some one-size-fits-all advice.

"The idea is not that there is some pathway everyone should follow," Case said. "It's more like a series of lily pads. Each step leads to the next step, and it's not clear as you take those leaps where each one is leading, or even if it is leading somewhere in particular. The people who ultimately thrive don't just have a raw talent in terms of intellect and hard work. They supplement that with a curiosity and hunger. They want to take on some new sector and become an expert in it. They develop great networks and people skills. Every day they try to learn something new."

As I interpret this, Case was saying there's a risk in taking these ideas around being a Pareto-optimal glue person with a growth mindset the wrong way—as a kind of paint-by-numbers guide to becoming the sort of person who will thrive in the messy world of twenty-first-century business. Essentially, Case was preaching the virtues of developing an approach to learning and experience that allows a person to jump to wherever the next promising lily pad might be, to backtrack as necessary, to move forward without necessarily knowing exactly where it's leading.

This idea seemed powerful. A couple of months later, I saw how it can work in practice, when I flew to Bentonville, Arkansas, and met Daniel Eckert.

At the time, Eckert, with his compact frame, well-tailored shirt, and intense eyes, was the senior vice president of Walmart Services and Digital Acceleration in the United States, the part of the company that works on many of the technological aspects of the shopping experience. We met at the headquarters of a company that, depending on the price of oil in a given year, is either the biggest or second-biggest in the world by revenue.[14] If you are familiar with the frugal corporate culture of Walmart, it will not surprise you that despite Eckert's senior executive status, his office was a windowless room with cheap furniture in a converted warehouse.

Eckert told me about his convoluted path to Walmart. He grew up middle class in upstate New York, where he was a high school wrestler, then studied at the University of Michigan, where he found himself with a hunger for public service. He signed up to become an officer in the US Marine Corps, which led to a four-year run as a logistics officer that included service around the world. As he was about to complete his commitment to the military—his wife, whom he went long stretches without seeing, wanted a more conventional life—Eckert started studying up on what use his skills might have in the business world. "I have this logistics background, which I think will serve me in good stead commercially, but I don't know, because I've been dealing with C-130s [a giant military transport aircraft] and helicopter parts and things we do in the Marine Corps fleet. I'm wondering, 'How is this transferable? I don't know anything about business.'"

His final deployment with the marines was to Norway, where during his downtime he picked up a corporate finance textbook and studied a range of business concepts on his own. When he was back in the United States, he tapped every acquaintance he could think of in pursuit of a job, before ending up as one of the oldest members of the new analyst class at the strategy consulting firm now called Accenture. (Most of the new hires were fresh out of college, around age twenty-two, while he was a comparatively grizzled twenty-six; his colleagues jokingly called him "the Silverback.")

Eckert sometimes found himself in over his head. One of his first projects involved valuation of a French chemical company, and the financial statements were in French, a language he did not speak; he bought a French-English dictionary and translated the statements line by line. But he outworked his younger colleagues and was doing well—and then an old friend called to ask him if he wanted to work together on a business plan.

The idea involved a new type of securities instrument that, by combining some of the more appealing characteristics of both equity and debt, would make it easier for people to hedge risks. They presented their idea at a business plan competition and only came in eighth; nonetheless, they received an offer from a group of investors to fund the business.

At that point Eckert had been at Accenture for only nine months, but the opportunity to start something new was too compelling to turn down. He and his partner soon learned, however, that introducing a new kind of financial product involved more onerous legal hurdles than they'd realized. "When we came in, I thought I had this great idea and we just have to fill out a few pieces of paper and off we go," Eckert said. Instead, he recalled, as they met with law firms the reaction was along the lines of "Do you know how hard this is? This is going to be impossible." But they persevered, and finally seemed on the verge of success—or at least clearing regulatory hurdles—when the winds shifted: Accounting scandals at Enron, WorldCom, and other companies in 2001 made the regulatory climate much more hostile. As their money began to run out, they concluded that the best option was to shut down the company, which they did on the day after Christmas that year.

This was a terrible time to be looking for a job, in light of the technology sector bust. Eckert's only prospect was part-time contract work helping some friends conduct due diligence on a company that was developing a better way to process oily wastewater from steel fabrication plants. It wasn't much of a job—but it allowed him to feed himself and be out in the marketplace.

By now, he was nearing age thirty, and his career path could be charitably called a disaster. Four years as a US Marines logistics officer, nine months as a strategy consultant, cofounder of a failed startup, and a few months doing something or other involving oily water: this is not the kind of résumé anyone would look at and say, "That's the guy I want to hire."

So when Jeff, his old boss from Accenture, called and offered him work at Chicago-based Bank One, then being led by an ambitious banker named Jamie Dimon, Eckert jumped at the chance. His job was part of what is often thought of as the boring part of banking, known as "treasury services"—making sure checks clear as they are supposed to, and helping big companies with the mechanics of cash flow. "I said, 'Oh, Jeff, did you just put me in the basement of the bank? Am I in the bowels of the organization? I'm never going to see the light of day.' Jeff said, 'Trust me on this one. I think there are some really interesting opportunities shaping up in this market.'"

Jeff was right. It was at this time that people were starting to turn away from paper checks and toward electronic payments. Tech companies recognized a potential payday in inserting themselves in the middle of the process, creating things like a Yahoo bill-paying service. The insight that emerged from Eckert's group at Bank One—and then JPMorgan Chase after Dimon engineered a merger in 2004— was that banks were actually better positioned than third-party firms to make online bill paying accessible and efficient. In fact, this would become a key competitive advantage for banks as more people worldwide started using broadband internet. Eckert's group would go on to build the digital infrastructure that allowed millions of Americans to pay their credit card and auto loan bills online. Eckert then moved on to HSBC, the global bank based in London, where he spent five years building a business in the United States with branded credit and debit cards.

At long last, Eckert had a more conventional résumé and career path—he had accumulated big-time experience and responsibility building innovative payment systems within giant banks. After his early years flailing around, he now had a track record as someone who could get hard things done at the intersection of digital technology and financial transactions, all in the context of a highly regulated, complex organization. He jumped across a series of lily pads, not always with a clear vision of where he was going, but ended up on the other side with a varied set of experiences across technology, finance, and regulatory compliance. He had become a Pareto-optimal executive, not by ticking off boxes or logging lots of years of experience, but by being open-minded about following opportunity wherever it arose.

That's when Walmart called.

Actually, the Walmart recruiter called three times before Eckert bit. He took a job in the company's financial services unit, focusing on its private-label credit and debit cards and building the division's fledgling e-commerce capabilities. But a bigger challenge arrived at his doorstep two weeks before Christmas in 2014, when the company's chief financial officer called Eckert with the type of request that, when it comes from the CFO, is really more of an order. "We're thinking about all the ways that digital could improve the shopping experience, and one of those experiences is checkout," Eckert recalls being told. "We're not quite sure how Apple Pay or Google Wallet or all these things might play out, but it seems like there's a way we might improve our checkout experience through payments. Could you do some thinking about it?"

Of course, Eckert agreed to take it on. Then the CFO added, before he hung up, "Oh, and we've got a board meeting in February, so maybe a white paper, six to ten pages, would be helpful."

It may seem odd to think of a company with 2.3 million employees and annual sales of half a trillion dollars—equivalent to the GDP of Poland—as an endangered upstart, but in certain ways that's where Walmart was in 2015. For all its scale, the company significantly lagged behind Amazon in digital commerce; Walmart was playing catch-up in any kind of commerce that didn't involve people coming into a store and picking goods up off a shelf. For years, the company had been focused on cutting costs, at a time when Amazon and other innovative rivals were investing heavily to make it as easy as possible to buy things online.

An innovative payment system using mobile devices, Eckert argued, would be a crucial part of Walmart's counterattack. It would introduce the company's mobile shopping app to millions of customers who thought of Walmart only as a physical store. It came as the company was embracing more fully than it had before the idea of "multichannel" or "omnichannel" sales—a world where people might buy goods online and either pick them up or return them in a store, or browse in a store and order an item on their phone to have it shipped straight to their house. Instead of being one on each side of a bright line, in-store sales and online sales were becoming part of a blurry mix, and Walmart's infrastructure in 2015 was not yet ready for it.

Meanwhile, more and more consumers were looking to use their mobile phones to make purchases, and a whole suite of companies from finance, technology, and beyond were introducing new products aiming to put themselves at the center of those transactions. To Walmart, that was a threat, creating a risk that it would lose control over its direct relationship with consumers. Walmart would rather not have Apple or Google standing between it and its hard-won customers, after all, and the ability to collect troves of data about its customers is a big part of Amazon's competitive advantage—one Walmart would rather not cede.

Eckert argued for creating what would eventually be called Walmart Pay, a mobile app—and the back-office systems to make it work—that would essentially serve as the glue connecting the different ways people might buy goods from Walmart, channeling transactions that take place online and in stores into one purchase history, connected to the consumer's credit card or bank account. It would make it easy for customers to return products or save receipt details. It could be a crucial piece of the company's broader digital strategy, which would eventually aim to let people use their Walmart app to wire money to family members far away or pick up prescriptions in Walmart's pharmacies. In a not-too-distant future when consumers might simply walk out of a store with a full basket and be automatically charged for their purchases, an app that the company itself controlled would prove crucial to making the process seamless.

About a month went by, and Eckert returned to his day job. Then he got a call from the CEO, Doug McMillon. "OK," McMillon said. "We're thinking that you could have an early prototype by August." Eckert's jaw dropped. He had sketched out a strategy for more frictionless checkout, but he didn't have any resources or staff to actually build the thing. "I'm actually not sure how we can make that happen," Eckert recalls saying. McMillon responded, "I still want you to target August for a working prototype."

They code-named the project CHICO, short for check-in-to-check-out. He quickly assembled a team composed of technologists who worked on the point-of-sales systems in the stores and the Walmart mobile app; teams from California, India, and Arkansas that had never worked together in the past were flung together. Add in some experts in creating intuitive user experiences in mobile apps, lawyers versed in the thorny legal and regulatory questions around privacy and data security, operations teams that would figure out how to teach the systems to 1.2 million Walmart store employees, and staff with deep understanding of payment systems and fraud prevention, and you had quite a large team—a 330-person task force, with 40 on the core team.

There were many possibilities of what failure could look like. Not delivering a working payments app would be one version of failure— but another would be delivering one so poorly designed that customers didn't use it. Yet another would be delivering a widely used app but allowing a data breach that could cause the company massive embarrassment and billions of dollars in losses. The old Facebook slogan of "move fast, break things" isn't particularly useful when you are a company the size of Walmart.

It's worth pausing for a moment to observe what a different way of working this was for a company where people spent decades climbing a traditional corporate ladder, trying to get a higher foothold in a rigid hierarchy. Instead, Eckert was being asked to take on a major project that was integral to the long-term strategy of the biggest company in the world. His title didn't change—he was still nominally in charge of the business offering cheap money-wiring services. Most of the people assigned to the project did not work for him in any formal, chain-of-command sense. Indeed, he was pulling in people from completely different arms of the corporate structure, many of whom had never even met before. The mission, coming from the board and the C-suite of the company, was straightforward: get this done.

The forty core team members assembled in Bentonville during the summer of 2015. They slogged through working lunches during twelve-hour days, dividing into smaller teams to attack different parts of the challenge. The drab office space in the corporate headquarters that they took over was quickly filled with whiteboards, which were soon covered with flowcharts and formulas and fragments of code as the teams seized the opportunity to collaborate face-to-face and worked furiously together for several weeks, before returning to California and India to continue pushing on their own.

Eckert is not himself a software engineer; the closest he came to being a coder was dabbling with Lotus database software while serving in the marines in the 1990s. A colleague named Brad Keefe was the chief architect of the app. What Eckert did have was an uncanny ability to keep everyone on the project pointed in the same direction and to break bottlenecks when they arose—whether it was conflicts between different engineering teams or bureaucratic constraints elsewhere in an organization so massive that the corporate headquarters alone employed nearly 17,000 people. His job was to understand the intersection between the technological challenges and the broader business goals of the organization, and keep the engineering work on track. It meant showing respect to the technologists and understanding their work even though he wasn't capable of doing it himself, resolving hard-fought disputes over questions like whether Walmart employees or customers would scan QR codes.

In effect, Eckert had to build a management structure for the project on the fly, even without the usual bureaucratic authority. "It very quickly became a question of how do you orchestrate a team within teams? What type of governance do you put in place? How do you manage these variable work streams across Bentonville, the West Coast, and India?" Eckert and the team created what they semijokingly called the "uber-program management office," a group that was responsible for continuing to push for progress across the whole task force. There was a meeting among the team leaders every Tuesday at 1:00 P.M., then on Wednesday a "leadership action scrum"—a gathering of a group of vice presidents and higher-ranking officials from various departments whose buy-in or help might be needed to overcome some obstacle or another.

It worked. Eckert's group delivered a prototype of Walmart Pay by August 2015, as the CEO had requested, and it was being tested in stores by October. By late 2017, it had reportedly surpassed Apple Pay in number of users, and represented an important part of the company's success at becoming a true rival to Amazon in the technologically advanced, brutally competitive world of twenty-first-century retail.

A more conventional management structure might have involved formally appointing a senior executive to be in charge of the new payments system and creating an entire bureaucracy underneath that person before coding a single line—hopelessly slow in the arms race for control of consumers' wallets. Eckert agrees it couldn't have worked that way. "All of the things we're doing in e-commerce require this, for lack of a better phrase, messy organizational design, because it's the only way you can move at speed. If you stick within your silo, you'll never be able to be able to get what needs to be done at the scale and speed you need it done."

Listening to Eckert talk about how he rallied this team of engineers and business professionals from three cities on two continents with different bosses to produce something that could compete with offerings by some of the most innovative companies on earth, I found most striking the thread that connected Eckert's speckled earlier career to his recent one.

When he was in the marines, he had the difficult experience of coming in as a second lieutenant just out of college acting as the commanding officer of marines who had been in the Corps for two decades or more. "As a twenty-one-year-old kid literally leading marines who are war fighters extraordinaire, what am I going to impart to them in terms of technical expertise? Probably not a lot. What I am there for, though, is to be responsible and accountable for everything they do and fail to do, and know that I will be there for them if we end up falling down."

Then there were the experiences of launching the failed financial products startup and working with the company trying to turn oily industrial wastewater into something useful. Those made him more comfortable with ambiguity, in addition to proving an amazing crash course into the nuts and bolts of running a business that sometimes people with a more conventional career path lack.

"Who would have thought that I would have learned on a subsistence journey"—recall that he took the gig only out of financial desperation—"for an oily water treatment concern? But here I am able to say, 'I know what a restructuring feels like, I know what a bank workout looks like.' I am struck by how few people have gone through these types of business interactions. I'm struck by some of my younger associates who come in and I say, 'Hey, we need to go negotiate this agreement,' and they're like, 'I don't even know how to do that,' and want to call in the lawyers immediately."

I left Bentonville confident that the act of following this circuitous, almost nonsensical early career path actually made him better able to navigate Walmart toward its twenty-first-century version than he would have been if he had started young at a bank or a retailer or a consulting firm or a tech company and steadily climbed the ranks. And that, I realized, was what Steve Case was trying to get at.

"In many ways, that old model is limiting, because of the way in which the environment in business is going," Eckert said. "Business is messy. The more experience and exposure you've had to different parts of the mess, the more you can actually build something of cohesion against it. Because you can take bits and pieces and say, 'I've seen that, and I've seen that, and if I put those two together, I'll have actually created something I can be proud of.'"

Laszlo Bock, Google's former head of people operations, has an admirably blunt way of thinking of it. "In retrospect, people are always crafting a narrative that draws a through-line, through the randomness of life, in all these random experiences," he told me. "But it's incredibly difficult to choreograph it up front. You instead should find things you believe will move you forward in some way, whether that's skill development, or stature, or the people you will get to know, whatever it may be. And the second thing is that the specific nature of the opportunity matters less than how hard you work at it and what you gain in terms of experience. And then you can figure out the narrative of how it all fit together with hindsight."

Still, as you choose which lily pad to jump on and which types of experiences you seek to combine to become Pareto optimal, it's essential to do so with a firm understanding of the economic and technological forces at work. The chapters ahead will give you that, starting with the lessons of big data for a successful career.

4

How Big Data Can Make You Better

INVERTED *MONEYBALL* AND THE PEOPLE
ANALYTICS REVOLUTION

On the day I met Brett Ostrum, he was wearing a black leather jacket and a close-cropped goatee, and the top and bottom panels of his laptop computer were covered with stickers that made it appear you were glimpsing inside the device to see its innards. Which is logical enough, because those innards are his responsibility.

We were in a conference room within the sprawling series of office buildings in Redmond, Washington, that are the global headquarters of Microsoft, where Ostrum's title was corporate vice president for Surface and Xbox development. He was responsible for a small army of engineers—seven hundred of them—who create the tablet devices, laptops, and gaming consoles that have recently been a key part of Microsoft's strategy to place its products more at the center of office life. It is a tough business, with technically complex products and brutal competition against Apple, Samsung, and many others. But in

2017, things were going pretty well for Microsoft's device business. The reviews of its latest products were strong: The newest Surface laptop was "the new de facto Windows laptop that most people who want a Windows laptop should get," *The Verge* assured readers;[1] the Xbox One S was "everything a game console should be: sleek, powerful and well-stocked," *TechRadar* wrote.[2] Ostrum might have been a hardware man in a software company, but his team's efforts were paying off.

Still, Ostrum saw a problem on the horizon, in the form of Microsoft's intensive surveys to monitor employees' well-being.

Ostrum's business unit scored above average in most areas that the surveys covered, and around the Microsoft average at nearly all the rest. But in one area, it was distinctly below par. Employees reported being much less satisfied with their work-life balance than their counterparts were elsewhere at Microsoft—satisfaction 11 points below average on a 100-point scale.

This was worrisome. The team included all sorts of advanced talent, from the chemical engineers who work on battery technology to the mechanical engineers who design hinges and casings to the thermal engineers who ensure that devices will dissipate heat effectively. Ostrum himself started his career working on silicon design, and his first job at Microsoft was as an electrical engineer helping design a computer mouse. He was a big believer that a team making hardware needed to be happy and motivated to do its best work—and that it would be a disaster to start losing talented, hard-to-replace engineers to competitors because their work was keeping them from seeing their families enough or was killing their social lives.

Ostrum did what managers have done when faced with a challenge since the dawn of the corporation. He called a meeting. Unfortunately, what Ostrum and his top lieutenants were doing was basically a matter of guesswork. The theories they came up with—developed out of anecdotal observation and intuition—didn't align with the data they had.

For example, one theory was that employees were being ground down by the international travel demands of their jobs. Members of the Surface and Xbox teams must frequently fly to China and other distant nations to meet with suppliers and monitor manufacturing processes. Even when not traveling, they often need to make phone calls late in the evening to Asia or Europe due to time zone differences. Maybe the dissatisfaction with work-life balance was rooted in the inherently global nature of the work.

Just one problem: the survey data, which was broken out by small teams—some of which faced greater burdens than others in terms of travel and off-hours work—showed no meaningful correlation between the teams that experienced the heaviest of those demands and those that reported the worst complaints about work-life balance. It seemed that people understood that some amount of grueling international travel and off-hours phone calls was just the nature of the job.

Or might it be a problem of some individual hard-charging managers asking too much of their staff? This, too, sounded plausible, but as Ostrum looked at the results by team, there was no obvious connection—aggressive bosses and laid-back bosses had unhappy teams in roughly equal proportions.

Ostrum was at a loss; his intuition hadn't revealed persuasive answers. That's when he remembered a presentation he had watched during an executive retreat a few months earlier, about the revolution in the ability to collect and analyze massive amounts of data that is remaking major industries, shaping everything from what television shows Netflix recommends to how energy producers make and distribute electricity. Could Microsoft use its ability to collect and analyze huge piles of data to solve the mystery of the miserable employees?

"The goal was to help my team to learn what was actually going on, versus our knee-jerk reaction," Ostrum said. "Sometimes that gut instinct can be very, very wrong."

MONEYBALL AND THE MARKET FOR TALENT

To understand the role that data can play in making people better at their job—as Ostrum was hoping to do—it helps to start in an industry that has been ahead of the curve in gleaning insights from numbers: baseball, which, of the major sports played around the world, is surely the most conducive to data-based analysis. And to understand what a corporate middle manager can learn from baseball, consider the experience of a man named Vince Gennaro.

In the late 1970s, Gennaro was a young economic consultant fresh out of business school who, in his day job, was assigned such tasks as helping Kimberly-Clark, the maker of Kleenex tissues, model the market for pulp and other raw materials. But his passion was baseball. In particular, he saw that the analytical tools he used at work could be usefully applied to his passion. During graduate school at the University of Chicago, he had developed a model to assess whether the record $3.35 million deal that the New York Yankees had given to the right-handed pitcher Catfish Hunter was justified, both in terms of the victories Hunter's presence on the team was likely to generate and the extra revenue those wins would ultimately mean for the Yankees franchise.

At the time, conducting almost any statistical analysis—say, running a multiple regression to calculate the relationships among a bunch of variables—was quite an ordeal. Today, you could perform that regression in a fraction of a second using inexpensive spreadsheet software on an underpowered laptop. In the 1970s, you had to reserve time to use the office computer to run the analysis, then tell the computer what to do with arcane, mostly forgotten programming languages. Gennaro took to putting the office computer to work toward his side project late at night when his colleagues had gone home.

What Gennaro realized at the time that most people who actually earned a living from baseball did not was that the key to assessing the value of a baseball player lay in calculating his "marginal revenue product," much as Kimberly-Clark might figure out whether it was worthwhile to upgrade to a higher quality of pulp or to hire an extra salesperson. Catfish Hunter, for example, in Gennaro's calculations, brought an extra 79,000 fans to Yankee Stadium during the first year of his five-year contract, which was worth about $680,000 to the team.[3] Gennaro tried to turn his avocation into a vocation. He called his company Sports Planning Associates and attended the Major League Baseball owners' meetings trying to drum up clients who might pay for these insights. *Sporting News* wrote about his efforts, in a story titled "New Rating System Puts $ on Player's Value."[4]

He didn't have many takers. "I was getting looks like I had three heads," Gennaro said. "Nolan Ryan, the Hall of Fame pitcher, saw it in the *Sporting News* and was intrigued by it and had me come in and talk to his agent, but his agent said, 'This makes a lot of sense, but I don't know that anybody on the team side is really going to understand it.'"

So Gennaro's hobby remained a hobby. He went to work at PepsiCo and rose through the ranks as an executive in the Frito-Lay division. He was the brand manager who launched Cool Ranch Doritos in the late 1980s, and by the late 1990s he was president of the $1 billion fountain beverage division. Then, in 2001, he retired—or, more precisely, stepped away from the corporate world to try to turn his original side interest into the next act of his career. A whole lot had changed in the interim.

While Gennaro was cadging time on the office computer to analyze baseball statistics, an army veteran who worked as a nighttime security guard at a pork-and-beans cannery in Lawrence, Kansas, was doing some hard thinking about some of these same questions. Namely, what lessons could statistics offer about how baseball games are won and lost, which players make the greatest contributions to winning, and the optimal strategies for maximizing the chance of victory?

His name was Bill James, and his work amounted to the start of an analytics revolution in sports. Baseball is a godsend for people who seek to use statistics to understand the world. A baseball game consists of a series of discrete interactions: a pitcher throws a ball, and a batter either hits it, or swings and misses for a strike, or stands still hoping that it will be ruled a ball. The sample size is large: a Major League Baseball team plays 162 games in each regular season, and statistics have been dutifully kept dating back to the nineteenth century. Through the end of the 2017 season, that added up to 214,651 games played, with batters facing pitchers nearly 15 million times and successfully hitting the ball into play 3.8 million of them.[5] Contrast that with other sports. For example, soccer features nearly continuous, fluid action in which it is hard to isolate the discrete actions of all the players on the field and their contribution to the ultimate objective of scoring goals and preventing an opponent from doing so. Soccer statistics, until recently at least, focused only on the rare moments when a shot was taken and defended against, leaving the other eighty-nine minutes of kinetic activity on the pitch largely unaccounted for.

But for all the data available about what wins baseball games, teams made awfully poor use of it when James—who had no formal connection to the sport—started his work. For example, a key measure on which batters were evaluated (and still are, at least among fans) was "runs batted in," a gauge of whether their efforts generated runs. Yet to perform well on this metric depends heavily on whether there are routinely other players on base ahead of you, meaning that a player's RBI numbers are in significant part a measure of how good his teammates are. Similarly, pitchers were often evaluated and ranked based on their win-loss record, which is as much a measure of how a pitcher's teammates were hitting that day as of his skill.

James's great insight was that much of the received wisdom about the game could be tested using a mathematician's sense of rationality and the voluminous statistical record—and that the results of those tests could be told with colorful, vivid language. He sold his first *Baseball Abstract* in 1977, and in annual editions of that book, he sketched out a series of analytical innovations that would eventually become part of the language of how even moderately sophisticated fans talk about the game. He concluded that the old wisdom had undervalued some skills, like the ability to get on base by being walked, and that traditional baseball strategy involved excessive use of tactics like base stealing and the sacrifice bunt. James became something of a folk hero for a certain set of sports fans who found clever analytical insight to be as thrilling as the action on the field. The term "sabermetrics" came into use for this body of inquiry, based on the abbreviated name for the Society for American Baseball Research.

Surprisingly, although plenty of people in professional baseball were readers and fans of the work of James and other like-minded researchers, it took a long time for these insights to be taken seriously as strategy advice—so much so that when a management group did embrace many of the lessons of sabermetrics, the story became a bestselling book and feature film. *Moneyball,* by Michael Lewis, told how Billy Beane, the general manager of the Oakland Athletics, fielded a competitive team despite having among the lowest payroll budgets in the league. By casting aside received wisdom about what makes a player valuable—in Lewis's colorful telling, ignoring grizzled veteran scouts who wanted to pick players based on gut instinct and intuition— Beane and the 2002 A's assembled a roster of inexpensive players who nonetheless added up to an elite team. After Lewis's book was published in 2003, "Moneyball" came to mean the savvy use of data to identify undervalued talent or other assets even in contexts far from sports.

What is not as well understood is how, even as the ink dried on Lewis's book—and certainly by the time the movie version came out in 2011—the innovations Beane used to put his team together in 2002 were being supplanted by new ones. An entire generation of team executives who had come of age with sabermetrics as a concept was coming to power in franchises; the success of the low-budget A's got everyone's attention; and the computing power to easily do more and more sophisticated analysis was becoming more widespread. Perhaps most significantly, where *Moneyball* was all about a team assembling a cheap but competitive roster out of necessity, teams with big budgets— most successfully the Boston Red Sox—were getting in on the party. Letting data drive decisions turned out to be the pathway forward for any franchise that hoped to succeed, not just something to be employed in moments of desperation.

An even more revolutionary step came at the start of 2015, when a system called Statcast went into use in every Major League stadium. A system of cameras and radar recorded every move on the field on every play, turning that information into an immense pile of data. Previously, statistical tables might record only that a pitcher threw a 92 mph fastball, which a hitter popped to right field, where the out-fielder caught it for an out. With Statcast, it would be known exactly where the pitcher released the ball and how fast it was spinning, how fast the ball came off the bat and at exactly what angle, and how efficient the fielder was in reaching the ball to catch it. The very first game at which Statcast was used generated about seven terabytes of data—by Gennaro's calculations, around twenty times the cumulative amount that had been collected on the 190,000 major league baseball games that had been played up to that point.

But data isn't the same as insight. It was up to teams to compete to make better use of the data. Want to figure out how much you should be willing to pay an aging player? A savvy team will pick apart different aspects of what makes the player valuable and look at the historical record of how quickly those pieces diminish with age—raw speed tends to go first, but the instinct to run toward exactly where the ball will land lasts longer. The strength to hit a baseball a long way will probably diminish in a man's thirties, whereas the mental acuity to decide in a few milliseconds whether to swing at a pitch ages pretty well. With a little bit of modeling, you can figure out whether a particular thirty-year-old centerfielder is likely to have five more good years or two, or zero, and make a contract offer accordingly. Or do you need to decide who to put in as a pinch hitter against a pitcher your team has never faced before? You can model the likelihood of your various players' success based on that pitcher's characteristics, much as Netflix tries to project what movies you will like based on the attributes of movies you have liked in the past.

The possibilities are endless, and use of this data—again, seven terabytes' worth for each of 2,430 regular season games a year—is in its early stages.

With this movement toward data-driven decisions in full force, Gennaro, having left the corporate world, started working on baseball analytics full-time. In the early 2000s, he began consulting for a few teams, appearing on television as an analyst, and teaching sports management at New York University.[6] At long last, the work he had done as a hobby as a young man was in major-league demand. It just took twenty-five years of patience. But even as Gennaro worked with teams to try to make good use of this data, he realized the Moneyball approach had another dimension, potentially more powerful, that tied back to his days in the corporate world. Just maybe, people trying to hit and catch baseballs can learn something from the people who sold Cool Ranch Doritos in the 1990s. In turn, people who want to thrive in the twenty-first-century corporate world may have plenty to learn from how the savviest baseball players are turning the data revolution on its head.

THE DIFFERENCE BETWEEN BUSINESS AND BASEBALL

As Gennaro took on more and more senior jobs at PepsiCo—by the late 1990s, he was running a 5,000-employee bottling operation in the American Midwest—he wrestled with the deep difficulty of identifying and rewarding good people. At that scale, just being good at strategic thinking and big ideas gets a manager almost nowhere; an idea is only as good as the people charged with executing that vision.

You could say the same about a baseball team, of course—a

stats-obsessed general manager doesn't win games, players do. The difference is that in baseball, the action takes place in plain view, there is a very clear definition of what constitutes "success," and it is relatively simple to calculate how much each person contributes to it. In the corporate world, especially for knowledge workers, this is inherently murky.

For relatively rote jobs, like factory line worker or barista, you can measure things like the worker's throughput and error rate. But who's to say which product engineer made the biggest contribution to a product's success or failure? Or whether a marketing associate really carried her weight or not, or if a shift supervisor in a bottling plant is better or worse than a replacement-value shift supervisor who could be easily hired? In a business environment, the work doesn't happen on a field for all to see—it happens in thousands of meetings and emails and conversations, most of them private and each with an ambiguous impact on the organization's ultimate success. Every day, you can know whether or not a baseball player contributed to victory on the field by looking at his statistics line; you have no way of knowing whether a brand manager did.

For all that murkiness, Gennaro devoted considerable effort to trying to use the same analytical, careful mindset he had tried to bring to baseball in his role as a food and beverage executive.

"I probably spent 25 or 30 percent of my time on things that were all about developing talent and doing in-depth reviews," he said. "That said, most of it was judgmental. It wasn't highly quantitative. Don't get me wrong, we were not just taking a 20,000-foot view and saying, 'Well, I have a feeling this person is all right.' No, we were evaluating a dozen attributes broken down, some subjective, some more quantified. How results-oriented were they? How did they react to adversity?"

Middle managers would evaluate eight or ten peers who had worked alongside them on how they had performed on each of several dimensions like those, adding more consistency and rigor to employee evaluations. The goal was to replace intuition with specific measures of success. Gennaro recalled once having an employee who was managing a Pepsi bottling operation in St. Louis that was facing big competitive incursions from Coca-Cola. "He was highly responsive to that," Gennaro recalled, "and he was responsive not in letting it produce anxiety, but rather it produced focus, it produced rational thought, it produced evidence-based thinking. All the things that you value when you're running a business. So as I would evaluate him, those sorts of things were admissible as evidence in his reviews and the dialogue we would have."

One of his obsessions was trying to use that kind of information—imperfect and subjective though it was—not merely to evaluate his workforce and decide who deserved a raise or a bonus but to help make people better at their jobs and more valuable contributors to the organization. "It is one of my real pet peeves," he said. "Too often we use this information in a strictly evaluative sense rather than a developmental sense."

But true as that may be in the corporate world, in the baseball world, the data revolution that transformed the game from a management perspective is also starting to change the game from an individual player's perspective. The best baseball players are using the data revolution to make their own performance better.

One of them is named Joey Votto.

LISTENING TO THE DATA, FROM THE BALLPARK TO THE OFFICE PARK

When Joey Votto was growing up on the west side of Toronto in the 1980s and '90s, he was athletic, but not very good at Canada's national sport of ice hockey. He later told an interviewer that as a teenager, a would-be girlfriend dumped him for being a lousy skater.[7] He was also never particularly numerate—math was not his strong suit—which would prove ironic inasmuch as his ability to learn lessons from data would later earn him more than a quarter of a billion dollars.

Votto was, however, extraordinarily good at hitting a baseball that had been hurled at him at high velocity—a skill that got him drafted by the Cincinnati Reds right out of high school, in 2002. As a minor-league ballplayer, he began obsessing over the statistics of the great hitters in the sport's history, especially Boston Red Sox great Ted Williams. After games, following the long bus rides and stays in unglamorous hotels that are mainstays of minor-league sports, he would watch that day's at-bats by the greatest hitters of that generation, like Barry Bonds, Todd Helton, and Manny Ramirez.

The goal in baseball is to score more runs than the other team, and the first step to scoring a run is to get on base. The two most common ways to get on base are to swing a bat, successfully hit a pitched ball into play, and run there, or to refrain from swinging on four throws that are outside the strike zone, at which point you get to walk to first base.[8]

One of the sabermetricians' earliest insights was that to walk to first is nearly as valuable, in terms of generating victories, as getting on base via a hit. By avoiding outs and getting on base, a player who walks a lot is going to make huge contributions toward winning baseball games.

This violated the ethos of old-school baseball people—the types of scouts Michael Lewis was mocking in *Moneyball*. After all, to take a base by walking is to succeed through inaction, to get on base because of what you didn't do (swing the bat) rather than what you did (knock the holy hell out of a baseball).

And while Votto can certainly knock the holy hell out of a baseball, that wasn't the skill that got him promoted to the major leagues in 2007, won him a Most Valuable Player trophy in 2010, and landed him a $251.5 million, twelve-year deal with the Reds in 2012.[9] Instead, it was his incredible skill at doing whatever it takes—including taking lots of walks—to get on base and not allow the other team to get an out that would bring the Reds' opportunity to score to a premature end.

"I think a very important part of a hitter's process is not swinging at balls and swinging at strikes," Votto told me in an interview in the fall of 2017, "so, if I'm not mistaken, I've done relatively well in that category."

Votto has done quite a bit better than just "relatively well in that category." And he does it, by his own telling, by paying obsessive attention to what the latest analytics insights tell him about every swing he takes, and the tendencies of every pitch he takes.

Essentially, he has learned and acted on the lessons of sabermetrics more successfully than nearly anyone else. An exceptionally patient batter, he has an uncanny ability to withhold his swing when the pitch is outside the strike zone and to keep at-bats going until he either successfully hits the ball or is walked. In the 2017 season, for example, he reached base on 45.4 percent of his at-bats, better than anyone else in the major leagues.

Imagine the strike zone—the area in which a pitch that isn't hit counts as a strike—divided into a 3 × 3 grid with nine panels. On a tablet computer, Votto monitors data about his rate of hitting pitches delivered in each box, putting in extra practice hitting pitches thrown toward any one where his hit rate slips. The idea is to ensure that pitchers can't seize the advantage by throwing the ball to an area where he is less likely to hit it; their job is harder if Votto has no weak places in the strike zone. He also monitors the rolling averages of the velocity of balls leaving his bat, and how often he swings at pitches that are inside or outside the strike zone in each direction. And those are just the basics—the uses of the data Votto is willing to tell a journalist about. "There's a gaggle of other things that are quite a bit more specific but that I don't want to share," he told me. You don't tell your competitors your best tricks.

Essentially, all those terabytes of data that Major League Baseball is collecting provide, for a player who knows how to use them well, an ongoing update of exactly what he is doing right and what he is doing wrong, an opportunity for real-time course correction as the

162-game grind of baseball season progresses. Votto is better than most at making use of it to improve his game.

Part of what makes this data tricky to use is that it is possible to overinterpret random statistical fluctuations. If a player has swung and missed on an unusually high ratio of outside curveballs over the last twenty at-bats, is it bad luck or a sign that he needs to change how he approaches the game? The key for Votto is to ignore small-sample statistical fluctuations except when they align with his intuition—when he feels as if something might be wrong, and even the small-sample data seems to affirm it.

"At times, when there's a blip, a spike one way or the other, I try not to buy into it too much," Votto said. "I mean, there's an intuitive side, which is based on feel and my swing and how I feel about the pitches or my game in general. And then there's the data and making good decisions and then taking a really big step back and looking at it all objectively. So if something stands out to me and I feel a certain way, plus the numbers bear it out, then I try to make an adjustment. It can be difficult, because oftentimes even something that has been a trend over two weeks, that's still too small a sample to react over. But when you're living it, it doesn't feel that way."

The data says that Votto's approach is making him more valuable to his team; there's a reason the Reds offered him that monster contract. From 2008 to 2017, his performance single-handedly generated an average of 5.4 more victories per year for the Reds than a "replacement player," an average first baseman of the sort that can be easily signed whenever needed. Of course, one of the challenges of being a more data-driven type of player is that focusing on the kinds of metrics that truly drive victory can mean neglect of the numbers traditionalists usually care about.

Votto faced that in 2013. He had recorded another typically excellent season, ranking seventeenth in the majors in wins above replacement. But the very thing that made him valuable according to the new generation of analytics—his ability to get on base and avoid causing an out—was under attack from people who saw limits in his approach. In particular, Votto's number of runs batted in was surprisingly low for such a good hitter. Votto ranked No. 2 in the majors in the percentage of the time he made it on base but was tied for No. 64 in RBI.

In the new wave of baseball analysis, RBI is a nearly useless statistic for judging the quality of a player. It depends heavily on circumstance and luck. A player who hits frequently with other players already on base will tend to have more RBIs, and that in turn depends on the skill of your teammates, where in the sequence of batters your manager places you, and luck in terms of when you get your hits. A more nuanced criticism of Votto—voiced with typical vehemence on Cincinnati-area sports radio—was that by swinging the bat so judiciously and thus being walked, he was costing the Reds runs (and himself RBIs) that would have led to more victories. Perhaps if he'd swing with greater abandon when there was a player on base, Votto could drive his teammates in, even if he himself made an out.

"He took heat from fans for years," recalled Lance McAlister, a sports radio host. "Honestly, it was a daily topic of conversation on my show." The implicit argument: that Votto's style of play was selfish. The bellower-in-chief was Marty Brennaman, who had announced Reds games on the radio since 1974. "He's not paid to walk," Brennaman told *Sports Illustrated*. "He's paid to drive in runs."[10]

In his years as a baseball player, Votto had been relatively reticent in his comments to the press, reluctant to establish himself as a public figure or get into disputes with his detractors. In the offseason between the 2013 and 2014 seasons, he finally had enough and defended his data-driven strategy.

"I've made a point when guys are on base to continue to stick to my approach," he said in a television interview. "A lot of people are not very happy with that approach because I'm not willing to hit the ball on the ground to a shortstop or pop the ball to a centerfielder to score that run like many people want. I'm more than happy to take my base."[11] This is essentially an empirical argument that goes to one of the early findings of Bill James and the sabermetrics crowd: that when managers encouraged players to trade an out for a run, they weren't sufficiently considering the value of extending the inning and potentially scoring many more runs. Votto made this more pointed when a columnist for *The Cincinnati Enquirer* pushed him on the issue a few days later. "It's better not to make outs than to drive in runs?" asked Paul Daugherty.

"No. Doubt. About. It," Votto told him.[12]

Later, on McAlister's show, he was asked what statistics he does use to evaluate how he's doing. If he's dismissive of the old-school metrics like batting average and RBI, what does matter?

"You know, it's going to drive a lot of people crazy when I respond, but I can't help myself," Votto began. "It would probably be 'weighted runs created plus,'" which he then briefly explained to what was surely a puzzled audience. Based on one of Bill James's statistical inventions, what baseball nerds abbreviate as "wRC+" incorporates the value of each of a player's hits and walks, including adjustments for the parks he plays in (it's easier to hit a home run in some than others, and the overall balance between hitters and pitchers in the league in the year in question.

There's no doubt that being a baseball player is a very different job from one in the corporate world. Votto does his work in front of tens of thousands of people; data about every move he and his competitors make is collected and available for anyone to analyze; there is a clear definition of what constitutes success and what constitutes failure. But speaking with him, I was struck by how many commonalities there are between his savvy use of analytics to be a better baseball player and what savvy professionals in the business world need to do to be more effective at their job.

In both baseball and business, there has been an exponential rise in the amount of data available and in the capacity to analyze it. In baseball, it's called "sabermetrics"; in business, it is sometimes called "people analytics." Most of that analytical work is on behalf of management, seeking to win games in baseball or create a high-performing organization in business. But a player, or individual employee, who can learn lessons generated by this data and analysis will have a leg up against the competition.

That revolution is a lot further along in baseball than it is in business, and Votto is further along than most other players at taking advantage of what information the data offers. "Votto is a bit of a savant on this stuff and very cerebral," Vince Gennaro told me. "This is one of the defining traits of elite players, the adaptability, the ability to understand what the data is telling them."

When I spoke with Votto about his use of data, what came through most was that his success stems not from any one trick or insight but from a mindset. "I pay attention to a number of different statistics, but I cannot pay attention to results," he told me. That might seem paradoxical in an industry where results—hits, home runs, victories— are everything. But inputs are not the same as outputs, and Votto has faith that if he gets the inputs right, good outputs will follow.

"I'm exclusively curious about the markers that lead to long-term success, but I pay no attention to counting stats, and I really try not to pay attention to rate stats," he said. That is, he's more worried about the underlying behaviors he can control: not swinging at pitches outside the strike zone; ensuring that almost every time he does swing the bat he makes at least some contact with the ball; making his swing equally effective across all quadrants of the strike zone so that there is no weak area a pitcher can exploit.

His approach to data is less about learning a single lesson and applying it, and more about always being ready to learn and adapt to what the latest evidence shows. "Where I try to use the numbers is to understand where the direction of the game is going," Votto told me. "I never want to be behind the curve. I always want to anticipate what's coming next and adjust."

Brett Ostrum at Microsoft wasn't trying to hit a baseball; he was trying to manage a large team focused on hard technological and business problems. Could the Votto approach—the dedication to studying the data and listening to what it teaches—really help?

WHAT WE CAN (AND CAN'T) LEARN FROM A FEW MILLION EMAILS

On December 2, 2001, the energy trading company Enron filed for bankruptcy protection. At the time, it was the largest bankruptcy in history. It set in motion an upheaval in the corporate world, triggering, among other things, the downfall of what had been one of the five major global accounting firms, Arthur Andersen, and a rewriting of American securities laws (resulting in what became known as the Sarbanes-Oxley Act). For our purposes, what is particularly interesting is that the following spring, federal energy regulators collected the email archives of about 150 senior managers at Enron from 2000 to 2002 and, as part of their investigation, published them for all to see. There were originally 1.6 million emails, though eventually the federal regulators would delete those that involved private information or were not germane to the business—bank records, conversations with spouses, travel confirmations, random spam—and hone them down to a few hundred thousand messages. Even after Enron was long gone, a mere footnote in business history, this data set represented something rare for all sorts of researchers: a rich, detailed source of data about how people in an organization behave when they don't think anyone is watching. Countless scholars of organizational behavior, linguistics, and other fields have analyzed the Enron emails. That makes them, to borrow from a headline in *MIT Technology Review,* the business equivalent of the DNA of Henrietta Lacks, a woman who died in 1951 but whose cells have been used in generations of biomedical research.[13]

A decade after the fall of Enron, a man named Ryan Fuller had an idea for putting the emails to a new use. He was a former consultant at Bain & Company who had founded a startup called VoloMetrix, based on a hunch that white-collar professionals' shift from paper to electronic communication offered as yet untapped opportunities to manage better.

"It wasn't all that long ago that everything was paper processes," Fuller said. "It was people writing memos. You could only really talk to the number of people you could call in a given day, or find in person. But all of these technologies like email and spreadsheets and calendar software that were proliferating made it possible for knowledge workers to do much more every day. So you had all these incredible productivity enhancers for the individual, but you didn't have any parallel evolution of tools for management. Every individual is doing more, but management tools haven't developed at the same rate, so there's some catch-up to do."

He and his colleagues theorized that by analyzing the big troves of data generated daily by these applications, they could develop deep insights into employee productivity. They had something of a chicken-or-egg problem, though: no organization would consent to hand over all its email or other electronic records to a newly formed company, but they couldn't prove their concept or trustworthiness without the data. "One of our questions was 'Why doesn't this already exist?' We thought it could be that either it's impossible to get the data out [from a technical standpoint], or the privacy implications are so strong you can't get around them," Fuller said.

Then they discovered the Enron emails, which were already public and so didn't present privacy issues. As a proof of concept, they crunched the correspondence of those 150 Enron executives and showed that VoloMetrix's technology worked to identify patterns of who was communicating with whom without endangering individuals' privacy.

That was good enough to get a 2,500-employee company to provide access to the metadata of its own internal email and calendar systems—how many meetings were held and with what combinations of participants, for example, and email traffic patterns stripped of information identifying the individual senders and recipients and of the contents of the message. The company's CEO thought it had a "meetings problem," as Fuller recalled, which is to say that its workforce was spending too much time in them. Fuller and his team at VoloMetrix set to work analyzing the data from that client and came in for a presentation. They had calculated to the decimal point how much time a typical employee spent in meetings, how many people were in the typical meeting, and how those numbers varied based on business unit and type of job, and were pretty pleased with the insights they had come up with. But that alone wasn't enough.

"We quickly learned that all that information was interesting but not actionable," Fuller said. "They said, 'Well, is that good or bad? Should that be lower or higher? How do we compare to our competition? What do we do now?' It was good validation that we were able to analyze the data, but it was also clear that we had to go deeper to help companies understand how to think about this data and how to utilize it to make it actionable. The problem was how to go from an interesting science project to something really compelling."

As Fuller was working with a few colleagues in a startup in Seattle, just a few miles away Dawn Klinghoffer was taking on the same questions, albeit from a very different perspective.

Klinghoffer was a college math major who had worked as an actuary in the insurance industry before she started in Microsoft's finance department in 1998, where she worked on the always-tricky task of allocating costs and revenue to different departments so that the profit or loss of individual business lines could be accurately calculated. Then, in 2003, a colleague came to her with a surprising proposal. The human resources department of Microsoft was trying to get better about rigorously measuring and analyzing the work of its then-55,000 employees. Klinghoffer joined a team aimed at doing that. "We were pretty fortunate in that we had a warehouse with more than fifteen years' worth of HR data," Klinghoffer said. But she soon realized she had the same problem as Fuller: "Reporting on data is great, and might tell you what has happened in the organization, but it doesn't tell you the why, and it certainly doesn't take it to the next level of understanding behaviors that impact performance, and why."

So, for example, it had been the conventional wisdom within Microsoft that an ambitious executive needed to spend time overseas in order to have long-term success. Analyzing the data, though, Klinghoffer found no solid evidence that this was the case; executives who spent time abroad on average had no more later success than those who stayed at Microsoft's headquarters. But she and her colleagues did find something interesting in this exercise: it turned out that a surprisingly high number of managers who did an international assignment left the company within a few months of coming back. That produced a useful insight: the company was doing a bad job of making sure executives returning from overseas assignments had an engaging job to come back to, leaving them in limbo for a few months upon their return—during which competitors were poaching them. "People would take these international assignments and then they'd kind of be hanging around for six months waiting for something to open up, and the thought was, if you're going to spend the money to put them overseas, you better have a path for them when they come back."

Later, they found two curious facts by looking at the same data on career paths and turnover trends. First, internal transfers could be very good for both the company and the workers: when people moved to another unit within the company, they tended to become more engaged in their work and ultimately become more valuable employees. (I interpret this as further confirmation that a nonlinear career path is valuable in becoming a Pareto-optimal employee.)

Second, despite this good news about the value of transfers, they found in surveys that employees felt it was easier to quit Microsoft for another company than to make an internal move. After Klinghoffer's team produced that data, the human resources team did some thinking about how to change that pattern—and realized its own policies probably had a lot to do with it.

Microsoft's rules stated that you had to be in a current position for at least eighteen to twenty-four months, depending on the department, before you could apply for a new job elsewhere in the company, and you had to ask your manager's permission before interviewing for a new role. But when people explored potential new jobs outside the company, those rules obviously didn't apply—meaning someone looking for a change had active incentive to look *only* outside Microsoft rather than consider internal transfers. The company relaxed those rules, and the transfer rate increased.

Both of those lessons came from juxtaposing data on career paths with measures of future success, such as longevity with the company. But Klinghoffer was convinced that there was room to take this type of analytical approach to a new level. After all, Microsoft was one of the biggest makers of office email and calendar software—programs that inevitably produce a type of "digital exhaust" of metadata about how nearly every employee of the company is using his or her time. Could there be some way to put it to use?

Then, in 2015, she got a call from a business development executive within Microsoft. "Hey, we're going to be evaluating this company that works in workplace productivity and analytics," the executive said. "I understand that's what you do here, so I wondered if you could come to the meeting and help us evaluate this company."

The company was VoloMetrix. When Ryan Fuller showed up for the meeting, he thought it was a sales call—that he was trying to persuade Microsoft to allow access to data about its employees and pay for the insights VoloMetrix could develop from it. Actually, Microsoft was kicking the tires; it would go on to acquire the entire company, and Fuller and Klinghoffer became colleagues. Separately, Klinghoffer and Fuller had envisioned using email and calendar metadata—the digital exhaust created by what had become 118,000 Microsoft employees—to produce genuinely useful business insights. Now, they would work together to do it.

SABERMETRICS IN THE EXECUTIVE SUITE

One rough approach to using data is to plug hundreds of variables into a computer and search for any correlations. The risk of this data mining is that you will get statistical information but not insight. If people who come to work unusually early are also likely to write longer emails, it doesn't really mean anything absent some theory of the connection—and may be a spurious correlation driven by a few verbose people who happen to be early birds.

Good data scientists, like their brethren in the natural and physical sciences, have a method for testing insights from data. They start with a question that needs answering, then form a hypothesis—that early arrivers are more productive, for example—that they then test against the data to see if the evidence confirms or disproves it. In the context of the work Klinghoffer and Fuller do, it is a matter of juxtaposing the metadata of email and calendars—not the actual contents of messages or calendar appointments, but the communication and meeting patterns—with patterns of success or failure within Microsoft.

If you want to figure out which behaviors in a company predict and contribute to success, you first have to define "success." For managers, they concluded, "success" counted as things like survey evidence of high levels of employee engagement, and achievement of sales and revenue goals.

As Klinghoffer and Fuller pondered the questions the available data might help answer, they settled on some possibilities: Is there an optimal length of the workday in terms of productivity? Should salespeople focus on deep contacts with a few clients or shallow relationships with lots of them?

It is the equivalent of Joey Votto seeking to understand which behaviors would correlate with eventual success and focusing on those he could control. Every Microsoft employee might want promotions and higher sales, just as every baseball player wants to win more games. The question is what data you can optimize for at the individual level to improve the odds of that organization-wide success; answering it effectively is the key to getting a multimillion-dollar contract as a professional baseball player and to getting a promotion within a company like Microsoft.

After a few years of this work, Klinghoffer and Fuller had a few propositions that proved robust—ideas about the behaviors of effective managers at Microsoft that came through in the data and proved true regardless of exactly how it was crunched: currents that were evident across multiple years and across many units of the company, for example. These are the business equivalents of Votto's conviction that he should focus on getting on base and avoiding outs by any means—lessons that have proved robust across different forms of analysis.

Among the lessons:

Work hard, but not too hard. One striking finding was that the number of hours of work—as revealed by when an employee is using email or setting calendar appointments—is contagious. Workers tend to follow whatever their boss does. Employees of managers who put in something longer than the standard forty-hour week were more engaged and more likely to work more hours themselves. But taking this to extremes—for example, managers who frequently worked evenings and weekends—swung that effect in the other direction. Their employees may have still worked long hours, but they became less engaged in surveys. "For one company we looked at, for every hour a manager spends doing email or meetings after normal working hours, it adds up to twenty minutes per direct report as well, and that cascades through the organization," Fuller said.

Meet one-on-one with employees. Holding regular department-wide meetings might seem like good leadership, but it had little correlation with managerial success. By contrast, managers who had frequent one-on-one meetings—even short ones—with their direct reports were likely to have more engaged employees who went on to greater success. "Employees felt like they had more career opportunities if they had regular one-on-ones with their manager, presumably because they're actually talking about that when they meet with them," Klinghoffer said. "And they were actually more open to taking feedback than employees who met less often with their manager."

Always work on building your network within your organization. It turns out that knowing people across different departments of a company is important not just for an individual middle manager trying to get things done but also for his or her subordinates. People whose boss had a more extensive network tended to have longer careers within Microsoft. It seems there is something contagious, in a good way, about knowing lots of people. "The size and depth and breadth of individual employees' networks is very highly correlated with performance, with engagement, with a number of different outcomes," Fuller said. "Generally speaking, bigger networks are better, and small or shrinking networks are an indicator of something bad coming. Which makes sense, humans being social creatures."

Apart from the specifics of this advice, what is striking is how technology—the rise of big data—is making possible the kinds of insights that Vince Gennaro hungered for in his own corporate career in the 1990s but weren't yet ready for prime time.

Klinghoffer and Fuller became the leading internal evangelists for this approach within Microsoft, and in 2017 they spoke before the company's most senior executives at a retreat, explaining their approach and its potential and pitfalls. In the audience was Brett Ostrum.

THE MYSTERY OF THE MISERABLE EMPLOYEES

When Ostrum approached them with his problem, Klinghoffer and Fuller saw an opportunity to put their analytical tools to a new use: figuring out why many members of the Surface and Xbox development unit were less satisfied about their work-life balance than other Microsoft employees. The organizational analytics team set to work analyzing the aggregated metadata of email and calendar usage of those seven hundred employees, to try to identify the core problem and figure out a way to solve it.

The team's work first confirmed that the original thesis—that international phone calls and travel were the drivers of the dissatisfaction—didn't hold up. By comparing the digital calendars of people on different teams, and testing those results against the survey results on satisfaction, the team members disproved it. "The answer was no," Ostrum said. "When we looked at the data, international travel was not the thing that was driving our overall work-life balance result. It was not the thing that was really moving the needle."

To test alternate theories, they identified which teams had particularly bad survey results on work-life balance and then looked for how their work patterns differed from those of teams with average or good survey results. They mined calendar and email data to reveal what differentiated teams where people were unhappy from those where things were fine.

It seemed the problem must involve something about after-hours work—why else would the employees' dissatisfaction come through as giving low survey ratings to their work-life balance, after all? But no matter how they crunched the data, there weren't any meaningful correlations to be found between groups that had a lot of work to do at odd times and those that were unhappy. It was a process of iteration, testing the different theories around work travel and off-hours phone calls and demanding bosses against the realities of the cold hard numbers. The data provided a common language and measurement tool to test out different gut instincts in a more objective way, and most of them weren't borne out.

But one thing that the team's gut instincts were telling them did check out in the data: people were spending an awful lot of time in meetings. In the analysis of the employees' schedules, they found that the difference between the hardware unit and other parts of Microsoft with higher satisfaction around work-life balance wasn't more hours in meetings, or more meetings at odd hours.

They found that dissatisfied teams spent twenty-seven hours a week in meetings on average—but what really distinguished those teams was that their meetings tended to include a lot of people: ten or twenty arrayed around a conference table coordinating plans, not two or three brainstorming a solution to a problem.

The issue wasn't that people had to fly to China and make late-night phone calls. People who had taken jobs requiring that sort of work seemed to accept that as part of the deal. It was that their managers were clogging their schedules with big meetings, reducing available work hours for tasks that demanded individual concentration—sitting down, thinking deeply, and trying to solve a problem.

As baseball teams showed long ago, data alone isn't insight, but armed with data, the executives could ask better questions of employees to understand the source of frustrations—and test their answers against more objective information. Employees complained about the need to catch up on work that required solitary concentration during their off-hours because so much of their workday was scheduled with nonessential meetings, and that complaint aligned with the calendar and email data.

For Ostrum, this insight was more than just theoretical. As it happens, his direct reports constituted one of the teams that reported both unhappiness over work-life balance and twenty-seven hours a week in large meetings. Fortunately for him, the diagnosis also implied the solution.

Ostrum and his leadership team set out to tackle the problem, realizing that because they were a major source of the overload, they needed to be the first to make a change. Ostrum and the analytics team showed the affected managers the data and their insights about what it revealed, and urged them to do a self-audit of how many meetings they scheduled and ask hard questions about which were essential. On the employee end, they began to encourage employees to schedule time on their calendars for the kind of independent concentration that was being pushed into evenings and weekends by those meetings. Simply accounting for independent work time on a calendar—as opposed to leaving it blank, thus making it easy for a colleague to request a meeting during that time—meant they were guaranteed time at work for this activity.

Ostrum's next step was to track progress, which he did using the kind of analytics information that helped him follow through on the solution—the corporate-world equivalent of the data Joey Votto studies on a tablet every game day to understand exactly how he is succeeding or failing at hitting baseballs.

"I get a ping every week that says, 'Here's what your week looked like,'" Ostrum said. "It shows how much focused time you had, how many off-hours you were on email, both sending and receiving. That's what every individual gets, and sometimes it's alarming to see how much email you're doing over the weekend or late nights, so it's good for awareness."

Just as many people use a fitness app like Fitbit to monitor their health behaviors, an app called MyAnalytics that was introduced in mid-2018 as part of the Office suite offers nudges when people display habits that are suboptimal. It might inform you that "you e-mailed in more than 40 percent of your meetings last week" or "30 percent of your weekly meetings are recurring. Review your recurring meetings to make sure they're a good use of time."

Joey Votto's success did not result from a one-time dive into analytics. In any situation, people continuously evolve in response to change in their environment, so we have to constantly follow up by revisiting questions and asking new questions. As Ostrum sees it, we've only scratched the surface of what can be learned. The big question for the years ahead is how to empower employees to develop Joey Votto–level skill at mining analytics.

As in baseball, not everyone loves the idea that human performance can be reduced so easily to data. The key for people who want to succeed in this environment is committing to listen to what the data has to say, to study it, and—perhaps most important—to develop the very human analytical and interpretative skills to understand what it is telling us.

5

The Economics of Managing

WHAT WOULD YOU SAY YOU *DO* HERE?

Some young couples bond over movies or sports. In the mid-1990s, Susan Salgado and her then-boyfriend spent their weekends taking a two-hour bus ride from Bethlehem, Pennsylvania, where she was studying for an MBA and working at Lehigh University, into New York City, to eat in some of the city's best restaurants. They were particularly fond of two spots that generated a great deal of buzz in New York food circles—Union Square Cafe and Gramercy Tavern, located within a couple of blocks of each other just north of Union Square Park. Both restaurants offered food that was sophisticated without being fussy, and warm customer service even to a graduate student who took the bus there from Pennsylvania, which is something you couldn't say of many of New York's top restaurants in that era. And both were run by a restaurateur named Danny Meyer.

By 1999, Salgado and her now-husband had moved to New York,

where she was working on a doctorate in organizational behavior at New York University's Stern School of Business. With most of her coursework finished, she was trying to figure out where to turn her focus for her dissertation. She wanted to do field research rather than crunch data in spreadsheets, and she wanted to study how successful organizations can provide authentic and consistent experiences to their customers. Meyer's restaurants were a great example of that, she thought. One night she was eating at Tabla, a newer outpost of his restaurant empire focused on Indian food, and she saw Meyer standing alone, surveying the scene. She had read about him and had been eating in his restaurants for years, but they had never met. She approached him, told him about herself and her experiences dining at his restaurants, and made a proposal. For her dissertation, could she study Meyer's company to understand the inner workings of this small restaurant empire that seemed to have a knack for accumulating plaudits from both restaurant critics and enthusiastic fans?

Meyer was a little wary, as she recalls, but intrigued enough to invite Salgado in to meet with his partners. After some discussion they agreed, but suggested that for it to work, she would have to truly immerse herself in the operations. So in November 1999, Salgado went to work as a reservationist in a back room of Union Square Cafe, where she took phone calls for eight hours a day, listening to the pleas of New Yorkers desperate to get one of the hottest reservations in town and learning Meyer's delicate method of saying no in a way that left the customer feeling good. After eight weeks, she began doing shifts as a restaurant host, learning Meyer's distinctive way of greeting customers and making them feel at home, and after that she trailed waiters, food runners, bartenders, and others to observe how they did their jobs.

Salgado's work resulted in a 161-page dissertation entitled "Fine Restaurants: Creating Inimitable Advantages in a Competitive Industry." Her top-level finding: Meyer's company had generated a durable advantage over its competitors in the cutthroat New York restaurant scene through the culture it had created among its employees. There was, she argued, a positive feedback loop in place. When staff treated each other, and customers, with respect and empathy, it made all of them better at their jobs than they might have been elsewhere, and created a meaningfully better experience for customers than they would have been likely to find elsewhere. Or, in academic-ese, "Successful growth of this organization resides in the development of both a core identity that is unique, valuable and consistent across restaurants, and strategic identities that vary across restaurants and allow each restaurant to compete in its niche. The sustainability of this system is rooted in management's ability to successfully develop and transfer both core and strategic identities, and in the institutional practices that continuously support and maintain the identity."

That might have been the end of it. Salgado could have gone on to teach management at a business school. But she had fallen in love with the restaurant industry and the way things worked at Union Square Hospitality Group. And the company was on the precipice of a huge expansion. Meyer had signed a contract to open a restaurant in the Museum of Modern Art. He was starting a catering operation. And he had opened a hot dog stand in Madison Square Park that, although no one involved knew it yet, would go on to become bigger than any of his other ventures; it was called Shake Shack.

Salgado, who had also studied other well-run businesses that saw their culture break down as they expanded, was worried about Union Square Hospitality's ability to keep growing while maintaining the qualities that had made its first restaurants successful. "I came in with the hypothesis that Danny had systems or structures in place that allowed him to effectively transfer that culture to new restaurants," Salgado told me. "But that wasn't true at all. It was all Danny. And that's not sustainable. I said that if you are going to continue to grow this restaurant group, you will need to build an infrastructure to support that culture, or it will fracture." Salgado thought she just might be the one to help Meyer do it. Which is why, after finishing her doctorate, she abandoned an academic career to join the company with the title "director of culture and learning."

In the fifteen years that followed, Union Square Hospitality would go from four restaurants to sixteen, not counting what became of that hot dog stand. Shake Shack was spun off to become a separate, publicly traded company that had 188 restaurants by late 2018, stretching around the world.

There's a tendency to look at successful businesspeople, especially entrepreneurs who build a company from scratch, through the lens of their vision—and there's no doubt that Meyer has a compelling vision around food and customer service—but vision only gets a person so far. What really differentiates Meyer from the countless other New York restaurateurs who have had less staying power is his ability to turn that vision into something that could be institutionalized and replicated to extend far beyond himself—even if he hadn't fully figured out how to do that when Salgado first joined the company. Meyer might not phrase it this way, but his companies' successes boil down to understanding and applying the fundamental economics of management.

That, in turn, makes his career a case study that matters for anyone in the business world. In a professional career, we all will be managed, and many of us will at some point or another manage others, and the benefits of managing well, or working for someone who does, are greater than ever.

HOW DANNY MEYER WENT FROM ENTREPRENEUR TO CEO

When Meyer opened Union Square Cafe in 1985, he hoped to bring a new type of restaurant to New York. The city had top-quality restaurants that served excellent food, many of them in the French tradition—expensive and formal and not particularly welcoming. And there were neighborhood places that could be a lot more cozy and approachable but served pedestrian food. Meyer hoped to emulate what he had seen in travels to Paris and Rome—as he put it in his memoir, "refined technical service paired with caring, gracious hospitality, and soulful seasonal cooking."[1]

It was an instant success. From the early days, just juggling reservations and tables was a challenge; Meyer learned quickly the power of a complimentary glass of dessert wine to calm a guest irritated at the wait for a table. The plaudits rolled in—a positive review in *The New York Times* in early 1986 triggered a 60 percent jump in business. Meanwhile, Meyer was learning how to be a manager as he went along. Very much a hands-on boss, he interviewed each potential new employee, even the lowest-level busboy, personally. Others could screen for candidates with technical proficiency, but Meyer trusted only himself to judge whether they had the emotional intelligence for the job—the instincts to read whether the mood at a table is joyous or somber, to offer subtly different service to a publishing executive having a business lunch versus a couple on an awkward first date versus longtime friends catching up.

Meyer and his team created systematic processes for the kitchen and for the technical dimensions of service: the chefs wrote out their recipes rather than just storing them in line cooks' memories; a specially crafted manual spelled out how a place setting should look, the proper timing of when guests' cocktail orders would be taken, when a small bowl of olives would be delivered, and so forth. But Meyer didn't want waiters and hosts to just read a script and execute the correct steps of dining service; he wanted them to know how to improvise to give customers a warm, memorable experience. The hospitality elements of the business remained messy and improvisational.

"It was my way of saying, 'I'm casting the play here, and I know what kinds of people I want to hire and what kinds of emotional skills I'm looking for,'" Meyer told me. "But I had yet to put words to those emotional skills. At that point it was only an intuitive feeling. I wasn't able to say to people, 'Here are the six emotional skills we're looking for.' I was hiring people based on how they made me feel."

For nine years, Meyer worked to try to perfect Union Square Cafe but was reluctant to open another restaurant. His father was an entrepreneur who had experienced the pain of bankruptcy, something Meyer saw up close as a child. "I was probably around ten," he recalled. "I associated his bankruptcies with too much expansion. So a big part of me was shying away from being the big boss and considering expansion." Tellingly, it wasn't until after his father died that Meyer saw a new opportunity that was too good to refuse. Tom Colicchio was a rising young chef who wanted to start a restaurant that would create ambitious food in a warm, tavernlike setting. His vision and Meyer's were simpatico. Gramercy Tavern opened in 1994, to instant buzz and attention; underneath four stars, the cover of *New York* magazine the week it opened asked in bold letters, THE NEXT GREAT RESTAURANT?[2] "It's the $3 million offspring of the Union Square Cafe. And it opens this week," explained a subhead, which was on one level the best free advertising a restaurateur could dream of, and on another level wildly overpromising for a restaurant that was yet to serve a single meal and would take a year or two to find its groove.

Meyer was operating only two restaurants, but he could tell that something was wrong. "Even though the restaurants were only four blocks apart from one another, I was like a whirling dervish," he said. "Every time I went back to one restaurant, it had gotten off center. It was fine while I was there, and then when I would go to the other one, I would have to correct things that had gone wrong. The things that bothered me that slipped were how people were treating each other, the approach they were taking to guests."

This remained true even as he opened two more restaurants, Eleven Madison Park (which was sold to its chef and general manager in 2011) and Tabla (which closed in 2010). The latter was where he met Susan Salgado that night in 1999, when that problem was still very much unsolved.

The insight Salgado had in her dissertation was that Meyer's restaurants relied on what she calls a "three-legged stool" to thrive. They hired good people; they had good systems and structure; they maintained a good work environment. None of those elements worked in isolation. Having a good hiring process wouldn't help much if you had a toxic work environment; those good people would quit, or become more toxic themselves. And none of it would work if leadership didn't create an environment where employees could be engaged and successful. "They are so organized systematically," Salgado told me. "There are systems for everything. They know if someone has taken the drink order. At Union Square Cafe, we had little square pieces of paper that were old chopped-up menus. If a table was pretheater, we put a chit of paper underneath the salt shaker on the table. Everyone knew they were pretheater, so we would make sure they got out on time."

But process alone isn't enough. It takes a good work environment and culture to ensure that those systems work effectively.

We were having lunch at Gramercy Tavern as Salgado told me all of this, in early 2018; it might have been twenty-four years old at this point, but it was still full. A waiter presented us with that day's *amuse-bouche,* the small bite before the meal begins. It was a brightly flavored dip of lemon, green olive, and yogurt perched on a house-made cracker. Then, a few minutes later, another waiter brought two more of the same *amuse.* Somebody had screwed up. I asked Salgado what had probably happened, and what the consequences were.

"One of two things happened," she said. "Either the first waiter didn't key in that he had delivered the *amuse,* or the second waiter misremembered which table he was supposed to deliver it to. But the really important thing is that the second waiter went back to the kitchen to figure out what had happened." In a toxic workplace, whichever one messed up would have incentive to try to hide that fact so as to avoid being screamed at—which, in turn, would make it less likely that the problem would be corrected and more likely to happen again. At the Union Square Hospitality Group restaurants, she said, a culture of empathy and trust means that the waiter who messed up would be more likely to be up-front about it. All three legs of the stool work together: because it's not much fun to be yelled at, a good waiter would be more interested in working there than at a place with a different culture, and when a mistake is acknowledged, it's more likely to result in tweaks to systems and processes to ensure that the double delivery of an *amuse-bouche* doesn't happen again. A good culture reinforces good hiring and good systems, and vice versa.

After joining the company as director of culture, Salgado worked to formalize all of this so that it could be replicated far beyond the limits of Meyer's personal ability to meet with people. Indeed, a big part of the job was figuring out and formalizing what Meyer would *not* do.

"When I joined, Danny had to be part of every decision," Salgado told me. "The menu price was changing by fifty cents on brisket at Blue Smoke"—a barbecue restaurant that Union Square Hospitality opened in 2002—"and the general manager had to ask Danny first. At a point that is disabling because he doesn't have the bandwidth." So they sat down and made a list, dividing business decisions into three categories: those that Meyer would always be involved with, those he would be informed of but not asked to weigh in on, and those that could be completely delegated, made by others without Meyer being consulted or even informed.

Meyer had to learn to discipline himself not to micromanage, especially on aesthetic details. Whenever he went into one of his restaurants, his immediate temptation was to point out small problems to staff so they might get fixed—a framed picture slightly askew, a light fixture set a bit too bright. But this was an operational mess. When he would mention these things to line-level staff, all other work in the restaurant would halt as they tried to fix the problem to please the big boss, and the authority of that restaurant's manager would be undermined. He learned to point out aesthetic and other problems he noticed only to the manager, who could perform triage and direct resources to fixing only the most important problems.

Salgado led the creation of a series of training sessions in a classroom they constructed in the restaurant group's headquarters overlooking Union Square. They focused not on front-line staff but on middle managers—the general managers and assistant managers and such who, as the company got bigger, were the crucial link between Meyer's philosophy of service and the product being delivered in those far-flung restaurants. The focus in these sessions was not on the technical aspects of delivering efficient service—after all, those were different in each restaurant, with the mechanical details of how things worked at Blue Smoke bearing little similarity to those at Union Square Cafe. Instead, it was on a broader organizational philosophy and on a mindset conducive to learning and collaborating. "The bigger you get, the harder it is for people to remember why these things are so important if you don't keep talking about them," she said. "Leaders in the company have to understand what their role really is, not just in terms of managing but in terms of making people want to do their jobs. Managing tasks and delegating and making sure the systems work, that's one part of management. But making people want to go above and beyond is what requires true leadership and inspiration, and that was what we focused on, the emotional piece of leading."

Salgado turned what had been a philosophy embedded in Meyer's gut into a formal curriculum that middle managers across the organization could be trained on, in sessions full of simulations of how to handle potentially hard situations: reprimanding an employee who keeps making mistakes; preemptively noticing a customer growing frustrated; mediating the inevitable disputes between front-of-house service staff and back-of-house kitchen staff.[3]

The idea of teaching and trusting middle managers extended to financial concerns. During this period of rapid expansion, Ron Parker led operations for the restaurant group. He had once dreamed of being a celebrity chef and had worked in some of the best kitchens in New

York, but eventually found more stable work overseeing catering and events. Before joining Union Square, for example, for a time he oversaw the forty-six concession stands at the US Open tennis tournament. He was very much a Pareto-optimal executive, conversant both in high-end cuisine and in workflow and process. (Presumably not many people are fluent in both how to make a foie gras torchon and how to design an efficient kitchen workspace by modeling it with three-dimensional design software.) In recalling the company's growth path, Parker emphasized the importance of entrusting middle managers—restaurant general managers and assistant managers—with enough data and other information to truly understand the moving pieces of their business. Successful owner-operators have a tendency to hoard that information, to be the one person with all the relevant information for major decisions. But part of the key to leading an organization of meaningful scale is trusting others with that information.

"It's something that I wish I was trained on when I was starting out as opposed to having to figure out," Parker said. "The constant mantra: whether you're an executive chef or you're a floor manager, I want more people to have access to the financial data, because then you can actually drive the business as opposed to the business driving you. And if you ever leave the industry, you will know how to read a [profit and loss] statement. I feel bad for any restaurateur who still feels that they don't want anybody to know how much profit or loss they have. You should want them to know how profitable or unprofitable you are, because then they can help impact the business positively."

This transparency ties in to compensation, too. The company has been building a series of pay bands, to offer workers more clarity about what advancement might look like within the organization, and how greater responsibility will be compensated. It's essential, Parker argued, that people understand that even a very good pastry chef will make less than the executive chef, no matter what their relative culinary skill, based on the economic reality that desserts account for only around

3 percent of a high-end restaurant's revenue. "It's an 'aha' moment, because if you're already at the top of what your job pays, your options are either to be proud that you've reached the top of that band or, if you want to advance further, to work on how to broaden your expertise to create more value"—for example, by leading initiatives across the company in addition to performing a day job at a single restaurant.

As I spoke with Meyer, I was struck by what seemed like a deeper lesson of his evolution from the founder of a single restaurant to the leader of a sprawling, lucrative empire. He had a knack from a young age for a lot of the fundamentals of starting a restaurant—hiring the best chef, getting the design just right, creating a warm atmosphere for customers. But plenty of other people with similar skills launched successful restaurants in the 1980s. What was different about Meyer was his capacity to create an entire infrastructure through which *other* people could become more effective.

And that gets at the lessons Meyer's growth from solo entrepreneur to CEO of a substantial company offers for people trying to navigate industries that are in most respects completely different from the restaurant business.

A BRIEF HISTORY OF MANAGERIAL CAPITALISM

Every modern organization is run by an idiosyncratic pyramid of middle managers—team leaders and department heads and regional vice presidents and so on. Working for the right manager can be the difference between loving a job and hating it, being a superstar in an organization or someone in line to be laid off. And while many organizations have become better at rewarding and supporting "individual contributors" who simply do high-value work without overseeing others, rising in that management pyramid to oversee more and more people is the most tried-and-true path to greater responsibility, more money, and all the other benefits that come from being higher on the corporate ladder (or lattice, for that matter).

One thing I heard over and over again in interviews with executives for this book was the importance, in this fluid business environment, of understanding the economic structure of the industry, and the company, in which you work. How do you personally, whatever your job may be, contribute to the company's profitability? In some jobs, this analysis is easy. If you are an associate at a law firm, your contribution is driven by the number of hours you bill, multiplied by the hourly rate at which your time is charged to clients, minus the overhead involved in keeping you employed.

But what is the economic contribution of a middle manager, really? The job itself can seem like an endless stream of putting out fires, writing performance reviews, trying to give a stern warning to an employee who needs to step it up or a receptive audience to another who needs to vent. Then, at the end of a long week of work, it might not be at all clear what you actually created. If you are a software developer, you help create the product. But what if you oversee a team of ten software developers, never typing a line of code yourself? To borrow from a consultant's pointed question to a hapless middle manager in the 1999 comedy *Office Space,* "What would you say you *do* here?"

To understand the answer, you need to know a little bit of business history.

As recently as the middle of the nineteenth century, what we now think of as "management" didn't exist. In previous centuries, even in the most advanced economies, nearly every business made only a small number of products in one place and consisted of an owner overseeing a single factory or farm, knowing the names of all the laborers. Consider that in 1470, the Medici Bank, the most powerful financial institution of its era, had all of fifty-seven workers, of whom a mere dozen were managers; now a middle-tier bank in some obscure region might employ thousands.[4] In 1776, in *The Wealth of Nations,* the great economist and philosopher Adam Smith, using the metaphor of a pin factory, explained how the division of labor can increase productivity;

notably, in his example of the awesome productive potential of specialization among workers, he wrote that a single person might be able to make only a single pin in a day, whereas ten workers each specializing in one part of the pin-making process might produce 48,000, thus increasing the productive output of each worker by a factor of 4,800. Now, of course, a factory floor with only ten people under direct oversight of the owner seems quaint. Smith presumably couldn't have imagined (to use a made-up example) a factory employing hundreds producing billions of pins and needles a month, under the oversight of a factory manager who in turn works for the executive vice president for sewing supplies of an industrial conglomerate headquartered thousands of miles away and owned by shareholders around the world.

The shift toward a world of large companies operating in multiple locations with layers of middle management standing between laborers and owners has its roots in technological change, especially around energy, transportation, and communication. The business historian Alfred Chandler Jr. told this tale in his 1977 book *The Visible Hand*, the title a nod to Smith's concept of the invisible hand. In Smith's era, coordination happened almost entirely through market exchanges. A tailor, working alone or with a small staff, would buy pins from that ten-person pin factory, along with fabric from a small textile factory, which in turn had bought wool from small farmers, and make suits one at a time. Eventually, something a little more complicated supplanted that system—a world in which large companies' goods and services were transferred in an internal market, overseen by paid, professional managers.

It started with the railroads. "The men who managed these enterprises became the first group of modern business administrators in the United States," Chandler wrote of the rail lines spread across the countryside of the United States and Western Europe beginning in the mid-nineteenth century. "Ownership and management soon separated. The capital required to build a railroad was far more than that required to purchase a plantation, a textile mill, or even a fleet of ships. Therefore, a single entrepreneur, family, or small group of associates was rarely able to own a railroad. Nor could the many stockholders or their representatives manage it. The administrative tasks were too numerous, too varied, and too complex. They required special skills and training which could only be commanded by a full-time salaried manager. . . . The railroad managers came to look on their work as much more of a lifetime career than did the plantation overseer or the textile mill agent. Most railroad managers soon expected to spend their life working up the administrative ladder."[5]

That pattern repeated with the rollout of the telegraph, the electrical power utilities, and other businesses requiring huge capital expenditures, a wide geographical footprint, and an army of capable managers. It is the innovation that allowed Sears, Roebuck and Company to become a retail titan in an era of small, family-owned stores, that separated Henry Ford's motor company from scores of small-scale tinkerers, and that made the early twentieth-century General Electric not just a skunkworks for Thomas Edison but a juggernaut that introduced lighting and home appliances to millions of households. You could expand the list to other advanced economies of that era. Britain was slow on the uptake, probably owing to its smaller and slower-growing domestic market and perhaps stodginess and traditionalism among its merchant class; Germany was behind the curve on consumer products but ahead of the curve on metals and advanced industrial goods. But by the First World War, the system of large, complex enterprises in which most future business careers would take place was predominant.

In those early years of managerial capitalism, a lot of the study of management involved applying engineering principles to try to make workers more effective. Frederick Winslow Taylor was the father of industrial engineering, an early management consultant, and an influential evangelist for "scientific management" at the turn of the twentieth century. But for Taylor and his intellectual descendants, managing workers meant treating humans as machines, and trying to figure out the optimal way to organize and run those machines. He used the example of the work of manually loading pig iron, the raw material from which steel was made. "This work is so crude and elementary in its nature that the writer firmly believes that it would be possible to train an intelligent gorilla so as to become a more efficient pig-iron handler than any man can be," Taylor wrote in 1911. Yet, he argued, the application of scientific principles could make a laborer dramatically more effective. He told it through a story about a Pennsylvania Dutchman he gave the pseudonym "Schmidt," who researchers figured out later was named Henry Noll.[6] In Taylor's telling, he asked Schmidt if he wanted to be a "high-priced man" making $1.85 a day, instead of being satisfied with only $1.15. Schmidt responded positively with dialogue that Taylor re-creates with a (condescending) Dutch accent: "Vell, den, I vas a high-priced man." But to make that princely sum, Taylor explained to Schmidt, "you will do exactly as this man tells you to-morrow, from morning till night. When he tells you to pick up a pig and walk, you pick it up and you walk, and when he tells you to sit down and rest, you sit down. You do that straight through the day. And what's more, no back talk. A high-priced man does just what he's told to do, and no back talk." By demanding that Schmidt work in exactly the ways "scientific management" prescribed, Taylor was able to increase how much pig iron he could load in a day from 12.5 tons to 47.5. He studied time and motion with stopwatches, understanding every moment of inefficiency, every unnecessary delay in how a worker might carry out his task.

You can still see the echoes of Taylorism in how, for example, companies optimize the layout of a factory floor. When Union Square's Ron Parker leads the design of restaurant kitchens, it is an act of Taylorism; he recalled, for example, that in designing the kitchen of the original Shake Shack it was important to put in separate griddles for burgers and buns, so the meat could be cooked and the buns toasted simultaneously, shaving a minute or two off average order times. But good luck applying this mechanistic "scientific management" to any area where the work isn't rote, predictable, and easily measurable—which is to say, nearly everything in the twenty-first-century service economy. Figuring out which algorithm is most elegant, or which marketing strategy most sensible, or how to provide consistently warm customer service in a high-end restaurant is a rather different question than how best to shovel pig iron.

Peter F. Drucker, the wildly prolific management theorist whose work spanned the latter decades of the twentieth century, coined the term "knowledge worker" in 1959 to describe the class of employees who were most crucial to shaping the fortunes of modern organizations. In the 1940s, General Motors concealed that one of its top executives had a PhD, such advanced education being considered embarrassing.[7] By 1967, when computing technology was by modern standards in its infancy, Drucker was writing presciently about how the ability to analyze and make judgments—and use computers to do so—would be a defining characteristic of successful business professionals of the future. He spent the ensuing decades refining his ideas around what the centrality of knowledge workers to a modern organization meant for the act of managing.

In one of his final books before he died in 2005, he keyed into one of the fundamental shifts that had taken place. "Fewer and fewer people are 'subordinates'—even in fairly low-level jobs. Increasingly there are 'knowledge workers.' And knowledge workers are not subordinates; they are 'associates.' . . . To be sure, these associates are 'subordinates' in that they depend on the 'boss' when it comes to being hired or fired, promoted, appraised and so on. But in his or her own job the superior can perform only if these so-called subordinates take responsibility for *educating* him or her. . . . Their relationship, in other words, is far more like that between the conductor of an orchestra and the instrumentalist than it is like the traditional superior/subordinate relationship."[8]

If those exact words had come out of Danny Meyer's mouth, it wouldn't have surprised me.

Drucker argued for treating knowledge workers as if they are volunteers, who need to know the organization's mission and believe in it, to "make productive the specific strengths and knowledge of each individual." And there, just maybe, is the common thread in what managers do—a connection between Taylorism's stopwatch-bearing taskmaster and Druckerism's symphony conductor.

What do managers do in a world of managerial capitalism? They make the people beneath them more productive than they would be otherwise.

THE STRANGE MATH OF PRODUCTIVITY

Productivity is a bit tricky as a concept. In the colloquial sense, we usually use "productive" to describe a day in which we worked unusually hard and got a lot done. In an economic sense, though, it means something substantially different.

To an economist, labor productivity is, quite simply, the amount of economic output attained relative to the time workers put into production—how much stuff is made for every hour of work.

Productivity isn't about how hard a person seems to be working; we've all known people who are constantly stressed out yet never get anything done, and people who might put in minimal hours at the office yet accomplish big things.

Given that math, for a manager, making an organization productive can take many forms. The ones that are most widespread in this era of managerial capitalism are these: Organize and incentivize people in ways that result in greater business success. Take people with relatively low levels of training or experience and put in place the processes to make their output more valuable than it ever could be in isolation. Turn some product that is valuable, unique, and artisanal into something that you can systematize and replicate.

That is just what Danny Meyer and Union Square Hospitality succeeded at doing. They developed a concept of "Enlightened Hospitality" and laid out the steps to bring it to a hospitality company. And it is heartfelt—they truly believe they have created an approach to the restaurant business that is better for employees, guests, and investors. But in an economic sense, what that culture amounts to— as Susan Salgado put her finger on in her dissertation back in 2003— is a difficult-to-replicate strategy that creates a sustained advantage in making the workers across the organization more productive. A waiter's job might look identical at Union Square Cafe and at a hundred other restaurants in New York with similar prices and menus. But the intricate combination of a thousand different choices made in how the restaurant is run results in Union Square being filled with more happy customers more of the time, which in turn means more sales per person-hour of labor, which means higher productivity.

Making your people more valuable—more productive in a true economic sense—is the north star of being a manager. Everything else, the stuff of thousands of books and articles about management, is mere tactics. The first step to either being a good manager or aligning with one is understanding that fact. Sometimes that happens in a business school or management training seminar. And sometimes it happens in a failing political campaign in a cold New England winter.

MATT MCDONALD AND THE QUEST TO LEVERAGE TALENT

American political campaigns have an uncanny resemblance to a fast-moving startup company. They start with nothing but a person's ideas and raw ambition (the candidate in campaigns, a founder at a company), and then must raise money and ramp up from nothing to an organization with a large staff and administrative hierarchy, all put to the purpose of beating the competition. The biggest of them are enormous; Hillary Clinton's 2016 presidential campaign had about eight hundred employees.[9]

It was in one such startup operation in the early 2000s that a young man learned about the economics of management the hard way. Matt McDonald was twenty-four years old and trying to figure out what to do with his life. He joined the campaign of Jane Swift, a Republican running for governor of Massachusetts.[10] He realized two things quickly: that there was an impossible amount of work, and that to have any hope of accomplishing the goals, he would need help. "There's an infinite amount of work to be done; it's just a question of how much you can pack in before Election Day," he said. "There's always another voter to be contacted, there's always another story to be pitched. So I think there is an assumed level of this sense of 'How do you leverage your time to be more effective?'"

The answer was interns. McDonald went around to College Republican clubs at nearby schools seeking out volunteers, who generally did not have any particular campaign-relevant skills but did have enthusiasm and a desire to pad their résumés. He trained them to monitor news reports and log voter contacts and otherwise keep the machinery of that campaign running. "If the expectation is that you have to do 110 percent or 120 percent of what you have time for, you can just work really hard," McDonald said. "But if the expectation is to do 200 percent or 300 percent, that's just not possible." By recruiting volunteers and training them to do the exact things that needed doing, he made it possible. He may have been twenty-four years old, but he was making the people beneath him more productive than they would have been otherwise, deploying volunteers as a force multiplier to enable the organization to create much more.

The Swift campaign faltered, and McDonald would go on to work for campaigns for George W. Bush, Arnold Schwarzenegger, and John McCain; he did stints in the Bush White House and at McKinsey. But the management lessons of those formative years on a failed campaign were evident fifteen years later, on a muggy Wednesday in June 2017 in Washington, DC.

About a dozen fresh-faced young adults—in their early twenties, most with newly printed degrees from good universities—took their seats around a conference table in an office building around the corner from the White House. They were newly hired staff at Hamilton Place Strategies, where McDonald is a partner who played a big role in shaping its organizational strategy.

Hamilton Place is one of the many public affairs firms you will find in Washington and other capitals; they help mostly corporate clients try to bend public policy in their preferred direction, particularly by seeking to influence media coverage. They analyze policy issues, craft press releases and opinion articles, build coalitions of support, and otherwise seek to inject their clients' views into the public discussion. McDonald began this orientation session by giving the new hires a window into the economics that shape their potential career path.

"Let's talk about the mechanics of growth here and how we think about it," McDonald said. "In professional services, your product is your time. It's how much you can produce in the time you are given. And the way that the firm and the people working in the firm get paid more is by increasing net productivity. So all the training and learning that you guys are going to do this week, that's all driven by the business model and the economics of this organization. This is true whatever professional services firm you go to, whether they say it explicitly or not."

He explained the structure of Hamilton Place and similar firms, and the economics that undergird it. At the bottom are analysts and associates, who do much of the work parsing data or crafting policy memos; they are expected to do 50 to 60 percent of the work on a project. In the middle are directors and senior directors, who act as project managers overseeing day-to-day service to a client; they do another 30 percent or so of the work. Above them are partners, who spend their time bringing in business and overseeing the work done for many clients at a time. For the entire business model of the firm to work, they should be contributing only the last 10 or 20 percent—perhaps guidance on the direction at the front end, and a final review to make sure the work is up to snuff.

Out of this economic structure flows the entire structure of how people get paid and how they can advance, as McDonald laid out that June morning.

"If you are serving two clients who each pay us $20,000 a month, and then next year you're serving two clients who pay $20,000 a month, there is no change in your economics or your role or anything," McDonald said. "The path to upward mobility in terms of both role and compensation is to either get our client to pay more or for you to be able to serve more clients. As you become more efficient at making those products, and at some point overseeing other people who make those products, that will make the totality of the firm more efficient. When we talk about all the training and teamwork, it's all good stuff, but I don't want you to mistake it for being done for fuzzy, warm feelings alone. It is also intrinsic to the business model of the firm and basically to any other professional services firms. This is how the economics of this works."

For example, he said in a separate interview, "if today you come in and it takes you forty hours to produce a twenty-page [PowerPoint] deck, and then next year you can produce the same deck in ten hours and it's better, then you're no longer serving two clients, you're serving three clients. And as you move from that zone of not only being able to make that deck faster, but then provide insight into other people and direction and guidance to leverage your time over, you're serving five clients instead of two or three, and you get paid more and you get more responsibility.

"I often see complaints of the variety that 'Hey, I've been at place X for five years and I haven't seen a raise,' and it's like, 'Well, what has changed in five years, and how are you more effective and more valuable in terms of what you're doing?'"

The way to do that at Hamilton Place consists, essentially, of becoming a Pareto-optimal employee. Those whose background is strongest in writing and communications need to force themselves to improve their abilities to do data analysis—for example, pulling information about an industry from the Bloomberg financial data terminal and manipulating it in Microsoft Excel to come up with useful insights. Those with a stronger quantitative background need to develop experience, for example, at becoming expert in some field of public policy and pitching reporters a story angle that clients want to be propagated.

Advancing, in other words, is not about racking up extra years of service but about using those years of service to become an employee who can provide the most value to clients, and then become a project manager who can in turn elevate the work of more junior, lower-paid staff—turning the raw talent of a new class of recent college graduates into Pareto-optimal employees in their own right. It's a lot more complicated than managing how an unskilled laborer loads pig iron, and the style of management much more closely resembles Peter Drucker's world than Frederick Taylor's. But the economics of it is not altogether different.

Ashley Smith graduated from Southern Methodist University in Dallas, Texas, in 2010; she had majored in finance and was interested in moving to Washington, so she applied for an internship with Hamilton Place, which represented clients in the banking industry. She was quickly promoted to become one of its first associates. At first, her work was mainly administrative—collecting news clippings, pulling together lists of reporters who cover various subjects, that sort of thing—and as she gained experience she was entrusted with more complex jobs, like crafting press releases or talking points for clients. That type of work is the bread and butter of public relations firms the world over, and plenty of people who start in those jobs do more or less the same for many years.

But McDonald and the other partners had a bigger vision for the type of firm that Hamilton Place might become, and Smith fit into it to a T. Their theory was that there was opportunity to be had in combining traditional public relations with policy analysis. And they had a theory that they could teach young, relatively low-paid workers how to do that analysis, and thus be able to offer a more valuable service to more clients relative to the cost. In effect, they would turn their mix of analytical and communications savvy into something replicable, by enhancing the productivity—in the economic sense—of relatively junior staff. It was the professional-services-firm equivalent of McDonald turning a bunch of unpaid campaign interns into a high-performing team, or Danny Meyer turning his preternatural gift as a restaurant manager into something that could be replicated across hundreds of locations.

"As the caliber of clients and the number of clients grew, it became much more systematic, more standardized," Smith said. "A lot of the culture was learning on the job. Matt taught us how to quantify qualitative information and present it to the client in a quantifiable way."

One day McDonald, the former McKinsey consultant, literally stood behind Smith while she manipulated a spreadsheet analyzing how different policy outcomes would affect the business of one client, cleaning up raw data the client had provided and turning big tables of data into coherent analysis, then turning that into a presentation with recommendations for the client.

"We were looking at the probability this change will take place and what the negative impact would be on the client's business in different scenarios," Smith said. "I remember one weekend I went in [to] try to replicate what we had done the day before so I would be able to do it in the future." Sure enough, Smith was soon able to do the same work on her own, and in time teach it to the newer, more junior associates. The firm, in effect, was becoming a machine for turning new, relatively unskilled college graduates like the ones who were at orientation that summer day into people who can create output with tremendous value to some of the largest companies on earth.

The fact that this has allowed McDonald and the other partners to spread their own expertise out more widely and make money off the labors of their more junior staff has surely been good for their own incomes. But it's wrong to think of this work to enhance productivity as selfish or exploitative; productivity enhancement cuts both ways. A more productive worker can ascend to more lucrative work. In her last couple of years at the firm, Smith—still only in her mid-twenties and only a couple of years removed from receiving step-by-step instructions on cleaning up spreadsheet data from a manager standing behind her—was running a team of four newer employees, teaching them the same processes and culture.

Smith might have started as an intern at a small Washington public relations firm, but because of the structure of the organization, she had acquired skills more akin to those of an analyst at an elite management consultancy, setting the stage for more lucrative jobs in the future. She eventually left to get an MBA at New York University's business school, and when I met with her in 2018 she was an investment banking associate at a leading Wall Street bank.

So the lessons from Hamilton Place apply equally whether you are directing other people in a leadership position or looking for a place to make your career.

If you're a manager, the pathway to success is to seek ways to elevate the capabilities of your staff, to offer transparency about what it will take to rise in the organization, and to seek to turn complex work into something that can be replicated and executed by more junior subordinates.

If you're an employee looking for a job, you should eagerly seek an organization with that type of culture—one where you will get the instruction and leadership to become a more valuable contributor, and where you will be rewarded as you rise and create more economic value for that organization and future employers.

And, it's worth adding, Hamilton Place offered Smith some lessons that she will take forward wherever the rest of her career leads. "By the time I left, I was helping to train people, guiding people, and serving as a mentor," Smith said. "What the experience taught me was [that] after you gain a footing in what you need to be doing, you can rise a lot faster if you can give guidance to the people below you."

In some ways, Smith was lucky to end up in the first job she did. She acknowledges that she more or less stumbled into it. But when it comes to creating the kinds of processes that constitute good management—that make employees more productive, and thus able to have better careers with higher incomes—a rapidly expanding body of evidence shows that not all companies are created equal.

MANAGEMENT AS A TECHNOLOGY AND THE BIG SORT

When Nicholas Bloom was growing up in London in the early 1980s, he had an uncommon obsession with the board game Monopoly. It might have seemed he was obsessed with making money. But what really captivated him was not figuring out how to make a great fortune for himself; it was understanding the mechanisms by which money is made.

After finishing a doctorate in economics at Oxford, Bloom went to work at McKinsey, the consulting firm. One day in 2003, Michael Porter, the influential Harvard Business School strategy professor, spoke at the London School of Economics about British competitiveness. Among those attending were John Van Reenen, an LSE professor, and John Dowdy, a partner in McKinsey's London office. They coincidentally sat next to each other and struck up a conversation about Porter's assertion that big-picture strategy was more important for overall competitiveness than the nuts and bolts of managing organizations. They both thought that the mechanics of management actually mattered a great deal, and that bad management practices might be holding back the British economy. Dowdy and Van Reenen talked about how to figure out if their theory was true.

Dowdy had been overseeing a project at McKinsey aimed at measuring the benefits of good management practices, which involved surveying approximately a hundred companies about what practices they engage in and comparing those practices with financial results. Bloom had been carrying out the work—and was on the verge of leaving McKinsey for the London School of Economics, where Van Reenen's office was down the hall. Bloom was able to serve as something of a bridge between the consulting world and the academics.

Scholars tend to view management more as the domain of management gurus who sell mass-market books at airport bookstores than as a subject for rigorous academic analysis and formal mathematical models.[11] "I'd give seminars presenting a paper about management, and when they saw the M-word in your title, people's view of your IQ dropped twenty points," Bloom joked. Conveniently, he added, Americans tend to mentally assign people with a British accent an extra fifteen IQ points. "So I'm about five down, but hopefully both prejudices collapse as the seminar goes on."

Still, he and Van Reenen decided that they might be able to learn something important about how, and whether, management techniques matter if they put the McKinsey survey methodology in place on a much larger scale. Maybe, with enough data, you could settle once and for all: Is there some secret sauce of good management that some companies have and others don't?

They came up with a plan. They would hire people—MBA students working part-time, as it turned out—to conduct structured telephone interviews with managers at midsize companies around the world, using what is called a "double-blind" technique. The interviewers didn't know anything going in about the companies they were interviewing, a step intended to prevent them from having any preconceptions. And the interviewees were given only a vague description of the purpose of the conversation—that they were part of a study about management practices. This was meant to encourage the managers being interviewed to be honest; unbeknownst to them, the interviewer was listening carefully and scoring their company on eighteen different management practices on a 5-point scale from "worst practice" to "best practice." For example, one of the eighteen was "consequence management." If, based on the interview, the best description of the company's practice was that "failure to achieve agreed objectives does not carry any consequences," it scored a 1 on that category; if the better description was that "failure to achieve agreed targets drives retraining in identified areas of weakness or moving individuals to where their skills are more appropriate," it scored a 5.[12]

Just setting the survey infrastructure up was a management challenge of its own; at the peak, there were forty interviewers working in a London office space, speakers of a wide range of languages who worked strange hours to match the time zones of the countries where their interview subjects were located. Bloom got his own taste of the difficulties of managing a large staff. "I had a couple of people who would mess about, and everyone else got really angry that they were getting paid the same as the guy two desks down who seemed to be on the internet all day looking at sports scores." It was hard work— in a full day, a staff member might conduct only two forty-five-minute interviews, spending the rest of the time trying to track down and persuade managers at firms in the sample to agree to have such a conversation—and the process involved some subjectivity, of course. But by the end of each interview, the result was a score of how close the company came to being run with what are widely acknowledged to be management best practices. From databases and public filings, the researchers already knew a lot about the companies' financial results.

With all that data, they could analyze all kinds of things: how the well-managed companies performed financially compared to the poorly managed ones, for example, and how management practices varied across countries. The first set of surveys was conducted in 2004, of 732 companies in four countries. By the time I met with Bloom in his office at Stanford, where he joined the faculty after his time at LSE, about 25,000 interviews had been conducted, covering firms in thirty-five countries.

Many interesting findings have come out of this work.[13] Sure enough, the firms that rate highest in their management practices have higher return on capital and are less likely to go out of business. Management practices seem to be strongest in some of the countries known for high competitiveness and high incomes, like the United States, Germany, Japan, and Canada—and weaker in places known to struggle on both frontiers, like Italy, Portugal, India, and Brazil. Interestingly, some of the countries with lower average levels of management quality have much stronger results at multinational firms' facilities within their borders, suggesting companies can export good management techniques. Bloom and his coauthors have drawn important broad-brush conclusions that are crucial to understanding careers in the modern economy.

Good management acts like a technology in and of itself. It is something that can be adopted and propagated across companies much as a new technique for smelting steel or testing machine parts might be. When best management practices are in place, the productivity of people up and down the organization is higher; each individual becomes more valuable than they would be in a more poorly managed firm. Higher productivity is an essential precondition to higher compensation.

Moreover, the Bloom–Van Reenen research shows that there is a wide distribution between well-managed and poorly managed firms even within a country, and within an industry. That ties in to how to think about a career all the more when you consider a different thread of research (to which, as it happens, Bloom has also contributed).

A powerful body of evidence indicates that certain firms are pulling away from the rest in the global economy. These "superstar" firms are more profitable and pay their workers better than other firms in their industries The next chapter will examine this evidence and its implications in detail, but I asked Bloom whether there might be a connection between that finding and his results on the idea of the role of management in shaping productivity. And it surely seems there is.

There have always been firms that were better run than others, presumably. What seems to be changing is that the relative reward for being at the well-run firms is rising. Which is exactly what you would expect if good management were a technology that had a particularly big benefit in increasing the productivity of people with high ability working together, which Bloom posits it is. The key idea is "complementarity."

"I watch a lot of soccer," Bloom said. "It's very obvious that there is a great complementarity between great players. Having Lionel Messi"—the brilliant Argentina-born forward—"is much more valuable if you have people he can pass to. So that could be the same story in firms, that complementarity has gone up." Maybe, in other words, when you have people with high ability who are well managed, the whole is not just a little bit greater than the sum of its parts but much, much greater, in the same way that an elite soccer player can achieve much better results with elite teammates.

"If you thought modern technology, being well managed, was really complementary with high-ability types, then it's going to make sense for well-run successful firms to hire more high-ability employees," Bloom told me. "You could see there being some firms that are winning everywhere. They're better managed. They have better technology. They have better employees that other employers are losing. If the marginal revenue produced by a high-ability person is increasingly higher in a good firm relative to a bad firm, then of course it will sort"—that is, the highest-performing people will sort themselves into the highest-performing companies—"because Google will just pay a higher premium compared to a less well-run firm."

That is precisely consistent with the pattern actually observed in most of the world's leading economies in the last few decades. "What's happening is, within every industry and region and demographic, however you break it down, it's a big sort," Bloom said.[14]

I asked him how, given these findings, he would advise one of his students at Stanford, or an ambitious niece or nephew, to manage a career. "Who you were employed by in an industry didn't matter that much fifty years ago, and now it seems to matter much more. So if it were my kids, I would tell them, 'Try very hard to get employed by one of the best-in-class firms in the industry.'"

That advice seems both obviously correct and rather limiting. By definition, not everyone can work at the handful of superstar firms that are the biggest winners in the big sort. We can't all work at Google or Goldman Sachs, just as not every young chef can get a job in Danny Meyer's restaurant empire and not every professional services company will offer young associates the opportunity to broaden their skills the way Hamilton Place Strategies does. The challenge is to navigate a career as it exists in the real world, where the ideal option isn't always available.

What do you do when you find yourself living in this world of superstar firms, aside from cross your fingers and hope for a job at one of the places where you'll be playing with the Lionel Messi or Danny Meyer of your industry? Three executives in Seattle helped me understand the options.

6

Navigating the Winner-Take-All World

─────

DO YOU WORK AT A WINNER, AN ASPIRANT, OR AN AFTERTHOUGHT?

Taylor Swift, the singer of infectious pop tunes, is estimated to have made $170 million in 2016. Several dozen more musicians earned in the millions of dollars.[1] Yet the median pay of the 40,000 people in the United States who made a living as a musical performer that year was $25.14 an hour, or about $50,000 a year.[2] They made a little bit more than tool and die makers and a little bit less than commercial drivers.

The highest-earning women's tennis player that year was Angelique Kerber, who made $10.1 million in prize money. The 100th best, a Colombian woman named Mariana Duque-Mariño, had earnings of $309,115, lucrative in the same way being a successful doctor or lawyer might be. The 1,000th best, a Belgian named Sofie Oyen, made a mere $2,678 in winnings; she would probably have earned more teaching retired dentists how to improve their serve at a resort.

In entertainment and sports, it's always been the case that the very best do radically better than people who are just a tier below them—winner-take-all, or, if you want to be more precise, winners-take-most.[3] One of the most important shifts in the business world over the last few decades is that the same dynamics increasingly apply to which companies prosper. And this has massive, and underrecognized, implications.

Nick Bloom's advice in the last chapter was to seek out those superstar companies and hang on for dear life. That can be good advice, as far as it goes—if your personality, your skills, your ambitions, and your luck in the job market all align. Frequently, however, that is not the case. Working at a large, profitable company has a lot of advantages. But for the right person at the right career stage, so does joining a more entrepreneurial upstart, or an established company that is experiencing hard times and is at risk of being one of the losers in the winner-take-all world.

The way to navigate the winner-take-all nature of modern business, in other words, is to understand the reasons for it, where your employer fits into that competitive landscape, and how to make the most of whatever advantages that position offers. This chapter is a guide to doing that.

FIVE FACTORS CREATING A POSITIVE-RETURNS-TO-SCALE WORLD

The great economic thinker Alfred Marshall, around the turn of the twentieth century, described the "law of diminishing returns," which was how things worked in agriculture and in heavy industries in which companies produce the same goods over and over again. The idea is that as a company gets bigger—stretches into new markets, taps new natural resources—its returns will fall. That new market will inevitably become more expensive to get into than a company's home market; the fourteenth-most-promising copper mine will be more expensive to excavate than the first. The more you sell, the more it costs to make each unit.

In the twenty-first century, Marshall's diminishing-returns world has been replaced by an increasing-returns world. There have always been some information-centric industries where this is the case. Once a movie studio has already spent $200 million to make a film in the United States, it costs comparative peanuts to bring it to China or Brazil as well. Oracle doesn't have to dig the fourteenth-best copper mine to sell another copy of its software; it just sells one more license of a product it's already invested millions in creating. A pharmaceutical company may invest a couple of billion dollars over many years trying to find the next blockbuster drug, but the cost of making each additional pill is trivial. Essentially, the potential profitability in those industries is limitless—if, and it's a big if, you succeed at being one of the handful of winners.

In recent decades, this world of increasing returns to scale seems to have spread into many more industries. You can see it in data on profitability, as the chart below, based on data crunched by economists Jason Furman and Peter Orszag, shows. As recently as the 1990s, the

The Rising Payoff of Being a Top Firm

Return on invested capital excluding goodwill, for U.S. publicly traded nonfinancial firms

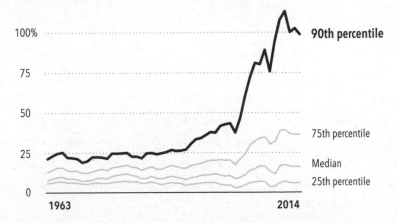

most successful 10 percent of publicly traded firms in the United States had returns on capital of around 25 percent, while for the median firm it was about 10 percent. The figure hasn't changed much for the median firm, but the top-tier companies are now achieving returns on capital of over 100 percent!

There are several reasons for this shift toward a winner-take-all economy. Here are several of the factors that I find most persuasive—and note that these are not mutually exclusive. Rather, each can reinforce the others to create an even bigger economic moat for companies in that top 10 percent.

Intangible inputs becoming more predominant. As mentioned above, information industries like software and movies have always had this winner-take-all element. But now things that are intangible—whether lines of code or giant pools of customer data or patents on some business process or just a well-respected brand—are becoming a bigger share of what it takes to make products in the modern economy, as opposed to physical capital. The software in a modern car is as important as the steel in its chassis; the customer data accumulated by a retailer is as important as its physical real estate. As Jonathan Haskel and Stian Westlake memorably titled their book on these effects, this creates a world of "capitalism without capital."

Network effects. Some products are more valuable the more people use them—meaning that the industry tends to converge toward a monopoly or duopoly, rather than a free-for-all of competition. This has long been true in software. I wrote this book in Microsoft Word in large part because my editors and other collaborators also use Microsoft Word. Even if I was persuaded that a competitor had created slightly better word processing software, I'd be reluctant to switch for that reason. Facebook became one of the most valuable companies on the planet heavily on the back of network effects—if you use the social media service, it is in large part because so many of your friends and family do. But network effects can also pop up in sectors that don't involve digital technology. As we'll see, network effects are popping up in some surprising places in the modern age.

Market power and contagious consolidation. When one industry consolidates for whatever reason, it can create greater incentive for those it does business with to consolidate as well, for fear of being steamrolled by a larger, more powerful, better-capitalized supplier or customer. One example of this is hospitals and health insurance companies in the United States. The more customers an insurer has in a given city, the more it can force hospitals to accept low reimbursement rates for treatment; the bigger the share of hospitals under the same corporate umbrella, the more they can stand together and push for higher reimbursement rates. On both sides, it creates an incentive to consolidate into as few companies as possible in a cycle that is either vicious or virtuous depending on how you feel about the value of bigness. You see similar dynamics with the giant makers of consumer packaged goods and retailers.

Crony capitalism and regulatory barriers. A company that is large and profitable has every incentive to use politics to entrench its advantage. The more a company makes, the more it can spend on lobbying and political donations to try to implement policies that help it, whether that means government-subsidized financing, intellectual property protection, or export subsidies. Even regulations that ostensibly rein in an industry can favor incumbent companies; for example, the banking industry opposed post-financial-crisis regulations in the United States, but a complex set of rules tends to favor large, successful companies that can influence the details of regulations and hire lots of compliance officers.

Antitrust authorities' tolerance of consolidation. Companies always seek to consolidate to reduce competition, and will do so as long as antitrust authorities don't stop them—and antitrust authorities have been more tolerant of consolidation in the last few decades. Airlines in the United States are a great example. Antitrust regulators did not stand in the way of Delta buying Northwest in 2008, or United buying Continental in 2010, or Southwest buying AirTran in 2011, or American buying US Airways in 2013. The result: a mere four companies accounted for 72 percent of market share in 2016 (the top four airlines had about 50 percent of market share as recently as 2007). In the technology sphere, there was barely a ripple when Facebook bought Instagram or WhatsApp, even as those acquisitions allowed it to solidify its hold on the social media and digital advertising market.

There are other excellent books worth reading if you want to evaluate the relative importance of these factors in creating our modern winner-take-all business world (a few are listed in the endnotes).[4] And there is an interesting debate to be had about the implications of this shift for workers and communities; there is evidence that by reducing the number of companies competing for workers, higher concentration of major industries may hold down overall wages, for example.[5] But for our purposes here, the question is what you should do about it. What does it mean that a small number of superstar firms are dramatically more successful and profitable than the rest? What should we make of the fact that the gap between the superstar companies and the rest looks more and more like the gap between Angelique Kerber and Sofie Oyen, or between Taylor Swift and your local wedding band? To find out, I spent some time looking at an industry where the rise of superstar firms is well established, to see what it has meant for someone looking to have a good career.

HILTON HOTELS AND HOW LODGING BECAME AN INFORMATION BUSINESS

There are hotels in every city of any size in the world. It is the ultimate business in which anyone with access to some capital and a little know-how can compete. It is an industry that rewards gumption and entrepreneurship. The lodging business, on its face, doesn't seem like some of the complex industries this book has examined. Unlike making aircraft parts or automobiles, it's about executing relatively simple functions—selecting a building in a good location for travelers, investing in comfortable beds and a nice-looking lobby, providing quality customer service that matches the level of fanciness expected by your target market.

And rooted as it is in real estate, it would seem like a classic negative returns-to-scale business: the more hotels you buy or build, the more you're spending and the more suboptimal locations you're going into. A hotel several miles from an urban center is the equivalent of the fourteenth-best copper mine.

The real estate piece of the industry really does seem to follow these rules, with ownership of hotels spread among an endless list of investors that includes real estate investment trusts, pension funds, endowments, and families who own and operate a motel under a franchise agreement.

But the management and branding of hotels has shifted in the other direction. In 1997, the five top lodging companies in the United States controlled 43 percent of hotel rooms in the nation, according to data and analytics company STR. By 2017 that had risen to 52 percent. Just three companies, Marriott International, Hilton Worldwide, and Choice Hotels International, control 2.6 million hotel rooms globally—15 percent of the hotel rooms in the world—and they're all headquartered within a twenty-minute drive of each other in the suburbs of Washington, DC![6]

The reasons for this shifting industry structure track closely with the five factors described above (some more than others).

While the physical capital of a hotel—the building itself, the furniture in your room—is a big part of selecting where you will stay on a trip, the intangibles have a value all their own, and this is where big hotel chains have an edge. If you reserve a room in a Hilton in a city you've never been to, you know you will be getting a comfortable bed and a certain level of service, based on decades the company has spent affirming that reputation (and requiring that its properties worldwide meet those minimum requirements). Then there's the technological component: Hilton employs software developers who have built and maintain a mobile app for easy reservations and check-in. Newer offerings let you use your phone as a room key and are seeking to supplement human customer service with artificial-intelligence-powered chatbots. These areas, unlike physical capital, are in the positive-returns-to-scale world: Hilton's brand reputation and its information technology are valuable, yet it doesn't cost much to extend them to the benefit of one more property. That reputation and technology might have taken decades and billions of dollars to build, but to enable an additional hotel to take advantage of them requires only the cost of putting up new signs.

Network effects show up increasingly often in the hotel industry as well. Loyalty programs reward frequent travelers with points that can be used for free rooms at other properties within a company. That means that the larger a company is, the more appealing it potentially is. If you are a frequent business traveler to Cleveland, why stay in an independent hotel when you could instead stay in a hotel where you will accrue points that might pay for a future stay at a luxury resort in Bali or a long weekend in Paris? And as frequent travelers choose among the major hotel companies, a bigger network is better.

For a prime example of how market power and contagious consolidation affect the industry, consider hotel booking sites. They have become a powerful middleman in lodging and other travel businesses; many people who are visiting a city decide where to stay by browsing the options on Expedia or Travelocity or Hotwire or Hotels.com or Orbitz. So a hotelier's fate depends significantly on how a property is featured and priced on those sites. A lone hotel is typically heavily dependent on the travel booking sites, and as a result is in a poor negotiating position; if it wants prominent play in search results, it must pay for the privilege. But big chains have a sales force and large-scale marketing operation of their own so are less dependent on booking sites. Hilton can run television ads (the actress Anna Kendrick was a recent spokesperson) directing people to its own website; independent hotels can't do that. And their negotiations with the bookings sites are more a battle of equals, because the booking sites need the big chains. If Marriott or Hilton withdrew its properties from the listings, those booking sites would no longer be useful places for travelers to make their plans. One piece of evidence for the contagious-consolidation argument: the five travel listing sites listed above are all part of the same company.

As for regulatory barriers and crony capitalism, the industry has tried to use political power to entrench the success of the largest hotel companies. In the United States, for example, the hotel industry has been in ongoing battles with Airbnb, with the marketplace for short-term rentals arguing that major hotel companies have benefited from state and local subsidies for building properties; meanwhile, the hotel industry has, with some success, pushed states and localities to enforce tax and land use laws more stringently in ways that might hem in that emerging rival.[7]

Finally, antitrust authorities have certainly been accommodating of consolidation in the industry, most notably with Marriott's 2016 acquisition of Starwood, a company that encompassed brands including Westin, Sheraton, and Le Méridien. That deal took time to work its way through regulatory approval in forty countries where the companies did business, but it eventually closed to create the world's biggest hotel company.

To understand what these shifts in the lodging industry mean for a person navigating a career within it, I sat down with Matthew Schuyler, the chief human resources officer for Hilton, in the company's global headquarters in a tower in McLean, Virginia.

Technology is changing the hotel experience inexorably, he said. When people are contemplating a trip, booking a room, even checking in, they are more and more likely to do it with their mobile device. That means that the people who actually operate the hotels—assistant general managers and general managers at a property, regional managers, and so forth—need a different mindset than in the past.

No one expects a hotel manager to understand the technical details of an RFID chip that enables a mobile phone to function as a room key. But he or she does need to be ready to embrace the implications of this and other technical advances that shift how the hotel delivers service. "When I'm interviewing somebody we're recruiting, what am I screening you for?" Schuyler pondered. "Culture fit, which is code for good judgment, that you'll get along well with others. That you're open to change, not change averse, and that you're adaptive and have the softer skills involved in leadership, that you can engage and inspire."

Joe Berger started his hotel industry career as a teenager in the 1980s, as a bellman in the Marriott hotel near Dulles Airport outside Washington, DC; it was a job in much greater demand in those days before widespread adoption of roller bags, he recalled, and paid a lot better than flipping hamburgers at McDonald's. He instantly loved the hotel business, and after studying finance in college returned to the industry on a management track with Marriott. He worked at Marriott hotels in Atlanta and Chicago, then moved his young family to Europe, where he did stints in Vienna, Munich, and Frankfurt. His next stop was San Francisco, where he would be the general manager of the Fairmont and later the Westin St. Francis, a monster of a hotel that was originally built in 1904, survived the 1906 San Francisco earthquake, and was later expanded to encompass 1,200 rooms.

After a couple of decades on the front lines of managing hotels, however, Berger moved up toward more corporate roles overseeing properties. He was a Pareto-optimal executive, combining his financial background with operational experience. He went to work for Blackstone, the private equity firm that owned the St. Francis when Berger ran it. Then, in 2007, Blackstone engineered a $26 billion acquisition of Hilton—putting Berger in a good position for a senior job at the company.

When I met him in 2018, Berger was president of the Americas for Hilton—meaning a big part of his job was identifying, developing, and promoting the hotel managers who would best propel Hilton's properties throughout the western hemisphere to success. And what he was looking for was rather different than the skills it took to succeed as a general manager in his younger days. "Today, a lot of our hotels are owned by private equity investors and others that act like private equity. You need to be able to speak their language. You need to understand their investment thesis. You need to be as good on the financial side as they are to meet their objectives. It might be 'We'd like to reposition this property up market, and to do that we're going to invest X dollars, and we need Y return, and our fund is chartered for seven years, and we need you to help us get there.' And the hard part about the job of a general manager is you've got to do that while also doing all the other things it takes to run a hotel. I think that's what makes this business so fun, that at the same time you're worried about return on [capital expenditures], you're just as focused on making sure the craft cocktails in the bar are creative and fun, and taking care of your team members and how you're servicing guests."

All of this means that to thrive, rising executives need to think about building their experiences differently. The success of the biggest hotel companies implies that the greatest opportunity lies within those large organizations, rather than with an independent property where growth opportunity will be limited. And making one's way within a Hilton (or Marriott, or Intercontinental, or Hyatt) requires becoming a manager within the "glue people" portion of the Pareto-optimal curve. "Today you really need to be able to move horizontally," said Berger. "I look at the business when I first joined as a bellman, or my first managing job, and this business has gotten a lot more complicated. You still need to be good at taking care of your team members, having a great bar and great restaurants, and creating that sense of theater, but there are also the financial components, the marketing components, the technology components. If you can't do it, you can't keep up today because everybody is pushing hard."

HOW FINDING A JOB IS LIKE INVESTING: GROWTH, VALUE, AND VENTURE

So given all that, nabbing a job at one of the preeminent, well-established, profitable companies in your industry would seem to be the best career advice, as Nick Bloom from Stanford suggested.

To which one might first reply, *Duh.*

And might next reply, *Yeah, but not everybody can work at the very best companies.*

Not every tech worker will snag a job at Google, Apple, or Facebook; not every banker at Goldman Sachs or JPMorgan; not every hotelier at Hilton or Marriott. It is true as a simple mathematical matter, but also true in the sense that at times it might be more desirable to take a job at a less-renowned firm rather than a name-brand superstar firm. Maybe that's because a less successful or well-known company is putting a better offer on the table in terms of compensation or responsibility (or is the only employer putting an offer on the table—most people don't get to pick which companies will offer them a job, after all). And not everybody is well suited, by personality and temperament, to work in these large, frequently bureaucratic organizations.

I wrestled with this conundrum for a while; given those realities, what really do winner-take-all effects imply for an optimal career? And

I realized that there is actually a handy parallel, from the world of investing.

There are two broadly defined types of stock that an investor might buy: growth or value. Growth stocks are the companies that, in the reckoning of investors, both are already successful and have bright futures. It is a category that includes most of the companies that would count as superstar firms, name-brand organizations that dominate their industries, are well managed, and are expected to continue churning out rising profits far into the future. But the fact that everybody thinks growth stocks are so desirable is precisely the problem: everybody wants to own them, and so their shares get bid up to premium levels. Their share price is high relative to the company's earnings, the book value of its assets, or whatever other accounting measure you prefer of comparing a company's market value to its fundamentals.

Value stocks, by contrast, are the companies that are disdained by the market. They may have shrinking market share, or a product being displaced by new technology, or legal troubles, or an incompetent CEO. These companies are disdained by the marketplace because they seem so flawed. And frequently the conventional wisdom proves correct: Their earnings may flatline or decline, bankruptcy or costly legal judgment may await, the CEO may turn out to be just as much of a buffoon as they think. But because conventional wisdom is pessimistic, their shares tend to be cheap relative to fundamentals. Each dollar you invest gets you more in annual earnings or asset value, because the smart money assumes that conditions will worsen over time.

Here's the thing, though. Sometimes a value company turns out to be not so bad after all. Maybe its market share stabilizes, the revolutionary new competitor is slow to take over, the lawsuit is settled, and the CEO gets replaced with somebody more capable. And not all growth companies will have as bright a future as everyone assumes; business history is littered with onetime superstars that fell.

If you could go back in time to 1968 and invest in any company listed on the New York Stock Exchange, with plans to hold its shares and reinvest its dividends until the 2000s, what company would you take? Perhaps something in software or semiconductors, to take advantage of the digital revolution that took place in that span? Or pharmaceuticals, to profit from all the innovation in medicine? Banking, to benefit from the remarkable surge in the financial sector in those decades? Those choices would all give you inferior returns to a company now known as Altria, then known as Philip Morris.[8] During that span, the scientific consensus around the cancer-causing properties of cigarettes became ironclad, tobacco companies faced multibillion-dollar lawsuits for covering that fact up, taxes on cigarettes were radically increased, and the proportion of American adults who smoke fell from around 40 percent to 17 percent.[9] Yet the stock returned 20 percent a year for more than three decades straight! The reason, of course, is that it was the ultimate value stock. The downward trajectory of the cigarette industry and its legal exposure caused Philip Morris's shares to be continually priced cheaply relative to its earnings and dividends. That meant those who bought and held the stock were constantly reinvesting dividends at bargain-basement prices.

And while Philip Morris/Altria is an outlier, over long periods value stocks have historically offered higher returns than growth stocks. It's true across different countries and different time periods: crummy companies that are cheap offer higher returns than great companies that are expensive. Investors are essentially compensated, in the form of higher returns, for investing in companies that aren't sexy and successful.

Then there is a third type of investment, companies that are neither successful high-flying growth companies nor troubled but potentially lucrative value companies. They are startups of various forms—companies that are in early stages and aspire to either become giants one day or be acquired for a lucrative sum. Startup investing, such as that undertaken by venture capital firms, has different dynamics entirely from buying either growth or value stocks on public markets. Venture capitalists generally aren't looking for modest successes. If they invest in a company when it is worth $5 million and it ends up selling to a bigger competitor for $10 million, it might seem like a win—after all, a 2x return on one's money is nothing to sneeze at. But the math of the industry, where most companies will fail, means an investment needs to attain more like a 20x, 50x, or even 100x return to count as a success. It is an investment style that veers toward either wild success or abject failure—buying into companies that will become the publicly traded growth stocks of the future or, more commonly, be sold to one of those established growth companies or, even more commonly, be unceremoniously shut down or sold at a bargain price.

Here's where the parallel between investing and careers comes into play. When you take at a job at a company, you are essentially investing in it—not with money, but with your time. Unlike stock market or venture investors, though, you don't get to spread your money around. As Ann Miura-Ko, a partner in the venture capital firm Floodgate, tells students in a class she teaches at Stanford, "If you go work at any company, big, medium, or small, you should think of it as having a portfolio of one. Your time is your most valuable asset, so if you're going to spend all your hours toiling, you need to be sure that work aligns with your goals."

That's why the "go get a job at a big successful company" strategy, while valid as far as it goes, misses something important about navigating a winner-take-all business world. Jobs outside those superstar firms can be fulfilling and lucrative if you treat them the way a savvy investor would—going in with eyes wide open about what you're getting, and why.

If you're working at one of the *winners* in the modern economy—organizations where you can go to work and have every expectation of having a bright future, a steady paycheck, and the opportunity to rise through the ranks—it's like being at a growth company. It has a very different dynamic than being at an *aspirant* company—a startup that hopes to one day become one of the winners (or, if it comes to that, be acquired by one). And that, in turn, has a different dynamic than being at an *afterthought* company, that is, a legacy company that is struggling; these are, in effect, the value companies in terms of career options—the fact that they are troubled can lead people to overlook their strengths.

To understand the trade-offs of these different types of firms, I spoke with three successful executives who don't know each other but whose offices were for several years only a few miles apart in the Seattle area. Each of their careers has focused on one of the three types of enterprises—and together they show the trade-offs involved in embracing a career at the modern economy's winners versus aspirants versus afterthoughts that every job-seeker should understand. We'll start at a company that we've seen in these pages already, one that embodies the powerful, successful incumbents who dominate the modern economy.

A CAREER AT A WINNER: NICK CALDWELL AT MICROSOFT

When Nick Caldwell studied computer science and electrical engineering at MIT in the early 2000s, opportunity seemed to beckon in every direction. A startup company he worked at during his junior year asked him to drop out of college to join it. He had friends who went to work at Google and other Silicon Valley upstarts, in the era when Google was very much still in its aspirant phase.

Caldwell's priorities were a little different. His parents were middle class—a public defender and a teacher in Largo, Maryland. He was staring at a pile of debt from MIT tuition bills. He wanted a job that would pay a steady and reliable salary, come what may, and allow him to pay down school debt and support a decent standard of living on day one.[10]

"My primary goal was that I needed to go and make money. That's why I did all this hard work in the first place," said Caldwell. "It seemed like in Silicon Valley I would have been working with some kid without a college degree who just had an 'I'm going to change the world' vision. It just sounded nuts to me. Even though I had an entrepreneurial spirit, I was always more grounded and practical."

So when a Microsoft recruiter showed up at MIT looking for interns, Caldwell was quick to raise his hand. It was, then and now, the consummate example of a superstar firm in the global marketplace. The year Caldwell joined, 2003, it earned $7.5 billion in profits (that year, Google scratched out only $106 million). Caldwell, an avid gamer, thought he was living a dream when his first Microsoft internship was in a unit that made tools for making computer games; he realized it wasn't for him when he learned that a woman down the hall had worked for years trying to optimize Microsoft's Flight Simulator program to make the clouds look more realistic. "She literally came in every day and just made clouds look fluffier or wispier, and I was like, 'This is so not what I thought making a game would be like.'"

He returned to Microsoft after graduation to a unit that was a more natural fit for his interests, focused on natural language processing— teaching computers to correctly interpret ordinary words and sentences. His unit focused on making the grammar checkers, proofreading tools, and the like that are so useful for making a document in Microsoft Word read correctly.[11]

So was it intimidating being a young, relatively junior employee in a massive global company? Not as much as you might think.

"The thing about a company like Microsoft is it's so big that it splits up into smaller organizations," Caldwell said. "Yes, there's more than 100,000 people there. But if you start looking at the org chart, things split up pretty cleanly. I was in the natural language group, and that split into four other organizations, and by the time you got down to me, my group actually felt pretty small and homey."

As an entry-level software engineer at an enormous, hugely profitable company like Microsoft, he had the luxury of focusing only on the software development tasks in front of him. He didn't have to worry about how Microsoft Office was selling that month or the market share of Microsoft Windows or how the company's finances were looking that quarter. It was managers several rungs up who worried about how the work fit into the broader strategy of the organization. By contrast, in smaller, more entrepreneurial organizations, even relatively junior people often have to worry more about how their work intersects with the broader business goals of the company. In a 100-person organization, what everyone does affects nearly everyone else. In a 100,000-person organization, there can be entire massive departments you know nothing about. Caldwell didn't meet anyone from sales and marketing until three or four years into his career when he was put in a program for high-potential talent that included roughly equal numbers of people from an engineering background and other areas like legal, sales, and finance. Essentially, the need to be a Pareto-optimal executive—to be skilled at navigating the intersection of these different specialties—happens at a more senior level the bigger and more established the company is.

There was, from day one, an exceptionally clear hierarchy. Microsoft even assigns numbers to different tiers of seniority, much as the US government does, starting at 50 on up; a recent college graduate who is a software developer will start at 59. Moving up to 60 signifies that you have a little more experience and can be trusted on significant projects, and comes with a little more money. It moves up from there. Levels 65 to 67 are for a "principal," typically doing work that impacts multiple teams. Above 68 reaches into titles like "partner" and people expected to have impact on the entire business.

"Did you ever play World of Warcraft?" Caldwell asked, referring to the immersive massive multiplayer game in which players adopt the avatar of a mythical creature. "You start the game and the first few levels are really easy, and you level up really quickly. Then you get to the middle, and every level you go up you need twice as much experience. And then by the end, it's astronomical. Like, you're in your house for months at a time just to get to the top level. The career ladder at Microsoft is kind of structured that way."

One of the great challenges in an organization like that is overcoming complacency. At one point Caldwell moved to the group working on Microsoft Office. "When I got into Office it was only the eleventh version, so we worked on that for about a year, and then it was time to work on the twelfth version. It's like you're shipping the same thing over and over again, at a time I wanted to make a difference by doing something new." Wanting to be entrepreneurial and working in a large superstar aren't necessarily inconsistent.

Around 2007, Caldwell was complaining to a mentor about the repetitiveness of the work and received an earful. "He told me, 'Nick, you need to stop acting like a manager and be a leader. Managers push work tickets across the board, and leaders take responsibility for what happens next.' He says, 'You can't stand here in my office complaining. You need to go do something about this, because you're actually a person who could make a difference.'"

It lit a fire under him, and he went straight to his general manager's office and asked for permission to form a team that would investigate options for a future product road map, which was granted. His team developed a team collaboration tool that was killed, but parts of it did ship in other Microsoft products—and the initiative got him on the radar of senior leadership.

That's how Caldwell was assigned to a project commissioned by Microsoft founder Bill Gates, trying to build tools to create data visualizations using plain-language commands. Caldwell was director of engineering; he helped put together a team of thirty people from across the company in a short span. It was in some ways the best of all worlds; he was able to try to build something new and exercise entrepreneurial muscles while also drawing a steady paycheck and leadership from one of history's most storied entrepreneurs. "When you're at a very safe company with options vesting, it is, for all intents and purposes, zero risk," he said. "You have to trick yourself into thinking it's a risk by moving around."

Caldwell eventually reached the rank of general manager, overseeing three hundred people in Microsoft's business intelligence unit. But after thirteen years at the company he feared he was becoming locked into the role of managing an ongoing business, rather than building something new. So he started looking around; in 2016 he became the vice president of engineering at Reddit, then chief product officer. Reflecting on his time at Microsoft, and its implications for others who find themselves at a superstar company, Caldwell described a tale of two types of careers.

"I'd run into two classes of people," he said. "One would be the iterate-and-optimize kind of person. They're fine working on Office 11, 12, 13, 14, and 15. That's their bread and butter. But for people like me, it was more like, 'How do you do something novel in a way that fits into this older product?' And it's a small number of people who are excited about that sort of thing, but if you can find them, and get those people together in the right way, that's where all the true innovation comes from." Even if one of your bets within such a company wins, you don't own upside from it; you are trading the potential of a big win for the safety net of a steady salary whether your product makes it or not.

In other words, being at one of the companies that is a winner in the winner-take-all economy means all the resources and opportunity in the world, and a life free of worries about where your next paycheck will come from. If you have an iterate-and-optimize personality, it can be perfectly satisfying. But if you don't—if you seek to build something new—being in a large, dominant firm means it's on you to push yourself toward opportunity and navigate bureaucracy effectively to build great products and have a truly fulfilling career.

A CAREER AT AN ASPIRANT:
AMY BOHUTINSKY AT ZILLOW

It was 2005, and everything was going right for Amy Bohutinsky in her life in San Francisco. She had just turned thirty. She was finally making enough money to get her own apartment, in Presidio Heights. She had lots of friends, and her sister lived in town and had young children. She had a serious boyfriend she was falling in love with. And she felt like she was getting really good at her job managing public relations for Hotwire, the travel booking site that she had joined shortly after its creation in 2000. But something felt just a little off. "It wasn't that hard anymore," she said.

Still, when Bohutinsky agreed to come to Seattle to meet with two of her former bosses, Spencer Rascoff and Rich Barton, about a new startup they were plotting, she had no intention of going to work there. If anything, she thought, perhaps she *might* consider starting a consulting business and doing work for the new venture on a contract basis. She showed up at a downtown office where Rascoff and Barton had assembled about a dozen employees; they couldn't even tell her exactly the new company's business strategy, in part because they had not yet decided what it was. All they had was a name, Zillow, and an ambition to transform the residential real estate industry. After two hours talking to them, Bohutinsky left for the airport. She called her boyfriend from the taxi, tearing up. "I'm going to move to Seattle," she recalled telling him.

In the conversations with Rascoff and Barton, she had been energized by the chance to be on the ground floor of building something exciting. Instead of being one cog in a huge organization, she would be helping shape strategy that could build a company from scratch into something meaningful. To do it, all she had to do was leave her life in San Francisco behind and take a 40 percent drop in salary. Her new pay package, as at many startups, was more tilted toward stock incentives than cash compensation, and Bohutinsky didn't even try to account for their potential value in her mental accounting, given all the unknowns. She and her boyfriend agreed that after a year at Zillow, if things were going poorly she would quit and move back to San Francisco, and if they were going well he would move to Seattle. He was the one who ended up moving.

On her first day at Zillow—there were about thirty employees by the time her start date rolled around—Bohutinsky showed up to find a desk with a computer still in its box. She had to unpack it and hook up the monitor on her own, because there was no IT department yet. It was the first of many realizations about what makes working at an ambitious young company different from being at a better-established company. When I met her thirteen years later, in early 2018, at Zillow's offices—now on the thirty-first floor of a high-end building with a view that stretches over Puget Sound to Mount Rainier on a clear day—Bohutinsky had risen from public relations director for a thirty-person company still figuring out its business model to chief operating officer of a publicly traded company with a $6 billion market value and nearly 4,000 employees.

When Zillow launched in 2006, it didn't have money budgeted for advertising or other conventional marketing efforts; all involved had learned the lesson of late-1990s dot-com companies that spent themselves into oblivion. That meant that the area Bohutinsky was in charge of—public relations—was doubly important; Zillow's marketing strategy was to develop buzz, and users, by telling an interesting story rather than by spending money on ads. "Part of the deal when I was hired was 'OK, you're the communications director, but that *is* our marketing,'" she said.

In larger organizations, including the one Bohutinsky was coming from, product developers tended to work on building a product, and then once it was ready to be rolled out the PR staff would work on getting media coverage or other attention. Marketing was a whole separate operation. What Bohutinsky found exhilarating about her job at a startup was that those silos simply didn't exist. She was in the room with Rascoff and Barton and the product team as they figured out what they were trying to build and how they would carry it out.

Their basic insight: there was a great deal of information about the housing market in places that were difficult or expensive to get to. Tax and property transaction records were buried across thousands of local jurisdictions' government agencies. Real estate brokerages and listings services were keen to control access to their databases, so that anyone buying or selling a house would need to use them. The vision at Zillow was that putting all that information in one place online, for free, with an accessible user experience and useful tools, could make the site a destination for anyone looking to buy, sell, or rent a house, or even people filled with idle curiosity about their neighbors. And, the founders bet, that large audience would prove invaluable to real estate brokers, mortgage lenders, and others seeking to provide services tied to housing, who would in turn pay big bucks to reach Zillow users.

During long hours trying to figure out what their first consumer product would be, the team realized that they had collected enough data to make a reasonably accurate estimate of the value of nearly any home in the United States, using a complex algorithm incorporating recent home sales nearby, earlier transaction records, tax assessments, and more. Bohutinsky was in the room as they worked through how they could create what became known as the "Zestimate," a tool that allowed people to find out how much their house—or their neighbor's, or their brother-in-law's—was worth, based on the latest transactions nearby.

In truth, the statistical model generated not so much a single estimate as a confidence interval. But Bohutinsky was in the room with product developers, helping work through how this offering could be communicated to the world, and they decided a single number—*Your house is worth $260,000*—would be more likely to attract interest than a mealy-mouthed *We can say with 70 percent confidence that your house is worth between $227,000 and $307,000.*

In the meetings Bohutinsky emphasized efforts to make Zillow a household name. She focused on the use of "Zillow" as a verb. She hoped that people might speak of "Zillowing" as the term for searching for a house just as they use "Googling" to mean conducting a web search.

The company set a lofty goal of reaching a million users a month within six months of launch. They hit that number in three days, and reached five million after a month.

The people who most thrive in startup environments are comfortable with ambiguity, with a lack of clear hierarchy or clear departmental lines. The payoff is that this very ambiguity allows you to get deeper, wider experience with crucial strategic questions than you would in a more established company. You get to see up close how the various parts of a company—product development, sales, marketing, finance, whatever—intersect with each other to a much greater extent than a person with a comparable level of experience would in a larger organization. "Being involved with product strategy is something I could only have experienced in a startup at the ideation stage," said Bohutinsky. "We were just a group of people in a room without a lot of walls or lines, and that set me up for a future of realizing I had a voice in what we created that wouldn't have been heard otherwise."

As the company grew, she became less the PR person assigned to try to get favorable media coverage and more part of the team shaping the strategy of the company. She lacked any of the traditional experience you would expect of a chief marketing officer—she had no MBA or experience as a brand manager for a big consumer products company, for example—but when Zillow began doing some more conventional advertising, that was the job she took on. She was in senior leadership as the company held its initial public offering in 2011 and when it acquired rival real estate site Trulia in 2015, nearly doubling overnight. Rascoff and Barton appointed her COO at a time when merging those two companies successfully was an urgent, bet-the-company operational imperative. I asked Bohutinsky why she thought they gave her a job for which she had such an atypical background and experience. "I think it came from years of me showing that if you give me something I don't know a lot about, I'll figure out how to tackle it and how to build the teams to go do it, and figure out what I don't know," she reflected.

That's the thing about joining an aspirant company. The cash compensation is probably going to be relatively low, and the stock options more often than not won't be worth anything (Bohutinsky was lucky in this regard). The hours will be long, the perks unimpressive, and you may have to set up your own computer. The real payoff is in the opportunity to learn exactly what you're capable of in an environment where the rules and procedures of a more established company aren't there to rein you in.

It can be a sink-or-swim experience in becoming Pareto optimal, a chance to learn how the moving pieces of a business fit together in ways that only senior, seasoned executives understand at the incumbent winner companies. Instead of thinking of your compensation as consisting entirely of an (underwhelming) salary and a (risky) stock grant, in an upstart environment, think of the learning experience you get as part of it. And with a little luck, you just may find yourself at the start of something big.

THE AFTERTHOUGHTS: MARK MASON AND THE ART OF THE TURNAROUND

When Mark Mason was growing up in Southern California, his family lived in an apartment next to a funeral home, which his parents operated. It was a tough business, offering empathy and help to people when they were dealing with the death of a loved one. Having seen how hard his parents worked, and how emotionally draining it was, Mason decided to walk away from the family business and become an accountant. As it turned out, he would spend much of his career in proximity to death anyway.

When he was a young accountant at Deloitte & Touche in 1990 in Orange County, California, a real-estate development client recruited Mason to become its chief financial officer. He joined the company just as a severe real-estate-driven recession was setting in. The company was functionally insolvent, and as it turned out, his job was to help engineer a turnaround—to sell off assets and restructure debts and try to allow the company to live to see another day. He learned a great deal in a short time about high-stakes negotiations and dealing with a company in crisis. They pulled off the restructuring, barely, though the experience left Mason ready to return to the safety of a job with a massive accounting firm where he might gradually continue his climb toward partner.

"I went back to Deloitte and took a step back to do that, both in compensation and stature," Mason said. "I think for me that was a great lesson, that often the right decision in your career is taking a step back to take a step forward. [It's difficult to do] because you get used to the compensation or the stature, but I've found a couple of times in my career that was exactly the right thing to do."

Taking that series of steps meant that by the mid-1990s, Mason wasn't just an experienced accountant but an experienced accountant who had also led the restructuring of a troubled company. It landed him an offer to be chief financial officer of Fidelity Federal Bank, a $5 billion institution that was in financial trouble, where he spent a year again selling off assets, raising new capital, and returning it to profitability. A few years afterward, he returned as CEO to that bank's parent company, yet another company at risk of failure and in which his charge was to make the best of that situation, whatever the "best" might mean—a true turnaround, an orderly bankruptcy, or a bargain sale to a competitor.

One of the most important lessons he learned in this series of jobs at struggling companies was the importance of due diligence—of doing work to understand just how dire a given company's situation is—and being realistic about what possibility an organization really has. "Every business can be turned, but there are some businesses for which the cost of turnaround is greater than the inherent value of the business," Mason said.

For example, he was president of a company called Tefco LLC that financed high-tech backup electrical generators for hospitals, prisons, and other institutions. But the high up-front cost of the generators turned off the would-be buyers, and the affiliated company that manufactured the generators ended up in bankruptcy in 2009. "There are situations where what it would take to get it back to a profitable position would be more than the future profits of the company could ever be worth," he said. "Your heroic efforts might be more than the situation deserves. And there are companies that are built upon honest people with good ideas with economics that can't profitably support that idea."

Which is how he found himself looking for his next job just when a financial crisis and deep recession were wreaking havoc on the US banking industry. HomeStreet Bank was a ninety-year-old family-owned institution in Seattle with about $3 billion in assets and, it seemed, about as many problems. Half of its loan portfolio was to homebuilders, with much of that backed by raw land. With home sales and prices plummeting, homebuilders could no longer cover their debts, and the value of the underlying land was plummeting, meaning the bank's collateral wasn't worth what it had been when the loans were made.

Oh, and the entire global economy was in free fall. Every Friday afternoon, American bank regulators pulled up in black Chevrolet Suburbans at the front doors of banks that they judged to be insolvent, then spent the weekend closing the bank down and transferring its deposits and loan books to a stronger acquirer—the goal being to ensure faith in the banking system by making sure customers never went a workday without access to their deposits. Regulators shut down 140 banks in 2009 alone, and HomeStreet was evidently high on the list of targets. "Every Friday there was a rumor from somewhere that we were being closed," Mason said. Anytime a customer who happened to drive a black SUV pulled into the parking lot on a Friday, it sparked fear. Mason thought the bank had a decent capital buffer and wasn't that close to being shut down; he learned from his regulators later that was not so. "HomeStreet was at the top of [their] closure list for many, many weeks," he said an official later told him. As a banking trade publication put it, "It seemed there were more regulators paying attention to HomeStreet Inc. than investors."[12]

One hazard of working at an afterthought company is that money is, almost by definition, tight. But Mason argues that small budget cuts won't turn a failing company around. By the time a company finds itself in dire straits, the travel budget has probably already been cut to the bone, blatantly unneeded workers already laid off, any lavish perks already reined in. In the case of HomeStreet, many of the 550 employees had savings in a company stock ownership plan—which, considering the bank was close to insolvent, meant they had lost a big chunk of their savings. But Mason had concluded from his previous work at troubled companies that holding on to most of those workers was essential. "First of all, you have to stabilize the employee base and not lose people. . . . So you have to be transparent with what's going down and what are the potential outcomes and why all of them have a potentially positive outcome for the employees," he said. "Typically, the problems with a company that is in a turnaround situation are the fault of prior leadership, not middle-management or the other employees. And when you change the strategy, people become better."

Mason's strategy instead focused on ripping off the bandage: selling off assets, recognizing losses, and insisting that staff not succumb to the "sunk cost fallacy." People are naturally disinclined to take big losses on loans they or their colleagues made just a few years earlier—they want to wait until the market turns around or the price of land returns to what seems fair. But in a crisis situation like HomeStreet's, time was not something in supply. "If we had held on to all that property, it would have come back in value," Mason said in 2018. "But we would have failed and not been here to reap the benefits."

Working at a troubled company, even if you're not in the executive suite, comes with an odd combination of traits of winner companies and aspirants. There is the uncertainty and risk of the aspirants, combined with some of the legacy process and bureaucracy of the winners. That isn't a combination that's great for everyone. But there is also something rewarding about making an established but challenged company the best version of itself it can be. And like the experience at aspirants, a company in decline can offer opportunities that a huge thriving company wouldn't; Mason was in his early thirties when he landed his first CFO job with a troubled real estate company.

"I think that you have to look at each job opportunity for its experiential value first," Mason said. Indeed, jobs at afterthoughts can offer experience, tools, responsibilities that you might not get in a normal situation, "because what happens in turnarounds is people get opportunities to stretch their capabilities and they have the opportunity, though it's far from assured, of having a much better experience and professional outcome than they would working in a healthier company." In desperate situations, a company's leadership may be willing to try more unconventional strategies and trust less-seasoned people than a profitable, dominant firm like Microsoft ever would.

Mason made a point of focusing on celebrating departments for intermediate successes in the overall plan of rebuilding the bank's capital ratio. For workers who had lost much of their savings and were terrified of losing their jobs in the midst of a recession, the goal was to make clear that there was a plan and that executing it successfully— pulling off a tricky asset sale with record speed, for example—would be rewarded. "After a while, if you're confident and keep pointing out where we're on target, where we're on the plan, where we're doing better than the plan, it helps people's confidence."

It worked. By 2012, HomeStreet's finances were sound enough that it was able to raise new capital, through an initial public offering.

As the housing market improved, HomeStreet became more aggressive, opening new branches and acquiring some smaller competitors.

Working at an afterthought company isn't necessarily a bad thing. It's just important that you understand the downsides (the tight budgets, the inherent risks) and care a lot about the things that can make it rewarding—the opportunity to be a value investor in your own career and show that an older brand has some life in it yet.

I left my conversation with Mark Mason confident about two things: that a career working at troubled, struggling firms was exactly right for him, and that it isn't right for everyone. But you would say the same of Amy Bohutinsky's career path, for which she uprooted her life and took a pay cut to join a thirty-employee company with no guarantee it would survive to its second round of venture funding. And you would say the same of Nick Caldwell, who spent the first fifteen years of his career incrementally climbing the ranks at one of the world's biggest and most profitable companies. And those are just three people who have each been quite successful in one city; you could also present cautionary tales of each scenario: someone who was made miserable by the bureaucracy while working at a winner; someone who was driven mad by the chaos of a failed aspirant; someone who was worn down by the dismal prospects facing an afterthought rather than invigorated by the possibility of turning it around.

No one type of employer is right for everyone, and for every stage of life. The key is understanding how a company you're thinking of working at fits into the winner-take-all world, and how it suits your personality, ambitions, and risk tolerance. You're an investor with a portfolio of only one stock at a time. It pays off to know what you're buying.

7

When Software Ate the World

AND HOW TO MAKE SURE
IT DOESN'T EAT YOU

When I started my first office job, I suddenly needed a more robust collection of professional clothing. So I did what many young men in that situation do and went to the store where my father went. That's how I ended up with a collection of dress shirts, blazers, and so on made by Brooks Brothers, the clothing company that dates to 1818, has dressed forty out of forty-five presidents of the United States, and by the turn of the twenty-first century operated stores around the world and a busy mail-order catalog business.[1] Brooks Brothers had a store a couple of blocks from my office, and I was able to get a well-made shirt for around $100 in 2000 dollars, which was a lot relative to my income at the time but seemed like a worthwhile investment. I may have been a mere intern, but I subscribed to the old line "Dress for the job you want, not the job you have."

A few years later, my income was a little higher, and I wanted shirts that might fit me a little better than the off-the-rack versions at Brooks Brothers, which always felt a little boxy on me. I found a Hong Kong–based tailor who visited Washington routinely and rented a hotel suite, where he measured me every which way, let me feel big stacks of fabric swatches, and took my order for shirts custom-made to fit my body and my style preferences. Six or eight weeks later, the shirts arrived, at a cost only a little higher than the Brooks Brothers shirts: $120 or so each, which seemed like a worthwhile splurge because they fit so well.

A few years after that, though, I discovered Bonobos, an innovative maker of men's clothing that made garments that were stylish and unfussy and, importantly, were available for sale through a highly efficient network of storefronts where you could feel and try on clothing before ordering it to arrive a day or two later. The shirts fit me nearly as well as the tailored ones, cost less—around $73 each—and could be ordered instantly online and delivered in a couple of days at no extra charge.

In 2017, two new developments in high-level corporate strategy, at two of the biggest companies on earth, unfolded that affected my sartorial choices.

First, Amazon began selling a line of well-made men's dress shirts under a house brand called Buttoned Down, available only to Amazon Prime subscribers. They cost a mere $40 and fit me nearly as well as the more expensive Bonobos offerings.

Second, Walmart spent $310 million to acquire Bonobos.

In less than two decades, I had gone from buying my shirts at a two-century-old traditional retailer to ordering from a specialty tailor to having two megacorporations, engaged in a battle to be the dominant retailer of nearly everything, fighting over my closet. In effect, Amazon and Walmart are both betting that they can make money selling me shirts by using software to better manage their supply chain, providing a better online ordering experience that will make me keep coming back, and use technology over time to better customize the apparel that is offered to me.

It may seem like a mere curiosity, but beneath it is something bigger. The shift is reflective of a shift in more and more industries—even seemingly very traditional ones like the sale of men's shirts—to being fundamentally about the effective deployment of digital technology. Almost every professional worker is in the software business on some level, even the ones who work at designing and selling men's shirts. That certainly doesn't mean everyone is or should be a software coder. But it does mean understanding and embracing the fact that competitiveness in the twenty-first century is more and more about who has the best software.

THE SOFTWARE ERA AND THE NEW TERMS
OF COMPETITION

In 2011, the influential venture capitalist Marc Andreessen published an essay in *The Wall Street Journal* titled "Why Software Is Eating the World."[2] He argued that every major industry was experiencing upheaval due to the rise of digital technology, and that the success or failure of a given company would be determined by how well it adapts to this world and leads this revolution. Reading the essay several years later, it is striking how many of the elements of his argument that were provocative at the time have become conventional wisdom. For example, much of the essay argues against the then-prevalent idea that technology stocks were in some new bubble. The day the essay was published, Amazon traded for $179 a share; seven years later, it would reach a price nine times as high.

But more interesting than stock market fluctuations are the ways that the forces Andreessen described have played out in the years since. As we've already seen repeatedly in this book, industries as varied as moviemaking, automobiles, and hotels—industries that would not be conventionally thought of as "the tech industry"—are defined more and more by who makes the best use of computing technology to provide products or services more effectively. Consider a few more examples:

- Disney in 2018 was seeing intense pressure in two of its traditional businesses: Fewer people were willing to pay the ever-rising prices to see movies on big screens, and younger people were less likely to subscribe to cable television, a driver of huge fee income for ESPN and other Disney-owned cable properties. Disney dealt with those challenges with a big bet on building a streaming service meant to rival Netflix. A century-old company that is best known for creating memorable characters that have become part of the fiber of the culture, in other words, will succeed or fail depending on its ability to build first-rate data compression, recommendation algorithms, and interactive user experience.

- Oil companies are in a computing arms race of sorts. With supercomputers, they can more effectively predict where it is worth drilling for oil and how to maintain their existing production capacity. An official of BP told *The Wall Street Journal* that the company was able to model forty years' worth of data on its operations in Alaska and has been able to maintain its 1,300 miles of pipelines with fewer costly in-person inspections, because the computers are better at predicting which pipes are likely to be corroding.[3]

- BlackRock is the largest asset manager in the world, with $6.3 trillion under management in early 2018. But it views its crucial advantage, and area for growth, not so much as the traditional business of buying stocks and bonds on behalf of clients as offering a data platform that allows clients to make better decisions on which assets they want. The company's Aladdin software was created as an internal risk management tool in 1988, and by 2017 was used by eighty-five institutional investors with $20 trillion in assets, carrying out 250,000 trades a day.[4] BlackRock CEO Larry Fink has said he expects license fees for Aladdin to account for 30 percent of the company's revenues by 2022.

• In 2017, John Deere, the maker of heavy agricultural and construction equipment, acquired a company called Blue River Technology. Blue River had little tangible capital but was an innovator in software that can identify weeds using optical recognition and machine learning.[5]

Which brings us to what this reality—that every company is in important ways a software company—means for managing your career. There is a temptation to go with a facile piece of advice like "learn to code," which isn't necessarily wrong, but is certainly incomplete. Many people's brains aren't wired in ways that will make them very good software developers, for one thing. And more and more low-end programming tasks are becoming relatively low-paid commodity work.

More fundamentally, each of these companies will continue to employ many, many people who are not software developers. The observation that "every company is a software company" very much does not mean "every worker's job is to create software." No matter how many petaflops of supercomputing capacity BP has, it still needs petroleum engineers and chemists and accountants. BlackRock needs traders who can put its financial data software to good use for clients. Disney needs brilliant creative minds to dream up the characters who will drive the next billion-dollar film franchise, and there's a good chance those will be people who don't know much about data compression or recommendation algorithms.

But that also doesn't mean nontechnologists can just ignore the increased primacy of digital technologies at the core of so many companies. I heard over and over again that they need to understand these shifts, and be eager and able to adjust their own ways of working, to be successful.

What does that mean in practice, and what does it mean for a person—especially a nontechnologist—navigating a career? To find answers, I visited another company engaged in the battle to supply my closet with dress shirts, one that is at the forefront of using software in making soft things that you wear.

SOCK HACKING AND BLAZER-MAKING ROBOTS

In 2007, Aman Advani was in his first job out of college, working as a strategy consultant. His job consisted, in no small part, of flying to the location of a client Monday morning and working eighteen hours a day before flying home Thursday night—then repeating the whole exercise the next week. Keeping well stocked with the formal clothes that were expected was, to use a term favored by young consultants, a "pain point."

"If you didn't get around to picking up your dry cleaning over the weekend, there was a chance you were searching for what clothing stores were open at six A.M. in Columbus, Ohio, so you could buy a shirt," Advani said. "You realize quickly what a pain in the butt it is to have to worry about ironing and dry cleaning and sweat stains, and by the end of the day you look like a total mess."

Advani may have chafed at having to wear dress clothes during long workdays. But the evenings were different. After dinner, he would put on gym clothes—often Nike Dri-FIT products—to continue his work in his hotel lobby. Those were far more comfortable. They stretched with his body and wicked sweat to keep him dry. He was convinced that comfort made him more effective. "At night, I'm just crushing it," he said. "I'm pounding through work at nine o'clock at night in gym clothes."

An engineer by training, Advani began experimenting with clothing hacks. One was a miserable failure: he tried applying tape to the inside of his dress sock so it wouldn't slide down over the course of the day. As it turned out, for any man who had hairy legs, this was a painful mistake. Another experiment worked better. Advani cut the foot portion off a pair of black wool dress socks and sewed the top onto a Nike Dri-FIT sock. To a colleague who happened to see his calf, it looked like he was wearing a standard formal sock, yet surrounding his foot was an advanced fabric that wicked sweat and provided more comfort as he walked.

A thousand miles away, Gihan Amarasiriwardena was doing eerily similar work.

A few years before, Amarasiriwardena was an undergraduate at MIT, studying chemical and biological engineering. He was a serious runner and was irritated that his dress shirts didn't wick sweat as well as his running shirts. So he sewed his own dress shirts with material from cut-up running shirts to accomplish that goal. In 2011, Advani showed up at MIT to get an MBA. A professor noted their similar interests and introduced them. They and their MIT classmates Kit Hickey and Kevin Rustagi soon went into business together, starting a Kickstarter campaign to bring a dress shirt using advanced fabrics to market. They named their company Ministry of Supply, a reference to Britain's World War II–era military supply outfit that doubled as the cover agency for a legendary inventor of spy gadgetry, Charles Fraser-Smith.

Some of the work they did as they built the company would be recognizable to anyone who has ever worked in the apparel industry. They traveled from their home base in Boston to the garment district in New York to identify manufacturers and distributors, for example. But much of what they were doing was implementing a strategy and a way of working utterly foreign to the industry.

For example, traditionally a designer would draw a shirt on paper, select a fabric, sew a sample, show it off on a model in a runway show, then make the shirts and distribute them to stores with grand hopes that customers will buy them. Ministry of Supply took to developing products the way a tech company would, with concepts like "minimum viable product" and "iterative design" and "a/b testing." It did small production runs of fifty to a hundred shirts, then tested which fabrics and designs resonated with customers before making more. "Industrial design is really built on this balance of aesthetic and utility, and that's the process we've been using," said Amarasiriwardena. "Build a prototype, test it, then use that feedback to create the next version. Very few fashion houses would show their product before it hits the runway. We're the opposite."

At Ministry of Supply, the design process is intertwined with marketing and production. From the beginning, the company has used 3D design software, including a package called CLO, the same type of software that movie companies like Pixar rely on. Rather than a designer drawing a shirt or sport coat with a pencil, essentially starting with how the garment will look, the process starts with a model of the human body. Each new garment is designed to test how it will move with a person's muscles and bones, and how it will react to body heat and sweat. "If we used a traditional design process," said Advani, "we would be using a physical mannequin to see how a garment will fit. But we're able to model how the garment is going to fit on a person when they're standing straight, then model when they move their leg. We can actually change the tension of the fabric and see how much force it takes to stretch and say, 'Actually this is going to be very tight in the rear, so we need to create a special panel here to release some of that stress,' and we can do this iteration without actually making a physical model."

In Amarasiriwardena's telling, the apparel industry has been so focused for decades on becoming more efficient by shifting toward places with low-wage labor—to China in the 1980s and '90s, more recently to Vietnam and Bangladesh and Ethiopia—that there has been underinvestment in seizing the benefits of advanced technology. "There's been a stagnation of the development of the apparel industry," he said. "We haven't been able to get that Moore's Law effect"—that's the awesome, exponential rise in computer processing speed in recent decades—"with clothing because it hasn't touched that digital era. But more and more we're able to make that happen on both the design and manufacturing side."

The most extreme example of this is a potential shift toward 3D knitting machines that are, in effect, robots that can do the job of a tailor. This technology was in its early days as of 2018, but Ministry of Supply is experimenting with it. In its store on Newbury Street in Boston, it has a $190,000 machine that custom-knits a blazer, a monster of a device with 4,000 needles that is so big the door to the store had to be temporarily removed in order to move it into place. Over time it should be able to customize to the size and color preferences of the buyer. It is not a stretch to imagine that the future of the high-end apparel business is about who has the best shirt-making robots.

All of that helps explain why Amazon and Walmart's digital units are trying to sell me dress shirts. An industry that has been dominated forever by craftsmanship and physical labor is turning into one in which information economies run rampant. The winners in the clothing business will not be those who are able to secure the cheapest labor or offer the biggest network of stores. Rather, they will be those who can make the best use of information to design garments, to integrate that design with production processes, and to use software to control that production. They may be big winner firms like Amazon and Walmart, or upstart aspirant firms like Ministry of Supply. And some of the existing companies at risk of becoming afterthoughts will either manage to reinvent themselves or limp along for a surprisingly long time. Amarasiriwardena argues that reinvention will be harder than it might seem.

"People ask us all the time, 'Why doesn't Brooks Brothers just do this?' or 'Why doesn't Banana Republic just do this?'" he said. "And the answer is that they would have to reconfigure their entire design and production process. No factory that makes a Brooks Brothers shirt today is willing to buy an ultrasonic welder, and we know that for a fact because we have approached and asked them all. Or in Gap's case, you're talking about moving a $16 billion company to an entirely new factory footprint. You're talking about hiring a design team that's half engineers and half traditional designers to come together. It isn't so simple. It's an ecosystem shift."

Regardless of exactly how the apparel industry shakes out in the years ahead, this much is clear: the terms of competition are shifting, and someone who seeks to have a vibrant career in the industry needs to change with them. What does it mean to work in the fashion industry in an era in which software is eating the world? Advani and Amarasiriwardena each came to the industry with an engineering background, but what if that's not your skill—if you are focused on another dimension of the apparel industry, such as the more purely aesthetic aspects of fashion?

As Ministry of Supply grew and expanded beyond dress shirts and socks, and toward more different garments and toward offerings for both men and women, Advani and Amarasiriwardena knew that engineering alone wouldn't cut it. They needed someone who understood not just the technical aspects of design but how to manage an entire line and develop good-looking clothes people would want to wear to work or for an evening out. So they hired someone with a long history in the fashion industry. As it happens, I had a bit of a personal connection to him, even if I had never heard his name. That's because Jarlath Mellett was in charge of the design of those Brooks Brothers shirts I wore to work back in 2001.

AN OLD-SCHOOL FASHION DESIGNER
IN THE NEW WORLD OF BUSINESS

Mellett first arrived in New York in 1981, with a scholarship to the Fashion Institute of Technology funded by the Wool Weavers of Ireland, which is his native country; nearly four decades in the United

States have only begun to take the lilt out of his accent. He majored in knitwear.

He bounced around New York fashion circles until in the mid-1990s he was recruited to become Brooks Brothers' first design director. The clothier was so traditional that it had more or less made the same suits and sweaters for generations with only modest alterations to reflect changing fashions. Mellett's office was literally above the store; the corporate headquarters were located above the handsome Brooks Brothers location on Madison Avenue in New York. His charge was to freshen the company's aesthetic—to add a bit of a more fashion-forward look to a company. "Once I dove into the heritage, I realized it was just a gold mine of fantastic stuff to play with," Mellett said. "All I did was tweak things. OK, let's brighten the shirts. Let's make the red ties brighter; let's match them with gingham shirts and make a table with twelve colors, with orange or purple or different shades of pink." They experimented with newer noniron fabrics and worked on adapting a company known for putting men in charcoal-gray suits to an increasingly casual workplace.

What hadn't evolved much was how the actual design work took place. Mellett would stand over a drafting board, sketching designs, then sew a sample garment. When the design of, say, a sweater was complete, he would send a package of hand drawings showing it from all different angles, and handwritten measurements and specifications, to the factory. It was no different from the design process he had been taught in school in the 1980s, and would have been a familiar way of working to anyone involved in fashion for centuries.

Mellett went on to a similar job with the clothing chain Eddie Bauer, then took charge of designing women's clothing for the fashion label Theory. It was the early 2000s, and how one went about designing clothing was shifting. He still designed garments by hand sketching, but a colleague would then transfer his design into design software on a computer, which in turn was used to create a single set of documents that could be shared across the organization, from supply managers trying to ensure they had the right fabrics to factories to the marketing department trying to sell the next year's line. "You would get yields of fabrics, you could do trim, the button, the zipper, the lining, you could figure it all out and have it all in one place."

But Mellett was getting burned out on the fashion world—the jockeying for status, the crushing sameness of making pretty much the same garments over and over while trying to make a big deal of minor shifts in color or material. So in 2005 he stepped away and started a firm designing home interiors instead of shirts and sweaters. That's what he was doing when he got a call in 2013 about Ministry of Supply. Advani and Amarasiriwardena asked him to take on a one-off freelance project, designing a men's suit. "I remember saying to myself, 'OK, if I like doing this project, I'll go for this job, but otherwise I have no intention of getting back into fashion,'" Mellett said. "What intrigued me was this ability to ask 'What can clothing be?' If you think about it, the phone has moved from the rotary phone to this phone"—he held up his iPhone—"while clothing hasn't moved that much, with technology in fabric, in design, in how it forms to the body."

As Mellett talks about his work as design director of Ministry of Supply, and its contrasts with his work in the same job at more traditional apparel companies like Brooks Brothers and Eddie Bauer, it becomes clear how much of the difference isn't really about the design technology at all. The 3D design software and knitting robots and advanced modeling of how a shirt will stretch when its wearer moves are all important—but he emphasizes instead the mindset underneath it. "We don't bring anything to market for the sake of doing something," Mellett said. "We've got to have evidence that our customer really wants that. We do a lot of field testing, a lot of listening to our customers, what is going on in their lives. You can experiment if you have a hunch of what they might want." In his previous life in fashion, designers almost never interacted with customers. "It was more like 'that was our bestselling sweater last year, so we should do the same thing.'

"Your dress shirt, who made that?" Mellett asked me. That day I was wearing a light blue shirt from Bonobos. "So, it looks like a pinpoint oxford, right? That fabric has been around since 1864 or something, and nothing has changed. Now I'm intrigued with finding fine-gauge machines that can knit fabric like that that's lighter but stretches amazingly well and moves with your body and wicks moisture away. That's exciting."

No one would confuse Mellett with a software engineer. In fact, he still prefers to do his first go at a design with a pencil on paper, which colleagues who are better versed in the 3D design software then draw digitally in order to begin the process of testing how the garment will fit, dissipate heat, and so on. But Mellett shows genuine respect and enthusiasm for colleagues and partners who have deep technical skills he does not. When they set out to design the robotically knitted blazer, he spent hours sitting with the coder who knew how to create instructions for the machine, experimenting with its capabilities and limitations. "You can see everything. You can zoom in, see how the needles are working, just amazing stuff. And then I think we had a sample two days later. The beauty of this—and I think this is the future, and I'm so excited about it—is customization. Eventually, everybody will have clothing to order in their size."

When he talks about the apparel business becoming a digital technology business, it's clear he's not taking any one element in isolation. It's not just the 3D design software or the robots, "it's a combination of everything—the best technology to communicate with your customer, the best technology to take all your customer information and use it in a way that enables you to give them what they really want," said Mellett.

It is a safe bet that many of the people Mellett studied fashion and design with in the early 1980s are long since out of the industry, and many more would struggle working at a firm where so much of the focus is on software and engineering as opposed to design in the more traditional sense. So what made Mellett different? After all, he still draws his designs on paper and couldn't write a single line of code.

Speaking to him and several of his colleagues, what stands out is that what Ministry of Supply needs him for is to fuse decades of experience making clothing that professional men and women want to wear with all its whiz-bang technology. The two founders are MIT-trained engineers—they need somebody with an eye for design who may not be a technologist himself but is genuinely open-minded and excited about the opportunities that new technologies create for clothing.

Thinking about Mellett's success made me think about the many people I've worked with in the media industry over the years; some of them have thrived as the internet disrupted our entire business model, and others have long since been bought out or laid off. The common thread among the people who survived and thrived wasn't necessarily an inclination to become technologists themselves; many of the most talented and successful internet-era journalists I've known don't know a thing about the underlying technology that makes words and images appear on their readers' phones.

Rather, what successful internet-age journalists have in common with internet-age fashion designer Jarlath Mellett is an underlying enthusiasm for the new opportunities that changing technologies create. Both are aware that you adapt to digital technology not by simply doing what you've always done slightly differently but by rethinking the entire process of how work is done. The successful media industry employees of the digital age don't simply do what generations of print newspaper people always did and publish those stories on the internet—they reimagine everything about the workflow and product to take advantage of the new technology. And the successful fashion designer of the digital age, like Mellett, will not be content to just tweak the color palette of the same shirts that his company has always sold but will rethink the entire design, production, and sales process from first principles.

In sum, as more industries become, at their core, software businesses, it doesn't mean that everyone should be a technologist. It does mean that everyone needs to be focused on making the most of those technologies.

THE AGE OF AI: THE ACCOUNTING CLERK AND THE GARDENER

As useful as Mellett's approach is for navigating a career in an industry being disrupted by the digital revolution, attitude alone isn't always going to be enough. The very nature of this revolution is that it is making certain types of jobs and skills obsolete in their entirety. Mellett's ability to adapt his way of working to the apparel industry as a software business wouldn't have been much use if suddenly software got very good at designing shirts, blazers, and dresses.

So where does that leave a person who wants to have a long and successful career in an age in which computers are getting smarter and robots more dexterous every day?

James Manyika spends a lot of time thinking about this question—both as a partner at McKinsey who studies the future of work and as the father of a teenager who will be navigating this world soon enough. Among other things, Manyika's team at the McKinsey Global Institute, the consulting firm's in-house think tank, has worked to unpack the details of what different jobs entail, to understand which ones are highly vulnerable to being displaced by machines and which are relatively safe.

A research venture called O*NET has worked for years examining each of hundreds of jobs and isolating the specific actions they include. So, for example, being a manager in a retail store might seem like a simple job. But O*NET breaks it apart into the twenty-one different tasks a retail manager is likely to carry out, the twenty-four different technology skills he or she needs, twenty-three different work activities, and so on. For almost any job you can imagine, it is essentially distilling a job into its constituent parts. Meanwhile, Manyika's team at McKinsey has worked to cross-reference each of about 2,000 different tasks against how effectively computers can carry out the task now and in the foreseeable future. The results add up to a map of which types of jobs are highly vulnerable to being displaced by digital technology and which appear relatively safe for now.

What is striking is the ways their conclusions are not a simple matter of "high-skill jobs are safe, low-skill jobs are endangered." In fact, the results are all over the map in that sense. The details of what a job consists of matter more than the overall skill level involved.

"Take an accounting clerk versus a gardener," said Manyika. "The first question is a purely technical one. Is the bundle of activities that go into being an accounting clerk easy to automate? That is a technical question, they are analyzing data, interpreting data, and so on. Do the same for a gardener. A gardener has to recognize objects, pick them up, manually clip the rose the right way. It would be very sophisticated robotics to be able to navigate a garden in an unstructured environment it hasn't seen before. And when you ask that question, you will conclude that the accounting clerk is actually easier to automate than the gardener."

That becomes even more true when you look at the economics of automation. "In the case of the accounting clerk, most of what you are automating you can do with a standard computing platform and software, and those costs come down all the time, whereas the gardener, even if you solve the technical question you'd still need to build a physical machine with lots of very complicated moving parts." Moreover, accounting clerks are typically more highly paid than gardeners, which makes the economics yet more favorable, and are more specialized, which makes them harder for an employer to find.

Finally, there is a "social acceptance" factor. Nobody really knows, or cares, how a company manages its books behind the scenes, but people might be discomfited if their neighbors had a giant robot gardener pruning their hedges.

Similar dynamics apply when you think about jobs that are similar in terms of education required and compensation. In medicine, contrast an emergency room doctor with a radiologist who studies x-rays all day. The emergency room doctor is more like a gardener, reacting to a fluid, changing environment, improvising, jumping from repairing a broken bone one minute to treating a heart attack victim the next to making split-second decisions on whether a given patient's ailments are mental or physical. No robot could do it in the foreseeable future (though that's not to say new digital innovations won't make emergency room doctors more effective). The radiologist is more like the accounting clerk, applying knowledge in a structured way that is prone to displacement as software gets smarter.

Or in the legal sphere, a courtroom lawyer who represents clients before juries is probably going to be safer than one who reviews contracts all day to ensure that i's are dotted and t's crossed—a more process-focused job.

The important idea is that the types of jobs that are at risk of being disrupted out of existence have things in common, and so do those that are comparatively safe. That leaves two options for a person navigating a career. One is to focus heavily on areas that have low probability of being automated out of existence because their demands run so contrary to what computers and robots are able to do—whatever the equivalent of the gardeners are in your field.

The other, of course, is to focus on being the automator rather than the automatee. That is, to be the type of person who is shaping the algorithms that enable computers to do the job that an accounting clerk or a radiologist or a paper-pushing lawyer focused on routine contracts could once do. It requires acting on the lessons about being a Pareto-optimal worker described in the early chapters of this book—

someone with deep knowledge in both accounting *and* software engineering, or medicine *and* imaging technology, or contract law *and* natural language processing. It's not easy, but it is a clear pathway to success in this world of more and more advanced artificial intelligence and robotics. "I'm always struck by how many of the people driving the breakthroughs have multidisciplinary backgrounds," said Manyika. "The supply and demand works in your favor, whereas it seems like it's easier and easier to get people with narrow specialties."

But what does it look like in practice to be at an organization doing exactly that—applying advanced digital technology to hard problems rooted in the real, rather than virtual, world? And how can people who come up through one specialty turn themselves into these types of multidisciplinary workers? What does it mean in practice to be an automator rather than an automatee?

A PROGRAMMER AND A BIOLOGIST
WALK INTO A LAB . . .

Erin Shellman studied economics and evolutionary biology as an undergraduate and then got a PhD in bioinformatics from the University of Michigan in 2012. Despite her study of biological science, though, she was never one for the lab; her passion was for processing information, using computers to analyze genetic code and other immensely complex bodies of data. "I was never a wet lab scientist, ever," she said—referring to what you're probably envisioning when you think of a laboratory for biological research. "Both my master's and PhD were coding-based programs."

That helps explain why, after completing her doctorate, she put those skills to work in a completely different arena. Her first job was for Nordstrom Data Lab, a unit of the high-end department store, where she worked on product recommendations, those algorithms that predict that a buyer of Hugo Boss sunglasses may also be in the market for a Michael Kors watch. She moved from there to Amazon

Web Services, where she analyzed many terabytes of data to detect how customers were using the cloud servers and thus how to engineer the services more effectively. She enjoyed the work at Nordstrom and Amazon, but did feel like it was a bit of a waste not to use all that knowledge of genetics and molecular biology she had gained during all those years in graduate school.

Shawn Manchester, by contrast, was very much a wet-lab kind of scientist when he was studying for his doctorate in chemical engineering at MIT. He speaks of the act of executing a "polymerase chain reaction," a technique to copy DNA, almost as an art form. "You can tell how long someone's worked in a lab based on the angle of contact between their pipette and the tube they're pipetting out of," he said. "If you're a novice, you do this," pantomiming a tilt of a thin glass tube. "And if you're experienced you do this," showing the right way. "You end up learning it almost as you learn to play the piano."

But as he was finishing his doctorate, he was tinged with fear. He had spent years of training to understand and manipulate the DNA of yeast. At a yeast genetics conference, he heard a cofounder of a company called Zymergen talk about building a platform through which researchers could order different strains of yeast, their genes manipulated as instructed.

"It scared the crap out of me, to be blunt, because this thing I was getting really good at was building yeast strains," he said. "And I realized that very soon, the ability to build a yeast strain was going to be something that a robot would do, and that I would have no job." What if you spent six years learning to play the piano just as someone was inventing a robotic piano player more virtuosic than you could ever hope to be?

If you can't beat them, join them. Shellman and Manchester both went to work at Zymergen, and I spoke with them in the company's headquarters in Emeryville, California.

The company was founded by Joshua Hoffman, a former consultant and banker; Zach Serber, a biophysicist; and Jed Dean, a biochemist. Many types of companies need to synthesize microscopic organisms, either for direct use in their products or to generate chemicals that are difficult or impossible to make any other way. That is important in the production processes for wine and beer, and the fragrances that make fine perfume; it is also a part of countless heavy industrial processes, including in agriculture, energy, and pharmaceuticals.

That research has traditionally been done in the Shawn Manchester, wet-lab way. It includes researchers in white lab coats who develop an idea of how a particular strain of yeast might be genetically engineered to produce a compound that would be useful in, say, the production of a new antibiotic. After a labor-intensive process of messing around with pipettes, hopefully held at just the right angle to avoid contamination, if they're lucky they'll have a promising advance; more likely they will have a useless result.

Human researchers are limited by their own intuition and instincts, and by the physical limitations inherent in the need to manually manipulate samples. A yeast cell might have 5,000 genes, each of which could be manipulated in countless ways. By combining machine learning and robotics, Zymergen can explore possibilities that would never even occur to a human researcher. Said Manchester: "Given the way that biology design happens, through random error and new genesis and evolution, it's probably the case that the best way to understand that is not through a rational human mind, right? It's probably the case that these machine learning algorithms are going to be much better at it."

Hoffman, Serber, and Dean bet that by applying the latest techniques in machine learning and robotics to this research in molecular biology, they would be able to come up with bigger insights, faster. Instead of individual researchers spending weeks testing their latest theory, robots could administer tests on hundreds of manipulations of, say, yeast DNA at once and calculate the results. And sophisticated algorithms could take the results of all that data and use them to discern the most promising areas for further exploration. In the most optimistic scenarios, it could amount to a revolution in materials science. "There has been a century of innovation in materials science based on what you can do with the molecules that are in a barrel of crude oil, but innovation has really dropped off in the last couple of decades," said Dean. "There just aren't really new materials coming out, because you can only mix and match the component parts in so many ways. But biology offers a whole bunch of new component parts for materials scientists."

Essentially, their vision was to put advanced computing techniques to work to solve what, for all their scientific complexity, are old-economy problems: how to create new materials that will be more useful to society. But to do it, they needed people like Erin Shellman, data scientist, and Shawn Manchester, biology researcher, to work effectively together.

"It turned out that all the molecular biology I had learned in grad school was valuable, but really importantly, it was not valuable alone, right?" said Manchester. "The only way to be successful in building out the platform was to collaborate really closely with people who did not speak the same language that I did."

Indeed, at Zymergen and other companies I spoke with, the idea of a language barrier came up again and again as one of the hurdles to bringing technology to bear on old problems.

"It was so easy for me to say stuff like, 'Make sure that you aspirate above the pellets so you only get a supernatant,'" Manchester said, "and some automation engineer is like, 'What are you talking about? That makes no sense.'"

When dealing with data scientists and software engineers from Shellman's team, Sheetal Modi, a biomedical engineer, said, it was particularly important to get at the root of problems rather than offering up too much technical detail. "I think a lot about talking to your grandparents or to a fifth grader and just sort of boiling things down to 'What is the core essence of what I'm trying to do?'" Modi said. "It turns out you can strip out a lot of the random technical details that are involved in something if you're really trying to get to the heart of the problem." Indeed, she said, that's what made Shellman good at her job—an ability to take in information from biologists and translate it to the software engineers and data scientists.

Judy Gilbert, the company's chief people officer, describes it as "helicoptering," moving up or down in the level of technical detail in any given conversation to match the person you're speaking with and the demands of the task at hand. "You're trying to find a common altitude where you can actually get stuff done," she said. "You might need to go down into the details to actually implement, or go up to tell the story to someone else and bring them in. What people are getting really good at here is figuring out what level of detail to operate at in any given conversation."

To do that effectively takes the right attitude. "You need to have a real humility, a really humble disposition, because you'll be humbled constantly," said Shellman. "It's not uncommon to be in a meeting with a roboticist and a mathematician and a biochemist, and everybody is an expert in their field, and you are there to learn more than anything. So if you come in with a fixed mindset, you're not going to have a good time here."

Dean, the cofounder, tells of one early revelation that this mix of humility, openness, and constantly helicoptering levels of technical discussion brought him. As a scientist, his instinct was to approach the question of how you genetically engineer new strains of yeast like a scientist working manually in a lab would: of the 5,000 genes in the organism, identify the ten most promising and manipulate them, and then the ten next most promising, and so on. But Shellman realized that the problem he was describing was more akin to a problem that software engineers had made a lot of progress toward solving a different way: searching the internet. "When you talk to the data science folks," Dean said, "they're like, 'Wait, you have 5,000 genes and near-infinite ways to vary them? We're not talking about some kind of rank-order problem where you go through the list in priority order. This is a search problem. We're talking about search here, because we don't know enough about the complexity of the landscape.'"

Molecular biologists like Dean and Manchester were able to make themselves the automators, rather than the automatees, in a mode of research that, whatever Zymergen's future may hold, is the future of industrial science. Data scientists like Shellman and biologists like Modi were able to deploy their software development and analytical skills toward fundamental research that could have long-lasting benefits for how humans live, rather than just optimizing a product recommendation engine or serving up advertisements a little more efficiently.

They've been able to do it by first looking around the corner to see coming disruptions and acting preemptively to be the drivers of change rather than the victims. And they've succeeded within this adjustment to biological research as a software business thanks to an open-mindedness and humility and an ability to adapt their communication style to match an interlocutor's level of technical expertise. Therein are lessons for anyone whose industry is poised to experience upheaval as computers get smarter—which is to say, for all of us.

8

Should I Stay or Should I Go?

One of Patty McCord's first jobs, in the 1980s, was as a recruiter for Seagate Technology, a leading maker of computer storage products. She realized quickly that the key to doing the job well was to come to truly understand the mindset of the highly sought-after engineers the company needed to create the sophisticated robotics required to make its hard drives. The more she understood their hopes, dreams, and habits, the more she could identify the right people and persuade them to join Seagate. She developed some tricks along the way. Networks of engineers would spread word of obscure, hole-in-the-wall restaurants in the strip malls where Northern California's best Korean hot pot or Indian lamb vindaloo could be found. McCord would go to these restaurants, many of which asked customers to deposit their business cards in a fishbowl at the front counter to potentially win a free meal. McCord would copy contact information off the business cards, identifying targets for recruitment.

What made her good at recruitment—understanding the mindset and priorities of top engineering talent—made her turn her attention as the years passed to more strategic thinking. She didn't want to just focus on filling an open slot; she wanted to understand the strategy behind making a high-performing organization in which those engineers and other talented people can make great products. So she joined Sun Microsystems, then one of the hottest companies in Silicon Valley, in a more strategic role,[1] and then a software company called Borland, and then a small startup, Pure Software, as its head of human resources. Its CEO was Reed Hastings.

Hastings initially hired McCord because of her recruitment background, viewing the process of attracting capable software developers as the main thing that a human resources department was good for. Over four major acquisitions and an initial public offering, McCord got an up-close view of all the strategic dimensions of building a large, profitable company. When the company was acquired in 1997, she and other senior managers were out of a job (though the recipients of nice severance checks), and she turned to consulting projects.

Until about a year later, that is, when she bumped into Hastings in the parking lot of an office supply store near Santa Cruz, California, the oceanfront town ninety minutes south of San Francisco where they both lived. He was buying a postage meter. He had been sending DVDs to himself to test whether they would break in the mail. It was the core of his new business idea—for people to get movies through the mail. It seemed ridiculous to McCord; this was an era of VHS cassette tapes and the dominant video rental chain Blockbuster. DVD players cost $1,000 and so were the province of wealthy tech geeks like Reed Hastings and very few others.

A few weeks later, Hastings called her late at night. He wanted her to join the company to run human resources. She recalls telling him: "Go back to sleep. It's just a dumb idea. It's the dumbest business idea

I've ever heard in my life. Second, I already did a startup with you. And third, I'm happy. I ride my bike to work. My kids know my name. There's no reason for me to do this." But, Hastings countered, what if they could create their dream company? If they could turn all the ideas about how to create high-performing culture from scratch, in contrast to Pure, where they had spent all their time integrating acquisitions and dealing with people and systems they'd inherited?

"So I told him, now I'm awake," McCord recalled. And that is how she joined a little company called Netflix.

THE CULTURE DECK AND THE MEANING OF LOYALTY

By the time I was speaking to McCord in 2018, on a patio at a coffee shop a few blocks from the beach in Santa Cruz, Netflix was one of the most interesting, respected, and valuable companies on earth, with a $139 billion market capitalization and remarkable power in the entertainment industry, which is what you get when you spend $8 billion in a single year on the creation of original programming.[2] With that knowledge, it is easy to forget how precarious things were at Netflix, and for how long.

When McCord joined the company in late 1998, the dot-com gold rush was under way, and the buzz around Netflix palpable; it might become an internet portal for movie lovers, something like Yahoo, its enthusiasts argued. But—and this was true of too many other exciting companies of that era as well—its underlying economics just didn't work. It was losing money mailing those DVDs to people, while also investing in employees to expand into other areas, like publishing movie reviews online and selling advertising on its website. It was all being subsidized by venture capital dollars that were running out by 2000 as investors realized how many of the buzzy companies they were investing in were a mirage. Netflix raised $50 million in April 2000, one of the last deals of that size to happen before markets completely closed, but it was clear that would have to last until the company was profitable. So the company needed to slash the rate at which it was losing money. To cut the "burn rate," McCord had to supervise the layoff of one-third of the staff, including virtually everyone involved in those noncore areas like content and advertising.

She was responsible for plotting out the severance packages and, most importantly, how to communicate about the layoffs. From her experience with layoffs at her previous jobs, she had a vision of how to carry it out. What McCord wanted to avoid at all cost was a drawn-out process of employees feeling uncertain about whether they were losing their jobs, combined with an extended, morale-sapping process of good-byes. In her experience, both the people being laid off and the people remaining benefit from a crisp, efficient process, painful though it can be.

At the time, the company was small enough to have weekly all-hands meetings in the parking lot of its Los Altos headquarters. One of those Friday mornings, Hastings and McCord announced not merely that layoffs were in the works but that layoffs were happening that day. "We're not going to stand there and tell them that every other person's going to go eventually," McCord said. "I'm like, 'Every other person is going to go, and if your manager calls your name to come into a meeting you're leaving. I have lots of Kleenex. I'm sorry.'" Managers were instructed to tell those who were being laid off in a direct manner and present them with a severance package that morning, then turn their attention to those who remained.

Still, the company was losing money. Salvation came in the form of cheap DVD players. That Christmas, the prices of the machines fell below $100, and Americans en masse gave them to each other as gifts. And included in most of those boxes—at this point cash-strapped Netflix's only meaningful form of marketing—was a ticket-shaped insert that offered a free trial of the DVD-by-mail service. The business started growing quickly—but cash was still tight. Seemingly every dime that came in went toward buying DVDs and mailing them to customers. Things were precarious; Netflix stayed tight-lipped about its explosive growth, as it didn't want Blockbuster or another better-capitalized competitor to come in and overpower it with deeper resources. Fortunately for Netflix, Blockbuster seemed to view it as an annoying gnat rather than a genuine competitor.[3]

As Netflix's growth became more solid, the company started looking toward an initial public offering, which would take place in 2002. Now, McCord and Hastings realized they had another problem. Their team consisted of dozens of devoted, enthusiastic employees who had endured the lean years, but not all of them were correct for their jobs in what was becoming a bigger company.

For example, in the early days, Netflix bought DVDs from a wholesaler, essentially paying the same price any neighborhood video rental store might have. Now it was becoming one of the largest buyers of DVDs and striking deals directly with movie studios. The person who was perfectly good at managing supplier relations in the earlier iteration wasn't the person you wanted negotiating a complex deal worth tens of millions of dollars with Disney or Twentieth Century Fox.

"I had done two IPO preps and realized a lot of these people were just wrong for what we were becoming," said McCord. "Our people love, love, love this startup with no rules, right? But now we're going to be a public company. We've got to talk about a lot of sophisticated big-company stuff."

That created a dilemma. Unlike two years earlier, the issue was no longer a cash crunch that necessitated layoffs. They had to decide what to do with people who were good, hardworking employees but whose skills and experience were no longer a match for what the company needed.

"We need somebody who's done sophisticated accounting, and the person in that job is wonderful and she works hard, but she doesn't really have the right skills. I need at least a CPA, and she doesn't have it and doesn't really want it. And she kind of wants to be a massage therapist." One option would be to put an employee like that on a "performance management plan," the corporate euphemism for a limited window given an underperforming worker in which to either improve or face dismissal. To McCord, that seemed just cruel—almost punishing an employee and dragging out an unpleasant situation even though the employee had done nothing wrong.

It was a formative moment for the company's culture. She and Hastings debated it as they drove together from Santa Cruz over a winding mountain road to Los Altos, over and over again. And in the executive committee, top leaders had long conversations about what to do with people like that accountant.

"We had endless, endless conversations about loyalty," she said. They had top executives who had come from industries where people habitually spend decades at a company, and only truly bad performance had historically resulted in a person being fired. The chief marketing officer was from Procter & Gamble, the iconic consumer goods company; the chief financial officer was from banking; the head of product was just, in McCord's recollection, a sensitive guy. The constant question, she said: "What about loyalty? What do we owe these people?"

McCord argued in favor of a swift, polite dismissal accompanied by a large severance check. The way she saw it, this approach might have been hard—both for the dismissed employees and their former colleagues—but it wasn't cruel. "What's really cruel is setting somebody up to fail," she said. She felt that too much of the corporate world had developed an unhealthy aversion to honesty in its relationships with employees. Even as business had become more cutthroat and the old norms around employer loyalty had dissipated, managers and recruiters had retained a habit of pretending that a person accepting a job would work at the employer forever. McCord has particular contempt for the tendency to refer to a workplace as a family. The day after the big layoff in 2000, she recalled, she stood on a chair and said, "We're not your family, OK? We didn't lose members of our family. We lost our colleagues and our friends, and they're going to go to work somewhere else, and they're going to live the rest of their lives, hopefully happy as clams. 'Family' is a bad metaphor."

This ethos became a part of Netflix's culture—the one that she had joined the company in the first place to help build. But McCord and Hastings weren't just debating these questions during their long commutes together and in executive committee meetings. They were also committing them to paper. They believed that the culture they were building at Netflix was something important and special—that they were creating an optimal environment for creative, highly skilled people to build fantastic products. They debated different metaphors for this high-performing organization they were building. If not a family, what? McCord recalls suggesting the parallel of a ballet company, top performers working together. Hastings suggested instead Olympic athletes—but the fact that so many Olympic sports are individual pursuits rather than team activities made the metaphor not so great for the collaborative world of a modern company.

They were happier with a different metaphor: a professional sports franchise—where it is understood that everyone must be outstanding at what they do, no term with a team lasts forever, and a person whose abilities no longer fit the team's needs will be politely, respectfully cut. So that's what made it into the slide deck that McCord and Hastings would present to new employees during onboarding sessions. It grew to over a hundred pages. Here are some highlights from that first version (which Netflix's leaders constantly revise).

Adequate performance gets a generous severance package.

We're a team, not a family.

We're like a pro sports team, not a kid's recreational team.

Loyalty is good as a stabilizer . . . but unlimited loyalty to a shrinking firm, or to an ineffective employee, is not what we're about.

To McCord's thinking, putting all this on paper, and showing it to newly hired employees, was an exercise in honesty. It made a reality that was implicit at many modern organizations explicit.

One morning in 2009, during their commute to work, Hastings mentioned to McCord a new product that he had learned about the night before. It made it possible for people to publish PowerPoint slides online. "I wonder what people are going to put up?" McCord asked. "I put out the culture deck this morning," Hastings replied.[4]

"Oh, God, why'd you do that?" she responded. The presentation itself was a little amateurish—it was designed only for internal use, after all. More importantly, she worried it would scare off candidates thinking about working at Netflix. Some employees who saw the presentation during their onboarding seemed to blanch at the implications of all this—but, she recalls, those were usually people who didn't end up working out. So she crossed her fingers and hoped that it might not be so bad.

Two things happened next. First, the Netflix culture deck, as it would be called, went viral. The original 2009 version posted to SlideShare reached 17.9 million views by the time I spoke with McCord in 2018. Second, people considering working at Netflix started discovering the presentation, and it shaped the conversations in their interviews, making them more honest about how a job at the company might fit into their broader careers. The candidates self-selected more toward those who found the Netflix culture appealing, and neither interviewer nor interviewee pretended that coming to work with Netflix would mean forming some lifelong bond.

THE END OF LOYALTY

Think about the Netflix story from the perspective of those people who were summarily dismissed in those different episodes. If you were an advertising salesperson for the company in 2000, or an underqualified accountant in 2002, you were lucky enough to be an early employee of one of the greatest business success stories of the twenty-first century. And yet you lost your job, through no fault of your own.

So is that the way it is now? Is every job and every organization fundamentally one in which a bunch of free agents are always coming and going, staying only as long as the firm finds them useful and the employee doesn't have a better offer? To use a different metaphor, an employee's relationship with his or her employer seems to have become less like a marriage and more like one in a series of hook-ups.

It sure feels that way sometimes. We've all known of venerable, successful companies announcing layoffs of thousands of people, and not even just when the company is in major financial distress. To take a semirandom example from the business headlines in early 2018, Kimberly-Clark said it would cut 5,000 to 5,500 jobs "in an effort to reduce expenses as it faced stiffer competition for consumer staples like tissues, paper towels, and wet wipes," as *The New York Times* put it.[5] That quarter, its sales were actually up 5 percent from a year earlier.[6] The shift away from employer-employee mutual loyalty and to a world more like the one described in the Netflix culture deck has been under way for decades. In 1998, for example, as aerospace giant Boeing faced tough global competition, its executives held a retreat where they decided to shift how they talked about the organization. "More team, less family" was the mantra, as described in Daniel H. Pink's aptly titled book *Free Agent Nation,* published in 2001, back when Netflix was still focused on how many DVDs it could mail.

For a few decades in the aftermath of World War II, large companies really did offer a paternalistic attitude; if you worked reasonably hard and kept your nose clean at General Motors or Eastman Kodak or any of the other giants, you were pretty well assured a job for life. There is some gauzy nostalgia for that era that is worth casting aside—among other things, that bargain was mostly available only to white men, and many companies were complacent and failed to adapt to changing technology and consumer demands.[7] But there is no doubt that something big has changed.[8]

There are several reasons. Globalization has meant that companies face more cutthroat competition, so there is greater pressure to constantly overhaul their workforce to keep pace with whichever company on the planet is the leader in their industry. Labor unions are far less powerful than they used to be. In 1985, 30 percent of employees in advanced economies were members of trade unions, falling to 17 percent in 2015; only Iceland, Belgium, and Spain had rising rates of unionization in that span.[9] And executives of publicly traded firms face more pressure than ever to maximize the value that accrues to their shareholders, even if that comes at the expense of the company's workers.

To see in practice how shifts in corporate governance make employers less focused on loyalty to their workers, consider the iconic Procter & Gamble. In 2017, the activist investor Nelson Peltz argued that the maker of Crest toothpaste, Tide detergent, Gillette razors, and many more consumer products was being mismanaged. His hedge fund, Trian Partners, waged a proxy battle for control of the company in which he released, among other things, a 94-page presentation articulating his case. One page pointed out, disdainfully, that of the thirty-three top executives at P&G, only three had more than three years of work experience elsewhere, and the average tenure at the company was twenty-nine years.

What in an earlier era might have seemed like a sign of a quality company—a place with mutual loyalty with its executives—is instead a data point presented by an investor seeking to overthrow the existing managers of the firm! Even more amazing is this: Trian narrowly lost the proxy battle among shareholders, but in a goodwill gesture, Peltz was given a seat on the board of directors. The fact that the shareholder vote was basically equally divided put the board and management team on notice that they needed to adapt many of Peltz's recommendations. Don't be surprised if those numbers on P&G managers and their longevity at the company look a lot different within a few years.

To understand how these shifts in the economy and corporate

governance have translated into a different reality for workers, imagine a hypothetical young, aspiring executive. We'll call the company LargeCo, and we'll call our young worker Bob. (Forgive the gendered nature of the name; during the heyday of corporate paternalism, almost all executive-track workers were men.)

Let's say Bob is hired into a management trainee program right out of college, at age twenty-two, at some modest salary—let's say $30,000 a year. (Assume all numbers in this exercise are adjusted for inflation.) Bob rises through the ranks, from trainee to junior executive to manager of a small team to head of a large department to perhaps division president or a job in the C-suite. Part of the common practice at companies in this era was to grant very steady, predictable raises based on years of experience. To keep it simple, let's say that LargeCo gives Bob a 5 percent raise each and every year. By the time he hits sixty-five and retires from his senior executive job, Bob will be making $244,490. So his earnings look like the smooth line in the chart below.

Even during the era of very loyal corporations, though, that nice linear pathway for earnings masked a different reality in terms of the value Bob actually created for the firm. It starts at the very beginning: in his first year, Bob probably isn't worth even the modest salary he's

Bob's Compensation History in the Old Economy

Annual pay, by Bob's age

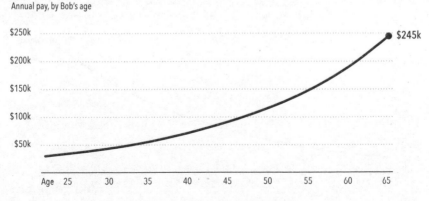

paid; maybe his actual value to the company in terms of additional revenue and profit is only $20,000. But as he learns the ropes, Bob's value soars rapidly. At age twenty-five, he's only making about $35,000 but is generating $50,000 in value! Essentially, LargeCo's investment in Bob is finally starting to pay off. That may remain the case for several years, until, perhaps, a recession rolls around and business dries up, making Bob less valuable; people just aren't buying the products his unit is selling. Then the recovery arrives, and profits soar, as does Bob's value. Maybe a few years after that, Bob experiences some health problems and can't put in as many business trips and late nights with clients as he once did, and his value falls relative to his earnings. But then his value rebounds, and once again LargeCo is making far more off Bob than it is paying him. Then, perhaps once Bob is in his sixties, younger executives are taking on leadership of the company and squeezing Bob out—but letting him keep his impressive title and salary, functioning as a somewhat underemployed elder statesman until he hits a proper retirement age.

The point is that in the loyalty era, employer and employee had an implicit deal: the employer would tolerate periods in which it overpaid the employee, but also the employee wouldn't bolt during periods when

Bob's Pay Didn't Always Match the Value He Created

Annual pay and value created, by year

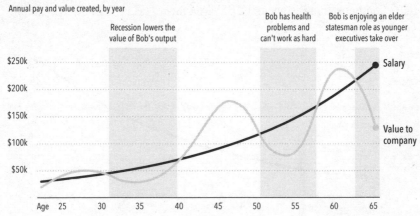

his value was far in excess of his salary. As it happens, on this chart, Bob's cumulative salary earned over the course of his career and his cumulative value created are identical: $4.53 million.

In an era of disloyalty, though, things work differently. At each of those points where Bob's value falls below his salary, the gray areas in the chart, he is at significant risk of being laid off. Because of the forces described above—global competition, lack of power among labor unions, and intense pressure from shareholders—Bob is likely to be laid off in his early thirties when that first recession arrives. If not then, his job is at risk again when he's unable to put in long hours due to health problems. If not then, the younger executives taking over the firm are likely to push Bob out when he's sixty-one rather than pay him a hefty salary for four more years to not do a whole lot of work.

This is just a simple model to describe what most people who have worked in a large company in the twenty-first century already know. But it's not enough to be able to identify the causes or describe the shifts. The question is what to do about them. And the answer is right there in our little chart about Bob and LargeCo.

THE TWO PRINCIPLES THAT MATTER: HONESTY AND RECIPROCITY

The implicit deal that Bob enjoyed during his career was that periods in which he was overpaid and those in which he was underpaid would more or less cancel each other out. The key for Bob's son or daughter now setting out on a corporate career is to have no delusions about what the implicit arrangement is today: we will keep you on staff so long as you are useful to our organization.

To have any hope of matching what their father achieved in lifetime earnings, Bob's children need to be more impatient and aggressive than their father was in times when their value is higher than their wages. That is—or should be—the flip side of knowing that your job is at risk when the reverse happens. That means working to have a clear view of the moments in your career when you have genuine leverage—when you have just led a successful project, or your particular job function has become much more important to the company's success. And it means when those moments arrive, asking for a substantial raise, and being prepared to look elsewhere if rebuffed.

This does not imply Bob's kids must become soulless mercenaries who will quit the moment some other employer offers a little more money or a slightly better assignment. It does imply they need to keep two big principles in mind as they make a series of crucial decisions about whether to stay at their current employer or go to a new one: reciprocity and honesty.

The truth is, many employers have kept some elements of the paternalistic, proloyalty model, to varying degrees. It is a continuum, not a binary choice employers make. The sensible strategy, then, is to make sure your degree of loyalty to the company is correctly aligned with the company's degree of loyalty to you.

Did the company help pay for some executive education classes, or entrust you with a project for which you were underqualified but that gave you the opportunity to grow? When the person in the next cubicle over had a young child and needed to leave early most days, how accommodating were the bosses? Does this organization tend to reward good performance with raises before people even ask for them, or only reward people when they have an offer elsewhere?[10] Perhaps most importantly, are layoffs rare and narrowly targeted for specific reasons, or a fairly routine business practice?

Reid Hoffman, the founder of LinkedIn, is blunt in his indictment of how many organizations approach the idea of loyalty. "Companies tell this fiction to employees because they know in some sense they'd like the employee to commit to them on a one-sided basis," he told me. "Which is frankly unconscionable. It's immoral. But also the employees know it, and sooner or later employees will come and say, 'Here's my two weeks' notice because I'm going somewhere else.'"

That doesn't mean employees should react by simply leaving a job whenever something better comes along. The more ethical approach, he argues, is to have some loyalty and dedication to each major project or assignment one takes on, and consider moving only when such a project is winding down. "We have this lie that it's still the 1950s or '60s and we're committed to each other for a lifetime, and because we both know it's a lie, we're not having the conversation. The whole point of 'the Alliance'"—Hoffman's construct for how employment arrangements should work in a modern organization, fleshed out in his book with that title[11]—"is to say, look, have the conversation, and do so in a very structured way in which you're being explicit on how you invest in each other, and if either of us break this compact within this timeframe, we suck. Then you could say you're betraying me."

As Reed Hastings of Netflix told me in an email, "Loyalty is not unlimited, like we think of friendship or a marriage. It is stability. So if a person has a bad quarter there is no hair trigger. Similarly if a company has a bad quarter. It's efficient to see each other through short-term blips, given the switching costs on both sides."

The idea of applying principles of reciprocity and honesty in how we think about loyalty also implies that the concept of loyalty should apply more to individuals than to large, faceless organizations. In the earlier era, it might have been completely logical for people to maintain a primary loyalty to the company, as the company could mostly promise they would have a steady job until retirement age and a comfortable pension after that. But at most organizations in the twenty-first century, no manager, no human resources director, not even a CEO can make that promise. They can't even be sure they'll still be in their job in a year. That means that loyalty to individuals within a company can mean more than loyalty to the company as a whole. When a particular boss ensures you get valuable experiences, promotions, and raises, you may well owe something to him or her and may want to think carefully before moving to a new team or a new company, even if the company itself doesn't show systematic patterns of mutual loyalty to its workforce.

Finally, there's compensation. The payoffs of a job take many forms, not all of them financial. It's hard enough to figure out how to value salary compared with performance bonuses compared with stock options in evaluating two job offers. It's even harder when you add nonfinancial dimensions. It could easily be worth sacrificing some cash compensation to take a job at an organization that entrusts people with new responsibilities and allows them to grow, or that allows a great deal of flexibility in hours, compared with one that locks people into the roles into which they are hired, or where bosses have strict expectations for how, when, and where people work. So think of compensation holistically—the full package of what you get out of a job. Still, the implications of the charts above showing Bob's salary are striking.

If Bob, in the modern economy, is at risk of being laid off whenever the value of what he produces falls below his output but doesn't otherwise adjust his salary demands, he has ended up in a heads-you-win, tails-I-lose situation with his employer. To maintain the same compensation over the course of his career that he would have managed in the old world, he will need to be a little more mercenary in those phases of his career when he is creating far more value than he is paid. It's no easy task, of course, to have enough information to know when those times occur, and when those moments arise either to secure an offer from another company or to deftly persuade a current employer to mark your compensation to market.

But choosing those moments to extract your value from the marketplace—when you're coming off the launch of a wildly successful product, for example, or when there is a boom in demand for people with your exact skills—is all the more important in this world where loyalty for its own sake is likely to go unrewarded.

Over the course of a multidecade career, you're likely to have a handful of pivot points that have an outsized importance in your long-term earnings and job satisfaction. Often they take the form of deciding whether to jump to a new employer or stick with the place where you already work. Should I stay or should I go?

There is a special place in hell for managers who try to use guilt and appeals to loyalty to persuade a person to stay in a job when it is a company that shows no similar loyalty to its workforce. The answer has to depend not on words but on how the company actually *behaves*.

Many of the people who have the most successful careers in this low-loyalty era understand this almost innately and have applied the principle of reciprocity and honesty along the way. Catriona Fallon is one of them, and her story shows a lot about how these principles can play out when those crucial career pivot points arise.

CATRIONA FALLON AND GETTING THE PIVOTS RIGHT

Fallon's career in the corporate world started with 1.75 seconds on a lake northeast of Atlanta in the 1996 Summer Olympics. She had devoted the previous six years of her life to becoming an Olympic rower, missing friends' weddings and birthdays, living in a group house 2,000 miles from home to train, and otherwise devoting every bit of her waking energy to try to win a gold medal for the United States. Her team—eight rowers plus a coxswain shouting commands—had been undefeated for eighteen months and was the favorite to win in Atlanta. But some subtle tactical mistakes doomed them. The Romanian team won gold; the US team came in fourth place, missing out on a bronze medal to Belarus by that slim 1.75-second-margin over a two-kilometer race.

"It was absolutely devastating," she said. "We made some of the wrong decisions. We knew it wasn't that we weren't fit enough. We made some of the wrong decisions in terms of the boat, the type of oars that we used. We lost it for ourselves."

She had a choice to make. At age twenty-six, she could buckle down and return to training for another shot at gold in the 2000 Olympics.

Or she could begin a more conventional career, aiming for a different type of success. What tipped the balance toward the corporate world? She "kind of decided it wasn't worth it" to invest four more years of sweat and toil in her Olympic dreams, she said. "In my view I had learned the lessons I needed to learn and I was going to move on to something else."

That something else, initially, was an entry-level job in marketing at Oracle, where she helped shape strategies for selling enterprise software packages—customer relationship management, strategic procurement, and the like—to large businesses. The work was fine, and before long she was running teams of three to five people, but she was soon trying to plot out where she wanted her career to lead. "I had that mindset of always asking, 'What's next? What's next?'" Fallon said. "And everyone above me who I respected, they had an MBA, they had some consulting experience. And they had pretty interesting careers."

That's how she ended up at Harvard Business School in the fall of 1999, and then at McKinsey as an associate in the San Francisco office after graduating in 2001. She learned the rigorous, methodical approach to analyzing problems facing large companies that makes leading consulting firms a breeding ground for future executives, and had a spectacular view of the Golden Gate Bridge while doing it. But the dot-com bust and accompanying recession meant that there wasn't enough work to go around. As is the habit of big consulting firms with too little business for their employee count, job cuts were planned, with the San Francisco–based technology team particularly hard hit, Fallon included.

It was an early lesson about a central reality of the modern economy: even if you do all the right things, you have to be ready for roadblocks. In Fallon's words: "Even with an MBA from Harvard and a job at McKinsey, you might get laid off. So don't go spend your signing bonus, because you might need to live off of it for a while."

She found her next job in the research department of the investment bank Piper Jaffray. Instead of helping companies solve complex problems, she was essentially on the other side of the table, trying to judge which software companies had good prospects and which did not. She had a crash course in financial modeling. And she soon learned how important the communications dimension of the job was: she spent perhaps half her time talking to corporate executives trying to glean any detail that would be helpful in making her projections and models more accurate; the other half was communicating those conclusions to investors looking for advice on where to put their money. Fallon enjoyed the work and was doing well. But after two years, a former colleague left for Citigroup and encouraged her to come along as well.

On one hand, Piper Jaffray had given her a start as a research analyst, and taken a chance on her despite her lack of experience, at a time when she very much needed a job. In the old world of mutual loyalty, this might be the kind of moment when she would stay put out of a sense of obligation, confident it would be repaid later. But that is not the world we inhabit. Citigroup was offering a bigger platform, greater exposure, and the opportunity to advance in a larger organization. It also paid more money, which Piper couldn't match. "They said, 'It's a great offer, good luck,'" Fallon recalled. Given that her boss had been a strong backer of her advancement, Fallon applied the principle of reciprocity. She gave him an unusually long notice before actually departing, to help him get through quarterly earnings season and have more time to find a replacement. "He was a very supportive boss, so I didn't want to leave him in a lurch."

In four years at Citigroup, Fallon built a reputation as one of the top analysts on software, media, and advertising. The money was good, and she was proud of her work. But she hungered for the opportunity to become an operational manager, overseeing a team; even as a senior research analyst, she oversaw only one other person. Meanwhile, a global financial crisis erupted that threw the future of the banking business into doubt. It might seem like the safest thing in the world to join a megabank like Citi, but in 2009 it reduced its employee count by 57,500 people, an 18 percent drop in a single year.[12] "So much was unknown in the industry, it was like a funeral march," Fallon said. When a recruiter approached her about a job that would involve more operational management, she didn't hesitate to take the leap. It might have even saved somebody else from being laid off involuntarily.

Fallon's new job was at hardware giant Hewlett-Packard, as a director in strategy and corporate development, a role that was something of a combination of her previous two lines of work, stock research and management consulting. Her job was to study competitors' strategies, examine companies HP might wish to acquire, and report to top executives and the board of directors about what she found. Typically, when a person is poached to join a new organization, it is to do something similar to what she has already done—most employers don't want to take a chance on someone new to both the company *and* the job she'll be doing. Following this pattern, Fallon was essentially taking a set of skills she had acquired elsewhere—skills at parsing the strategies, strengths, and weaknesses of tech companies—and putting it to work to help HP executives understand their competitors and potential acquisition targets better.

But—another common pattern—it is easier to try new things when you are already inside an organization and trusted by key decision makers. That played out in Fallon's next two jobs within the company. First, Fallon helped oversee investor relations for HP, and was thrust into understanding communicating with the external world. She would write scripts for the chief financial officer to use during investor conference calls and prepare her for the likely questions she would get from analysts. It was a time of crisis. In 2011, chief executive Mark Hurd was accused of misusing company resources and misleading the board about his relationship with a contractor; the board forced him out. For Fallon, it was a crash course in how the elegant models she had spent her career crafting are of only limited use when it comes to the messier world of crisis management.

Her next job was a big promotion, to a role in which all of her previous experiences were pulled together in one position. The job was vice president of strategy and financial planning in worldwide marketing. Fallon was finally overseeing a large team, at a time when new CEO Meg Whitman had an aggressive program of cost cutting in place, and she was earning her chops as a manager. "I was learning how to navigate a large marketing organization, how to influence decision making, how to build credibility and support for things."

In effect, HP had offered her just what you would want from an employer: the chance to grow and develop new skills. In an earlier era, rising executives who had landed a job at an employer like that wouldn't walk away lightly—they would set their eyes on more and more responsibility and potentially stay for decades. Yet Fallon moved on after four years. Why did she take the call from a recruiter asking if she might join a software company called Cognizant Technology Solutions as chief of staff to the CFO?

"I could have continued to make jumps that would have taught me more and more about HP's business," Fallon said. "But I don't think I was going to go on to be a general manager in a year"—having profit-and-loss responsibility over a business unit, that is. "And from my first day at HP there was continuous cost cutting. I was doing some of it, helping them figure out how to streamline or optimize an organization." It wasn't clear how long the path to running a business at HP would be. But it was obvious that there was no inherent reason to think that staying loyal to the company would be rewarded down the road; indeed, she could have ended up caught in the next wave of cost cutting. It was plain that the job she was being offered at Cognizant could offer a straight path to becoming a chief financial officer, or even CEO, one day.

From the beginning, her job at Cognizant was meant to be a limited-term assignment—a prime example of the "tour of duty" concept for managing a career discussed previously. She was to spend roughly eighteen months overseeing the integration of a handful of companies that had been acquired—a specific (hard) task, with the understanding that once it was done she would either need to find some other appropriately challenging job to do within the company or move on. "This culture stemming from the management team was very transparent, and very supportive of career progression." The money was good, but here, too, part of the compensation was the ability to develop experience across more of the skills needed in a CFO.

It worked. It was a winding path with many stops, but Fallon was now prime CFO material, with experience across all the different aspects of the job. She first went to a company called Marin Software in that role, then to Silver Spring Networks—where she had an experience that is perhaps the ultimate embodiment of the fluid meaning of loyalty in twenty-first-century business. She joined Silver Spring in March 2017 as CFO. Six months later, a rival called Itron made an acquisition offer that was too good to refuse, buying it for $830 million, a 25 percent premium above where its stock had been trading.

There's a reason senior managers are offered golden parachutes in these situations; shareholders don't want a CEO or CFO to fight an appealing acquisition offer just to save their own jobs. In this case, Fallon helped negotiate a deal that would leave her jobless yet again, though not without a lucrative payout for her several months of work. As it turned out, she stuck around for several quarters as the general manager from the acquired company to oversee the integration, leaving her with even more thirst for an executive role beyond just overseeing finance.

If you looked at Fallon's résumé and didn't know much about how the corporate world works, you might see just a slew of similar-sounding jobs. But if you pick apart the actual skills she was developing at each step on the way, it makes more sense. By the time she became a CFO in 2015, she had deep experience in corporate strategy *and* financial analysis *and* external relations *and* marketing. A lot of her moves were pretty much lateral in terms of title, pay, and prestige. But each of those lateral steps allowed her to gain experiences that made possible the rocket-ship ascent later. There's a parallel with her time as an elite rower. "Even when I was rowing, I knew I wanted to go the Olympics, but I would break up separate goals. What do I have to do first? Well, first I want to break seven minutes on the erg"—that is, to row the equivalent of two kilometers on a painful machine in seven minutes. "Then you need to improve it by twenty seconds to six-forty and improve on it. I always had intermediate goals. If I set the goal too far in advance it's too foggy. I have more clarity about what is immediately in front of me—the next six, nine, eighteen months. I know what I'm looking for to tell me if I'm moving ahead or learning more."

The thing is, she couldn't have done it if she had erred in either of two directions—showing excess loyalty to employers that were not going to let her propel forward, or showing so little loyalty that her mentors and bosses felt she didn't get the job done or viewed her as unreliable. Hers is a story of always rowing forward, stretching to get where you want to end up.

THE PRICE OF HONESTY

Why did the Netflix culture deck achieve such massive reach? After all, 125-slide presentations about human resources policies loaded with amateurish graphics are not normally the stuff of viral sensations.

It's hard to prove, but I think it's this: the relationship between employer and employee that Patty McCord and Reed Hastings laid out in that document was a more truthful description of how most organizations work in the twenty-first century than the kind of talk you more normally hear from recruiters and executives. And as brutal as its description of the Netflix culture can sound the first time you hear it, it essentially codifies principles of honesty and reciprocity in the relationship that amount to a truer version of what is fair and just and ethical than the kinds of lies around loyalty that are still common in the corporate world. People can more easily stomach being fired because their company's needs have changed if they haven't been lied to all along about the nature of that relationship.

In 2012, Netflix was in the midst of yet another reinvention, the one that would turn it into an entertainment industry juggernaut. Production was under way on *House of Cards,* the company's first blockbuster original programming. The DVD-by-mail business was being spun into its own subsidiary, aimed at extracting as much profit as was left in a shrinking unit while executives focused their attention on the fast-growing streaming business. And for Patty McCord, the principles she had codified in the culture deck were becoming personal. As she recalls it, it was becoming clear to both her and Hastings that she was no longer the right fit to be the chief talent officer for the company that Netflix was becoming—that her career in the tech industry and in startup environments didn't match well with a global entertainment colossus.

"That breakup year was really painful. I mean, I was just exhausted. I had been there a really, really long time. And so sometimes it's just time to start over." I asked her how Hastings told her it was time for her to take a generous severance and move on. She paused. "Oh, how did he tell me? I don't know. We both sort of saw it coming, you know? Come on, we worked together every day, and that whole period was really hard. When people ask me this, I'm like, 'You want to go talk to a stranger and tell them about your breakup, every last detail, who said what, how it felt?'"

What happened for McCord next is, to me, the more interesting story. She walked away with a nice payout and dignity. She began advising startup companies on their culture, wrote a book detailing her case for a more honest understanding of the employee-employer relationship,[13] and started taking time to enjoy the sunshine in Santa Cruz. She and Hastings still bump into each other in town now and again, always a reminder of what a relationship with a boss really is. "Our original executive staff was together for ten years," McCord said. "That's a long time. You know, it's important to know that your colleagues aren't family. But you can be really close friends with the people you work with, forever, for the rest of your life. But it has all the give-and-take that comes with a friendship. And it means you're not stuck with each other. And sometimes it's not pretty."

9

What Is a Job, Anyway?

HOW THE CONTRACTING ECONOMY
CAN FIT IN YOUR CAREER

In the summer of 2017, I spoke with two women for a story that was eventually published in *The New York Times*.[1] One was named Gail Evans. She grew up poor in Rochester, New York, and as a young woman in the 1980s she earned a living working in the evenings as a janitor at one of the most innovative, respected, and profitable companies of that era: Eastman Kodak. The work was grinding, but Evans was ambitious; she took college classes during her off-hours. Then a remarkable thing happened: a manager was implementing a newfangled spreadsheet program in order to track inventories and needed to train the tradition-bound workforce to use it. Somebody mentioned that Evans had been taking classes in computers, and she was drafted to run the training. When she finally finished her college degree, the company hired her into a professional-track role. Just fifteen years after that, Evans was the chief technology officer of the entire company, and she subsequently has had an excellent career with high-level jobs at companies including Bank of America and Microsoft.

The other woman I spoke with was named Marta Ramos. She lived in San Jose, California, and she worked as a janitor at one of the most innovative, respected, and profitable companies of this era: Apple. The work she did was awfully similar to the work that Evans had done back in the 1980s—vacuuming carpets, taking out trash, wiping down bathrooms. Even the pay, in inflation-adjusted terms, was about the same, though with a far stingier benefits package in the modern era. The bigger difference was that Ramos had almost no interaction with anyone who worked with Apple, and not really any advancement opportunity at all. She worked for a janitorial services contractor and saw no meaningful path toward anything more.

The article that told their stories achieved huge reach. I think part of the reason was that people who work in modern business know that the shift toward greater use of contracting, outsourcing, and freelance work is pervasive and is affecting the career options of most everyone. The outsourcing of janitorial services and other low-end work, like security guards and cafeteria staff, is only a vivid example of a development that affects all types of workers.

It's hard to overstate how profound the change over the last four decades would seem to someone from, say, the early 1980s. Just among the tech giants of Silicon Valley, traditional employees may develop software, but it is often contract workers who test it for bugs; contractors review social media posts for potential violations of terms of service; they work as recruiters trying to attract the next wave of engineers. Apple makes billions of dollars selling phones that are assembled by a different company, Foxconn.

My story about Evans and Ramos was focused on the implications of these shifts for overall inequality, which I'm persuaded are substantial.[2] But this also has potentially radical implications for a person navigating a corporate career. The very definition of a "job" is more fluid than it once was. Major companies put all sorts of work on a continuum in which only a subset of the workforce is full-time employees. So how can, or should, these nontraditional arrangements fit into an ambitious person's career? To answer the question, it helps to start with why these arrangements exist in the first place, which, as it turns out, is a more interesting question than it might seem. And it starts with the even bigger question of why *firms* exist in the first place.

THE THEORY OF THE FIRM AND THE AGE OF OUTSOURCING

Why do companies exist? This is the kind of question that might seem glaringly obvious to most people but is something economists have spent generations arguing about. You could imagine there being some pristine state of nature in which all work takes place as separate transactions. Instead of having a company with employees who come to work every day and receive a paycheck for their troubles, every task could be accounted for individually. The closest this comes to existing in reality may be something like a small network of freelancers who take projects and collaborate on a project-by-project basis.[3]

In the 1930s, a young British economist named Ronald Coase traveled across the industrial heartland of the United States studying how manufacturing companies worked. He sought to understand why, exactly, firms were organized as they were. His big insight was that corporations exist in part because the transaction costs of this hypothetical market-based system were too high. For example, in my job at *The New York Times,* I receive a paycheck every two weeks, in exchange for producing a steady supply of content about economics. If instead I had to negotiate my compensation for each piece, all the time and effort my boss and I spent haggling would be time wasted.

But that insight alone doesn't answer the question of why companies exist in the form they do. After all, almost all companies rely on some mix of full-time employees and other forms of labor. The pages of the *Times,* to continue that example, include articles written by both full-time staffers and freelancers. When a company hires an outside consultant or a law firm, it is essentially doing the same. You can broaden that question beyond labor. What other inputs does a company make itself, and which does it buy? Companies are always making decisions of this type. When should a company develop software tools for its workers to use in-house, and when should it buy software off-the-shelf? Should a company that manufactures ballpoint pens buy the plastic shaft of the pen from a supplier or make its own from scratch? Or should it manufacture raw steel itself? Each of those cases is a question of whether a particular input should be produced internally or instead rely on the external market.

Oliver Williamson built upon Coase's work, fleshing out the rationale for these "boundaries" of a firm.[4] The key, he argued, depended on how effectively a contract with an outside entity can be crafted and enforced. A typical middle manager makes thousands of separate decisions over the course of a month, and it would be impossible to spell out the contours of each of them in a contract.

And then there's the "holdup" problem. If every worker were a freelancer, and every input bought on the open market, you would have a perpetual risk of business partners exploiting the fact that you need them. If I worked for the *Times* entirely on a freelance basis, what would stop me from doubling my price just at the moment there's huge news and they most need my services? In effect, the more specialized knowledge and ability are involved, and the more mission critical the work, the less inclined a company should be to use contract work, because it will be more vulnerable to being taken advantage of.

All of this suggests that companies should keep functions internal when they're core to the organization's future and when successful fulfillment is an ambiguous concept. Conversely, for things that are less important to the company's success and where it is easier to craft a contract that covers the bases, it can make more sense to try to outsource on the open market.

That's the theory, anyway. It won both Coase and Williamson

Nobel Prizes in economics. And it goes a long way to explaining the difference between Gail Evans and Marta Ramos. Janitorial services are a prime example of a form of outsourcing that makes sense under this theory. Apple does not derive any of its strategic advantage from having a particularly good method for cleaning its offices every evening. It's easy to craft a contract that makes clear what the janitorial services company needs to do to get paid. Apple doesn't need to worry about a "holdup" problem; if the janitorial company were to jack up its prices, Apple would just switch to a different company. Most Apple employees wouldn't even notice the difference.

Notice that this list doesn't even include a mention of compensation. In theory, at least, there's no reason that a job that is outsourced should pay less than a comparable job that isn't. That implies that old-school companies were overpaying some of their workers relative to market rates before outsourcing their jobs—which would seem to be irrational on the face of it. Yet there is compelling evidence that, at least with low-skilled work, outsourcing does depress wages. Economists Arindrajit Dube and Ethan Kaplan found in one study that outsourced workers in the 1980s and '90s resulted in a wage penalty of 4 to 7 percent for janitors and 8 to 24 percent for security guards.[5] Deborah Goldschmidt and Johannes F. Schmieder found similar results using German administrative data, reporting a 10 to 15 percent drop in pay for low-skill jobs that were outsourced compared to those that weren't.[6]

The explanation may be about psychology and culture rather than strictly about economics. If you're a CEO of a big, profitable company, you probably aren't going to worry too much about cutting costs by paying your security guards and janitors the lowest possible wages, but once you outsource those functions and make it someone else's problem, your procurement department will push hard for the lowest price possible.

In effect, the rise of contracting and outsourcing work has created a bifurcated labor market. On one side, there are people with advanced skills, good pay, and lots of opportunity, and on the other, contract workers who are viewed as a cost to be minimized. There is an obvious implication for an ambitious person navigating a career: stay away from contract work if at all possible. While there is definitely a good bit of truth in that narrative, it oversimplifies things. I've known people who have had brilliant, rewarding, lucrative careers being part of the nonemployee workforce as independent contractors or freelance workers. So how do we make sense of that? When and how can the nonemployee life be part of a great career? The answer can be found in some flaws in that academic understanding of the theory of the firm. As is so often the case, the real world is a little more complicated— and so, then, are the implications for workers navigating it.

RULES ARBITRAGE AND OTHER REAL-WORLD REASONS TO OUTSOURCE

Matthew Bidwell was steeped in all this theory-of-the-firm stuff when he was a graduate student studying management at MIT in the early 2000s. But as he worked on his dissertation and then taught at business schools, first at INSEAD and then Wharton, Bidwell found something rather different.

"The way academics think of it, what gets done in-house and what gets outsourced goes back to Coase and Williamson," Bidwell said. "Can you write a good contract? Does either party have to make a big investment in the relationship? Is it hard to fire each other?" But, he said, "the first time I taught a class of MBAs, I was shocked. It was the area I knew best, and the set of ideas I was least able to persuade them of."

For his dissertation,[7] Bidwell embedded in the information technology department of a large (unnamed) bank and did surveys and structured interviews to understand why they made the decisions they did in terms of outsourcing some functions but not others. And the nice crisp theoretical story wasn't backed by the data. The ability to craft good contracts or the importance of the project didn't necessarily predict whether it would be outsourced.[8] Instead, it came down to internal politics.

Outsourcing, for one thing, made what Bidwell called "arbitraging internal rules" possible. The bank had much stricter rules around hiring employees than it did signing either independent contractors or contracting with a firm to do work, in part because firing an employee who was no longer needed was more costly and disruptive than terminating a contract. As one manager explained to Bidwell, "The buckets are not the same, and the approval process and bureaucracy for a vendor is far less difficult than it is to bring on an employee."

Moreover, contracting with outside firms sometimes served as a mechanism to force the internal "clients"—business units, like the bank's consumer lending department—to be clearer about what they needed. When bank employees were working on a project, those internal clients might change their requests constantly, whereas when the work was contracted out, they were forced to specify their needs up front so those could be enumerated in the contract.

And, importantly, the internal politics played out in the form of tension between senior managers, who were focused on minimizing costs, and project managers, who just wanted the best resources to get the job done. So on projects where the work was viewed as relatively straightforward, the senior managers would push to outsource the work to overseas markets with lower labor costs—even though this meant much bigger logistical and communication challenges for the project manager. On more complex jobs, the roles were reversed— often it was the project managers who wanted to hire sophisticated (and expensive) systems integration contractors to guide the work, with senior managers balking at the cost.

Power over this process, meanwhile, depended on how much political clout a given manager had within the firm. "There is one desk that made nine figures for the firm last year and has their own developers that have worked for them for years," one technology manager at the bank told Bidwell. "If they don't want to use [offshore vendors], they can't be made to. Conversations usually end with 'How much money did you make for the bank last year?'"

I suspect these observations from Bidwell's research will ring true to anyone who has worked in a large corporate setting trying to decide what types of work to contract out and what to assign to employees. Yes, the simplistic story of "keep core competencies inside and outsource the rest" can help explain it. So can the Coase-Williamson "outsource it if it's easy to craft a contract."

Those rationales for using contract work also contain bad news for contract workers: they imply that cutting costs is a primary reason for moving certain kinds of work outside the boundaries of the firm, and that the depressed wages and benefits that researchers found in the realm of janitors and security guards should also be expected for those doing more skilled work. They also imply that an ambitious person should only accept contract work as an absolute last resort—that the only pathway to good compensation and a bright future lies in the traditional job on the payroll of a large, profitable company.

But the real-world idiosyncrasies of what drives contract work that Bidwell observed suggest that it may not be that simple. Just maybe there are pockets of the contracting economy in which the work can be as remunerative and offer as much long-term opportunity as any conventional job. Sure enough, you can find intriguing examples of more innovative use of unconventional labor arrangements in some surprising places—including at a company at the forefront of an earlier wave of outsourcing that was purely about cutting costs.

GE, GENIUSLINK, AND VARIABLE VS. FIXED WORK

General Electric was a pioneer in shifting work away from employees on its direct payroll and toward various contract arrangements. Dating to Jack Welch's run as chief executive in the 1980s, it was an innovator in moving rote functions off the company's books, outsourcing information technology work to contractors in India and other low-wage countries, and generally undoing the traditional focus on having everyone who helps make GE products receive a paycheck from GE. "To those who know their IT outsourcing history," *CIO* magazine once wrote, "GE and offshoring are practically synonymous."[9]

It worked, as far as it went. Welch's push to get noncore, back-office functions off GE's payroll—and often, performed by lower-wage labor—was part of his successful effort to cut costs and focus on growing the most profitable parts of the business. Without doubt, the company in its modern incarnation is still very much focused on squeezing costs wherever possible—all the more so after a financially disastrous 2017. But that's starting to mean something different.

The Welch-era strategy was about shifting work from highly paid full-time employees in the United States to lower-paid employees of a contracting company in India who did pretty much the same work for a fraction of the cost. Now, GE is focused less on simply paying lower wages for rote functions and more on creating the technology to eliminate those rote functions entirely. At the same time, the nature of the business and the technology underneath it have been shifting in ways that make a different type of contract workforce more desirable. The jet engines, electrical turbines, and other products that the company makes become more technologically complex each year, and the engineering teams that make them are often in need of very advanced, very specialized help in some area of robotics or artificial intelligence—but sometimes only to solve a single discrete problem, not as an ongoing job. Meanwhile, in the commercial arena, GE has long been a huge customer of very expensive consulting firms like McKinsey and Bain—but sometimes the types of questions they have been hired to take on could be better answered with other approaches. If you're trying to sell equipment to electrical utilities and need to analyze pricing strategies, maybe a short-term contract with a utility CFO who is between jobs could generate more useful recommendations than a dozen young MBAs slaving away for six weeks.

Many companies aspire to be the dominant platform to match freelance workers with companies that might wish to engage them. Thanks to the internet, it is easier than ever to find someone with just the right technical expertise or history to provide temporary help.

In 2013, Dyan Finkhousen, a veteran of GE Capital, was assigned to try to help the company take advantage of those possibilities in a more systematic way. She leads what the company calls GeniusLink, a platform meant to help managers across GE use the potential pool of global freelance and contract talent more effectively. It has even run projects to crowdsource solutions to hard technical challenges; on one such project, a young Indonesian engineer named M Arie Kurniawan figured out how to cut down the weight of an engine bracket by 84 percent, for which he was paid $7,000.[10]

That may sound a little pedestrian at first, but when Finkhousen talks about how the company seeks to use that talent pool, it becomes clear how radical its implications could be. "Think of the base unit of work no longer as the job and the full-time employee," she said. "Think about the base unit of work as the task and the skill set.

"I look at it this way," she said. "To be successful as a business leader in GE, we need to step back and completely invert the way we are thinking about resourcing our business. First, before we even think about people, we need to think about what can be digitized, what technologies exist that could deliver this." That is, first figure out if the job you're trying to do can be automated. "Step number two, [we] should look at everything that remains, and think about the variable resources that could drive better cost, speed, or results for what remains." "Variable resources" here is the term for various kinds of contract work, meaning that use of it can ramp up and down depending on needs. "Then, and only then, should we be looking at what fixed resources we need to have on board as our full-time employees." She argues that only work that is needed on a sustained basis for more than a year should be executed by full-time employees. Almost anything else, aside from the most sensitive mission-critical work, is fair game for alternatives to full-time work.

The compensation varies widely, both in amount and how it is structured. For people with the most in-demand skills, like high-level software engineers or seasoned corporate executives, it can work out to $300 an hour or more. What Finkhousen was describing is not simply pushing big chunks of the company's work toward a contract workforce to save money by paying people less, like the 1990s-style GE outsourcing to India. Rather, it is something broader. In a corporate world where more work is project- and task-based, GE is trying to better align its use of talent with the vicissitudes of the company's needs. Given that its management practices have historically been copied across the corporate world—the Indian outsourcing wave of the 1990s is a prime example—it is a hint of what is to come in many places.

This implies that more of the work to be had will consist of various freelance and contract arrangements. It also implies that those aren't necessarily dead ends like Marta Ramos's experiences as a janitorial contractor. So in what situations, and on what terms, can contract work be a perfectly viable pathway for an ambitious, skilled professional? What are the trade-offs, and how can one fully exploit the benefits while minimizing the costs?

To find out, I met with a young freelance technologist who was making that life work well for him; his story is instructive. But first I met with his agent.

A SOFTWARE ENGINEER WALKS INTO A TALENT AGENCY . . .

Michael Solomon discovered as a young man that there was an industry where he could wear jeans to work, have fun, hang out with rock stars, and make a good deal of money. As a manager in the music industry, he helped guide the careers of John Mayer, Vanessa Carlton, and other popular artists. Until, at least, the onset of file sharing, which made the once-lucrative business of selling music on CDs obsolete—resulting in considerably slimmer pickings for anyone trying to make money in the music business.

In 2010, Solomon's company created a mobile app for Bruce Springsteen superfans in partnership with Springsteen and his management team. It fell to Solomon to hire some freelance software developers to build the product. He located the right people and then had what seemed a strange experience as they struck a deal. "They didn't represent themselves well in what I thought was going to be a negotiation," Solomon said. "We started with a lowball offer, and they just accepted it. I thought there would be a little bit of back-and-forth." Solomon's team felt bad, thinking that they were exploiting the engineers' lack of negotiating prowess, and ended up bumping up their compensation anyway.

As the project progressed, at one point the engineers went silent, providing no updates and not responding to emails. It turned out they had hit a technical roadblock and didn't want to admit they were having problems until they had solved it.

It occurred to Solomon and his partner, Rishon Blumberg, that those freelance engineers could have used the same services they provided to musicians. Performers rely on their managers to negotiate a price and effectively run their business. These engineers needed someone to play that role. From that insight was born 10x Management, a firm that represents high-end technical talent. The name comes from the notion, commonly understood in tech circles, that the best software developers are ten times more valuable than a run-of-the-mill developer. "We realized that there's a cycle in every industry where there is talent, whether it's musicians or actors or athletes," Solomon said. "There's a period of time where they get exploited pretty badly, and then there's a period of time where market forces happen, either because agents and managers come along to help keep people from being exploited, and then the other side is unionization, which hasn't happened in this industry yet."

His clients live all over the place; one prefers a beach in Thailand. Many of them have worked on staff at one of the name-brand tech companies like Apple, Google, or Facebook. The companies that hire them typically do so to solve some hard technical problem. When I met with Solomon in early 2018, for example, blockchain technology and cryptocurrencies were in high demand, so the small number of engineers who knew blockchain backward and forward could land lucrative contracts with any company considering an initial coin offering or other initiatives.

Solomon describes the thought process for a company thinking of hiring one of his clients versus a conventional employee: "With startups, they may think paying $200 an hour to a freelance developer seems really expensive, so they're going to hire someone full-time, and they have a $200,000 a year budget to hire them, which works out to $100 an hour. But how long have you been looking? If it's eight months, how much product have you not built in those eight months? And when you find that person for $200,000, how long will they stay? How much equity are you giving them? How much rent are you paying for their workspace? How does paid vacation factor in?"

Add it all up, and before you know it a couple hundred dollars an hour for a talented engineer on a limited-duration contract looks like a value play.

But the real question I had for Solomon is how the equation looks from the perspective of the worker—in the case of his clients, people who have plenty of options in terms of conventional, good-paying jobs. What are the trade-offs? For whom does this life actually make sense—what are the personality traits and ambitions that make a person who has the option of a high-paying corporate job better suited to a career more like a gig-centric rock star's? To answer that, I visited one of Solomon's clients a few thousand miles away, at the best Nepalese restaurant in Salt Lake City, Utah.[11]

WHAT HAPPENS WHEN A GOOGLE ENGINEER GOES FREELANCE

Sam Brotherton grew up in a small town called Conyers, Georgia, where he developed a deep enthusiasm for mathematics; he spent his weekends at math competitions, racing teams from other schools to solve problems. "I was a nerd," he said. "I mean, I still am a nerd, but I was really a nerd in high school." It was enough to get him into Harvard.

Brotherton wasn't terribly focused on his future career when he was a college student, but he did need some spending money. He applied for a part-time job with a small market research consultancy and quickly realized that by developing more sophisticated programming skills, he could increase his market value. He taught himself the programming language Python, and before he knew it was making enough money in his part-time job to be the envy of most college students. "If you could work at the library for fifteen dollars an hour or learn some computer code and make seventy-five dollars an hour, it's going to be the latter," he said. After finishing college in 2012, he moved to Los Angeles, where the woman who would become his wife was in graduate school, and soon took a job doing data science work as one of the first few employees at the anonymous-communications app Whisper. After a year of that, he decided the startup life wasn't for him. He wanted more structure, and he was more inclined to go rock climbing on the weekends than have work deeply entangled with his social life, as is common at tiny companies with close-knit teams like early-stage Whisper. So he applied for a job with Google; with his background in the hot field of machine learning, the Los Angeles–based natural language processing team was quick to hire him.

Google's reputation as a paradise for its engineers is well earned, in Brotherton's telling. The free (delicious) food and other perks are well known. So are the company's relatively high pay and good job security. But for the kinds of people with the mental wiring to be top-shelf engineers, the biggest appeal is all that you can learn from the people around you. "They really have an engineering-led culture to the point that they basically hire tens of thousands of smart people and let them do pretty much whatever they want, and then you get Google Search and Gmail and Google Maps," Brotherton said. "You get a lot of misses, too, but it's a wonderful place to be as an engineer."

He learned a great deal in a technical sense—he worked on the Knowledge Graph, Google's structured reproduction of the world's knowledge that powers its products' ability to respond with the right answer if you type "when is the next flight to New York" or "what is the capital of Mozambique." But the most important education Brotherton received was about how teams work at a first-class organization. "Basic things like how to treat your co-workers, how to motivate people, that's not something you learn when you're working independently at all. It's something you do learn when you're working as part of a team. Management doesn't have to be a bad thing. It doesn't have to be an authority figure telling you what to do. It can just be someone who enables you to do the things that you would be doing otherwise and takes the roadblocks out of your way. I would say that I really internalized that while I was there."

Listening to Brotherton describe all the awesome things about working at Google, I was a little confused. Why would he leave behind a high-paying job at a world-class organization with a boss he really respected to become a freelance software-engineer-for-hire?

Part of it was about geography and lifestyle. Brotherton and his wife lived in Culver City, which was only about six miles from Google's Venice offices, but the drive could take forty-five minutes; the commute grated. He wanted to live in a smaller town, particularly as they geared up to have a family (their first child was born in early 2018).

Brotherton was also starting to see the limits of a career in a large company. He didn't aspire to become a senior executive of the company, with all the sacrifices that would entail in terms of quality of life. "I was starting to get bored," he said, "because you're in this tech utopia, and you can work on anything you want, but you don't get the same sense of driving toward completion that you would at a company where every single project mattered."

Still, the idea of quitting such a safe job in favor of the unknown was slightly terrifying. Brotherton lined up a couple of contracts through his LA tech world connections before resigning. He bought a house in Salt Lake City and in early 2016, after less than two years at Google, went to his boss to resign from what had been in many ways a dream job.

In the ensuing two years, he worked with Solomon's company, which connected him with more potential clients. When Brotherton first struck out on his own, he sought $150 an hour from the companies that contracted with him; like any good agent, Solomon upped his rate, to $250 an hour, and also handled the messy business of collecting when a client was slow to pay. The projects have varied. One particularly interesting one was with I.am+, a maker of premium headphones and other music-related hardware that was founded by Will.i.am of the hip-hop group Black Eyed Peas. Brotherton worked on the software that enables the earphones to understand voice commands, which was subsequently licensed to Deutsche Telekom AG to power a customer service chatbot.[12]

So what are the trade-offs of this type of high-end gig economy work that Brotherton has chosen? He thinks about it a great deal.

What he loves the most is the freedom—the sense that he can choose what he works on and when. He took advantage of the fantastic ski slopes near Salt Lake City to go skiing forty times during the winter of 2017–18—not something he could have done if he had been on the payroll of a large company that expected him to be in the office on a regular schedule for meetings.

The flip side of that is that he sometimes misses the rhythms of an office. While he often ends up collaborating with others, including some other contract programmers with whom he maintains a loose ongoing professional relationship, the vast majority of his work is solitary. Solomon describes a bit of a paradox in terms of what it takes to have a viable career as a contract engineer. A successful contractor needs to be extroverted enough to succeed at dealing with customers, but not so extroverted that they become lonely without the social aspects of a more standard office invironment.

"If you really crave being on a team and being surrounded by people, and need that constant feedback or validation, I don't think this is for you," Solomon said. Conversely, if you are a total recluse, it won't work either. "You do have to have good soft skills. You're not going to be in the closet coding and just have to talk to one other engineer. You're going to be dealing with a customer, which could be a CTO or an engineer who speaks your language, and in other cases may be a nontechnical person who's relying on you, and you need to have enough of a backbone to push back when there's a mistake being made." Big companies have so much need for programming talent that a skilled engineer can get away with being a bit antisocial.

For this career path to make sense, you need to be enough of a loner that you don't miss the trappings of office life too much, yet not so much of a loner that you can't successfully interact with your clients.

The other great trade-off is that contract work doesn't offer the same sense of purpose and identity that being an employee of a high-quality organization would. Brotherton jokes about how, when he went to his five-year Harvard reunion, people would stare at him blankly when he said he was doing contract engineering work, presumably silently wondering if this was a euphemism for "I'm unemployed." He is not the type of person who is hung up on status markers, but even he admits that when he came back from the reunion he pondered whether it would be worth exploring becoming a remote-work employee for a name-brand company.

Also, contract work like this offers no practical path to the executive suite; if you aspire to run some large organization, you're infinitely more likely to get there by managing bigger and bigger teams on the staff, not by executing some project—even a very important one—on a three-month contract. Essentially, Brotherton has to derive his identity and self-worth from things other than an impressive company that pays his paycheck—his family, his recreational activities, the inherent satisfaction of solving hard technical problems. That isn't for everyone.

Then there are the financial dimensions. Brotherton said he's making somewhat more than he did as an engineer on Google's staff—but it comes with considerably higher risk. It's easy to imagine a scenario in the next recession in which Google does not lay off skilled engineers but demand for contract work dries up. So, Brotherton said, he focuses on saving more than he would have when he was an employee.

He and Solomon both mention the importance of doing the accounting right when comparing the compensation between a conventional job and the contract lifestyle. How much would an employer subsidize health insurance? What is the value of the employer's contribution to your retirement plan? Are you properly valuing paid vacation, sick leave, and parental leave? Then there are the inevitable expenses: Brotherton has to buy his own computer and software, and pay an accountant to do his more-complicated taxes, and Solomon's firm receives a commission. In effect, the gross income one earns as a contractor has to be substantially higher than an equivalent regular job would provide to be financially equivalent, and it rests on the shoulders of the would-be contractor to get the math correct.

Finally, there is a benefit to traditional employment arrangements that is hard to measure, but one a would-be contractor has to think carefully about. Part of being on the staff of an established company is the opportunity to stretch one's experiences and abilities in new directions. All of the recommended ideas to turn yourself into a Pareto-optimal employee discussed earlier in this book are easiest to do when you are on the payroll of a company. The experiences and abilities you're developing are *part of the compensation you're receiving in your job.* So, for example, if you're a good engineer on staff at a company, you might be given an opportunity to take on a project in some different sphere that is a little out of your depth. You might be encouraged to interface with sales and finance and the marketing dimensions of a new product, which can enable a path toward more senior jobs. It is by having those cumulative experiences over the course of a career that we become more capable employees.

But with contract work, companies only want to hire people who have a proven ability to carry out the job at hand. They have no incentive to invest in the contractor's long-term development. They don't care if you end up as a Pareto-optimal contractor the way they care about developing Pareto-optimal employees. So that burden rests on Brotherton and people like him—to educate themselves about the state-of-the-art technology, to constantly cultivate new skills. One way Brotherton does this is by carefully choosing which contracts to sign, based in part on whether it will expose him to an emerging technology that might have long-term value for his skills. Ironically, he said, the fact that so many people in the freelance tech economy think this way means the compensation can actually be better for working on old, outdated technology than on the latest and greatest.

As I was heading back to my hotel after dinner with Brotherton, I thought a bit about Gail Evans and Marta Ramos. While it's clear that contracting and outsourcing can be a tool for companies to minimize costs and in the process leave workers with less-fulfilling opportunities, it's also clear that's not the end of the story. In reading Matthew Bidwell's research on why companies contract out some types of work and not others, and talking to Dyan Finkhousen at GE about how crowdsourced work and other alternative models fit into the company's future, and speaking with Solomon and Brotherton about the real-world trade-offs of being a tech contractor, a common thread appears.

When you're evaluating whether to take on contract or freelance work as a step in a professional career, everything is situational. What is the nature of the opportunity—*why* is the company contracting out the work? Does it match your personality and ambitions? Have you properly calculated the true value of the compensation, and discounted for the trade-offs around identity and learning opportunities and the rest? If so, contract away.

10

A Quarter-Million Hours

———

AND LIVING A PARETO-OPTIMAL LIFE

The core idea behind this book, as you know if you've read to this point, is this: the economic landscape has evolved in ways that favor large, global, digitally advanced companies; to thrive in that world, an ambitious person must understand how different types of functional expertise fit together; the best way to achieve that is to have a somewhat winding career path that allows exposure to multiple types of expertise. In the previous nine chapters, we've explored the forces that have created this economic backdrop and, given those changes, the ways that a thoughtful person navigating this world can achieve the best odds of success.

It's worth stepping back to ask: What does "success" even mean?

The title of this book was chosen carefully, and with a little bit of intentional ambiguity. In the early planning of this project, I was thinking of writing a guide to compensation in the modern economy—what it takes to get paid. But the more I thought about it, the more I realized this was too narrow. Sure, there are people for whom maximizing their earnings and getting rich is the definition of "winning." But not everyone puts riding on private jets and affording a massive vacation home as the fundamental goal of a career. Others may derive their satisfaction more from a sense of empire building—running some large organization.[1] And of course, for others, a successful career may mean something simpler even than that: the ability to do engaging work, with enough compensation to live comfortably, and enough free time to enjoy more relaxing pursuits. Sam Brotherton in the previous chapter is an example of someone who defined success that way.

I included "How to Win" in the title of this book because winning is a sufficiently subjective concept to encompass all of these priorities and others. The ideas explored in the previous nine chapters are useful whether your ambitions are for a big executive office or reflect a different set of priorities. I think that crystallized for me early in the reporting of this project when I sat down with a man named Nick Lovegrove.

WIDENING THE BELLOWS

Lovegrove joined McKinsey as a young consultant in 1982, when its London office was a sleepy outpost with its headquarters in an old Mayfair gentleman's club near St. James's Palace, at the beginning of a career with many zigs and zags. He would become a leading consultant on European media strategy during the tumult of that industry in the 1990s, then worked as a policy adviser to British prime minister Tony Blair in the early 2000s, then led McKinsey's Washington office for six years, followed by late-career stints in public affairs at Albright Stonebridge and then Brunswick. I met him because he wrote a book, *The Mosaic Principle,* that overlapped with the themes in this one.[2]

We talked about the inherent tension between being a specialist and a generalist in the corporate world—the ways the technological complexity of modern business requires deeper specialized knowledge, yet paradoxically can offer the greatest rewards for those who can combine threads, see linkages across specialties, speak different languages, and translate between tribes. Talking about the different phases of a successful career, Lovegrove uses the metaphor of a bellows, one of those devices that you widen or narrow in order to push air into a fire.

"There are periods in your career when you want to push in the bellows and narrow your focus because you really need to get smart about something," he said. "Then there are periods when you want to broaden out and release the constraints somehow."

In the early 2000s, as Lovegrove was hitting his stride as a media industry consultant, the industry he made his living advising was on its knees. "The media work dried up. The dot-com bubble, the boom-and-bust just kind of wrecked the business models. Nobody had any money. They were all just stranded. So you find yourself thinking, 'What I know about has no commercial value right now.' In consulting, if you focused on something that goes out of fashion, is not in demand, then you have to broaden out. And that is the trickier part. The narrowing part is relatively easy. That's just like choosing a specialty subject, choosing a major. Once you've chosen it, you just do it for as long as you can. The broadening out is the harder part because you're trying to find a hook, a point of connection that enables you to evolve."

In his case, it was seeing the linkages between the policy issues at the heart of competition in the media industry: government regulations of the telecommunications and broadcast sectors. He refashioned himself as a specialist in the intersection of public policy and business more generally. That led to his work with the British government and then his move to Washington.

That capacity for personal reinvention, he argued, is part of what separates those with long, rewarding careers from those who find themselves stalled out or stymied. "In consulting firms, if there isn't any demand for a particular type of service, people have the choice of whether to reinvent themselves, reboot, or leave and go do something else. That language of rebooting was very commonly used. Later on, I spent a lot of time on evaluation committees at McKinsey, and we would commonly ask of somebody whether they had the capability to reboot. Have they rebooted in the past? Have they demonstrated that they can actually change their focus? I realize now we were sort of inherently asking, 'Did they have sufficient breadth to fall back on, to draw upon when they had run out of road in their own specialty?'"

That's where Lovegrove's bellows analogy and some of the concepts from the first part of this book intersect. What truly makes for a successful career—one that combines longevity and financial success with intellectual engagement and sense of purpose—is that ability to constantly stretch and pivot and apply skills honed in one job in some new context. It is a different way of describing the kind of zigzagged, winding career path that is described in chapter 3, which represents the best pathway to becoming a Pareto-optimal employee or, should you have management aspirations, a Pareto-optimal executive.

"The more I reflect upon it," Lovegrove said, "the changes in the business world since I've been in it, the last thirty years, have been greater than the thirty years before that or really any period you want to look at. This is a transformative period because of the computer and globalization. And that means the people who rise to achieve success are adept at managing that. They are probably rather internationally oriented. They are able to handle complexity. And they probably made significant career adjustments along the way. It's unlikely they would have just done one thing exclusively."

Lovegrove extends this idea far beyond the confines of career advice. He sees this approach to managing a career as intimately tied up with the broader realities of what it takes to have a fulfilling life. He emphasizes a strong moral compass, deep relationships with others, and cultivating broad intellectual interests.

Listening to Lovegrove sketch out this philosophy, I started to worry that the ideas in this book may be portraying career management through too narrow a lens. After all, if the point of this book is to talk about "winning" in the modern economy, and that isn't by definition limited to winning more power and more money, how do these concepts of Pareto optimality and understanding the economic backdrop in which we are all operating apply to life outside the narrow pursuits on the job?

The answer lies in some simple math.

THE PARETO-OPTIMAL LIFE

It is typical, in the United States at least, for a college education to conclude when a person is 22 years old. It is similarly typical for a person to retire at age 65. There is a lot of variance at either end, of course—plenty of people begin or end their working lives at a different age. But for that archetypical person, 43 years will elapse between a college graduation ceremony and a retirement party.

Those 43 years work out to 15,706 days, including the February 29 Leap Day every four years. Can't forget Leap Day.

If you assume about 8 hours of sleep each night, that leaves 16 waking hours a day. Multiply those 16 hours by the number of days during a working career, and you get 251,292 waking hours during an adult's prime working years. Let's call it a quarter-million hours to keep it simple.

During those quarter-million hours, a professional worker will pack in every boring meeting, every exhilarating discovery, every successful sale, every soul-crushing disappointment that work life can offer. But that's not all. That quarter-million hours will also include every date night with a future spouse, every afternoon spent watching your favorite sports franchise lose a big game, every starring performance by your progeny in a school play, and every Sunday afternoon spent napping on the couch.

In laying out the idea of a Pareto-optimal career, we looked at how the goal is to reach an efficient frontier, creating whatever mix of expertise is needed in your profession. You may not be the best corporate strategist in the world and you may not be the best software engineer, but, to return to the A. J. Liebling line, you have a bright future if you are better at corporate strategy than anyone who's a better software engineer, and a better software engineer than anyone who knows more about corporate strategy.

That idea of Pareto optimality is really about maximizing something against a binding constraint. But here's the thing: the quarter-million hours you have to work with during your professional career is the biggest, most binding constraint of them all.

The goal for any of us can't be simply to maximize on one frontier—to make the most money or have the most impressive title or oversee the most subordinates. The only remotely sensible way of thinking about a career is in Liebling-esque terms—to weigh different elements of your life goals against each other. It's an optimization exercise. It's not simply about making money; it's about making the most money you can contingent on also being a great parent and spouse. It's not about having the most impressive executive responsibilities; it's about having the most impressive title possible contingent on also working within an organization you're proud of and find satisfying.

I was struck over and over in my interviews with the people whose stories are featured in this book by how often crucial questions around career advancement butted up against deeply personal elements of life. Layered into so many of the conversations were aspects of juggling a career with personal relationships or the financial responsibility that comes with having young children. Career choices don't exist in a vacuum. We aren't robots that carry out a specified task for a specified reward. Your career is how you are going to spend some large chunk of those quarter-million hours, and the goal for all of us is optimizing based on what really matters to us.

Which gets back to why this book is about "winning," in all its possible meanings, not "making as much money as possible" or "becoming the CEO of a Fortune 500 company." Make no mistake, the people who succeed at becoming billionaires or make it to the tippy-top of the corporate world made some different choices in what they optimized than most people. Whether they sacrificed time with their families, or recreation, or sleep, or all of the above, they very likely used their quarter-million hours differently than the typical professional. And that's well and good, so long as they made those choices deliberately and with their eyes wide open about the nature of the trade-offs they were making.

A lot has changed in the twenty-first-century economy that makes the career landscape something our grandparents would barely recognize. Those shifts, and their implications for navigating a work life, are what this book is all about. But even as technology and the competitive landscape change all around us, that hard constraint of a quarter-million hours isn't going to change. So what really counts as winning in the winner-take-all world? It is being thoughtful and making a series of choices that ensure that after your quarter-million hours are done, you can look back at the trade-offs you've made—between work versus leisure, money versus personal satisfaction, and so on—and be comfortable with your choices.

In the introduction, I argued that the modern economy is like a vast and stormy sea, and each of us managing a career is trying to sail a small boat that is tossed around by forces beyond our control. But we're better off when armed with an understanding of winds and currents, which this book has aimed to provide. The seas may not be calm, but you're better off knowing the challenges you'll face.

Happy sailing.

Appendix

The Takeaways: *What to remember from this book*

Introduction

The twenty-first-century economy increasingly favors large, complex, technologically advanced firms. This book is about how to navigate that reality.

The people who are most likely to thrive in this environment embrace the fluidity of digital-age business as an opportunity and are careful students of the economics of their industry. Ambitious low-level and midlevel people need to understand business dynamics that were once only the focus of senior executives.

This is an ability that anyone can cultivate, with the right mindset. Adaptability and capacity for reinvention are things we can develop, such as by stretching ourselves into new areas in low-stakes settings like college or early-career jobs.

This book is intended to help ambitious people navigate a career in this changing economy, much as a sailor must understand winds and currents.

Chapter 1:
Rise of the Glue People

The types of organizations that are dominating the modern economy are dramatically bigger and more complex than their counterparts of past generations, combining lots more people and lots more advanced skills.

This means that it is impossible for any one person to have a deep understanding of what goes on in every part of these organizations, and it makes effective teamwork harder.

That in turn means that people who can bridge the gaps between different types of expertise have become particularly valuable. You want to become one of these people, who can be called "glue people" because they help teams stick effectively together.

A first step to becoming a glue person is to understand how your function fits into the broader landscape of your organization. Make sure you understand how your company makes money, and how your role and the roles of adjacent departments help further that cause.

There are also bad kinds of glue people—people who gum up processes with extra bureaucracy without actually helping propel projects forward. You don't want to be that kind of glue person.

What is the difference between good and bad glue people? The good ones are Pareto-optimal employees. These are people who could not possibly have greater ability in one area relevant to their jobs without sacrificing something in another.

Organizations need people at the middle of the Pareto curve, who have a fair amount of ability in two or three areas; these are often general managers. They also need people who go very deep in one area and have only a bit of exposure to another, but these people have to be extraordinary at their jobs.

The key is that if you are underneath that curve, figure out the quickest way to get out to the optimal frontier, either by becoming even better at your main area of focus or by broadening your experience in a second or third area.

Chapter 2:
Becoming Pareto Optimal

Figuring out what mix of expertise and skill to cultivate to become Pareto optimal in your industry can be challenging. Ask yourself what combinations of abilities are likely to be rewarded by the marketplace, and cultivate those you lack.

Combining skills that aren't often found together in the same person can be particularly valuable: an engineer who's developed sales ability, for example, or a finance professional who understands software development.

Monitor job listings of the companies that are considered cutting-edge in your field to see what types of skills, and in what combinations, are likely to be in high demand as the rest of the industry catches up.

These ideas apply even more strongly if you aspire to be a senior manager. C-suite executives almost by definition must understand multiple areas of functional specialty and how they intersect.

People who want to ascend to CEO and other top jobs must seize every opportunity along the way to stretch their experience across different functional areas (marketing, finance, operations, and so forth) and different geographies in order to be a compelling candidate.

Chapter 3:
The Power of Mindset

There are lots of incentives in a career to specialize, to become better at whatever we're already good at. But there are often surprising advantages to being a generalist who moves between different specialties; it often pays to focus on building muscles that are weak instead of those that are already strong.

The idea of a career ladder is outdated. Rather than a linear path to the top, successful careers today tend to follow a "career lattice," in which sideways or even downward moves across different disciplines are not just acceptable but often crucial to eventually rising higher.

When you weigh a job opportunity, don't look only at your chances for promotion. Look at what it can offer you in skills and experience that will put you in a good position to have interesting options no matter how the economic winds shift.

Think of each job as a "tour of duty" of two to four years in which you aim to accomplish a specific task or gain a specific type of experience or skill, after which you will find something new to accomplish, whether at the same employer or a different one.

Train yourself to have a "three-year itch" in every job. The first year, in a new job, you're learning your way around. In the second year, you're making change happen. In the third year, you're coming into your own, and it's time to seek out discomfort and push for new experiences.

This ties in with the idea of a "growth mindset," which is often discussed in a psychological context. It is the career management version of an approach to the world that involves opening your mind to new experiences and rushing toward the unfamiliar.

Don't think of these steps in a career as some paint-by-numbers sequence of jobs you can plot out in advance. You have to make a series of jumps, as if hopping from one lily pad to the next, without being totally sure where it's all leading.

In any given job, what really matters for your long-term growth is what you gain in terms of experience. You can figure out a coherent narrative through-line of your career with the benefit of hindsight.

Chapter 4:
How Big Data Can Make You Better

The explosion in computing capacity has made possible much richer analysis of how people work and what makes people in a professional setting successful.

While most of this work is driven by senior management and aimed at making organizations more successful, it generates lessons that individuals should use to make their own performance stronger, much as baseball players can use advanced statistical analysis to improve their results and increase their value.

Good ballplayers focus on the inputs that are within their control and tend to generate success over time, rather than end results. Similarly, look for data that tells you what actions are likely to lead to future success and behave accordingly.

For example, a major software company came up with these practical lessons from this big-data work that are likely to apply in other business settings as well:

- There's a sweet spot for workweeks in the forty-to-fifty-hour range. Managers who worked much more than that, especially evenings and weekends, tended to have less engaged employees.

- If you're a manager, having frequent one-on-one meetings with your direct reports, even if they're short, tends to lead to both them and you being more successful over time.

- Work assiduously to build your network within your organization; the more people you know, the more likely you are to be happy and successful.

Keep an open mind and listen to what data and analytics are telling you about your performance. It won't always fit your gut instincts, and might not always be comfortable to hear.

Chapter 5:
The Economics of Managing

The role of a manager is to make his or her employees more productive, in an economic sense—to produce more economic value for any amount of work.

In an information economy, that usually doesn't mean just pushing people to work harder; it generally means creating a system that causes their work to create more value than it would in a less effective system.

Achieving higher productivity, in an economic sense, is crucial to achieving higher compensation. Therefore, as a worker you should seek out managers and systems that will elevate the value of your work product, and if you become a manager you should seek ways to make your workers' labor more valuable.

Differences between well-managed and poorly managed companies are large and persistent. Good management is essentially like a technology that some organizations have and others don't.

That tends to create winner-take-all effects in modern business, a cycle in which the best-run firms are the most profitable, and therefore through reputation and high compensation can recruit the best workers, and thus entrench their advantages.

Seek out employment at those best-run, most-successful companies if possible, where you'll likely be working with other high-performing people who will complement your own skills to make everyone more productive.

Chapter 6:
Navigating the Winner-Take-All World

More industries are becoming dominated by a handful of large, highly profitable companies. There are several reasons for this.

- Intangible investments, like software and patents, are becoming more important to modern products than physical capital, like real estate and machines.

- Network effects are coming to predominate in more industries, situations in which the more people use a product or service the more valuable it is to everyone.

- Rising market power for big firms in some industries has created incentives for consolidation.

- Government regulation can entrench the advantages of large, politically connected firms and make it hard for competitors to challenge them.

- Antitrust authorities have become more tolerant of mergers among even very large firms in markets with relatively little competition.

The ascent of these superstar companies has meant higher demand for the Pareto-optimal glue people discussed in the first two chapters, given their technological and business complexity.

But that doesn't mean superstar firms are the only ones worth working in. Just as there are trade-offs to different modes of investing—growth companies, value companies, startups—there are trade-offs in working at different types of firms.

"Winner" firms are profitable superstars. "Aspirant" firms are startups that wish to become winners one day (or be acquired by one). "Afterthoughts" are struggling firms.

At winner firms, the profitable superstars, you gain the safety of a steady paycheck and know that if you do good work there is a clear hierarchy in which to climb. But it is easy to become siloed in a narrow area, and you have to work harder to find inner motivation and good mentors if you want to be entrepreneurial and push boundaries.

At aspirant firms, cash compensation tends to be low and stock compensation high-risk. There is little bureaucratic structure, which can be unnerving. But part of your compensation is in the opportunity to push your own boundaries more than you would at a more established organization.

At afterthought firms, there can be a combination of the

bureaucratic inertia of the winners and the financial risk of aspirants. Often, however, these companies have underappreciated strengths, and finding them and enhancing them can be rewarding, both financially and psychologically.

Chapter 7:
When Software Ate the World

Almost every major business is now, in important respects, a software business, from energy and agriculture to finance and media. To have a successful career in twenty-first-century business is to be digitally savvy.

That doesn't mean everyone needs to be a coder, nor should they be. There is still important room for nontechnologists in these industries, so long as they know how to work effectively in that environment.

The jobs at greatest risk of being displaced by artificial intelligence and other advancing technologies are those that involve any kind of repetitive process, as opposed to improvising and reacting to a fluid environment.

In seeking a career that is not likely to be displaced by technology, the options are either to focus on that kind of improvisational work or to be one of the people driving the use of advanced technology to supplant other jobs.

The key is to think ambitiously about how emerging technologies can make it possible to do traditional jobs more effectively, to become the person reinventing a traditional job rather than the person whose job is being reinvented.

To become the automator of an industry rather than the automatee, it is important to develop the skill of "helicoptering," moving up and down in level of technical detail so you can communicate with others with different types of expertise.

Chapter 8:
Should I Stay or Should I Go?

The idea of a job being a lifelong relationship between an employer and an employee is outdated, but our language about that implicit contract hasn't caught up.

Think of a job at a high-performing organization the way a professional athlete thinks about their contract with a team—a relationship of limited duration, which will end when the team's needs and the employee's abilities are no longer a match.

When you are at a pivot point in your career where you must decide whether to stay with an employer or leave for another offer, apply principles of honesty and reciprocity.

Some employers still do display more long-term loyalty and investment than others; match them in kind by being more reluctant to leave because a better offer comes along.

Chapter 9:
What Is a Job, Anyway?

One of the biggest changes in the corporate landscape over the last generation is more widespread use of freelance and contract talent, as opposed to full-time employees.

Whether a career in the contracting economy is appealing and potentially lucrative depends a lot on why companies are outsourcing that particular type of work.

One rationale for this contracting is that it allows companies to focus on their core competency; a side effect of contracting out noncore work is that it is easier to apply downward pressure on price, meaning lower wages for people doing the work.

But in practice, companies outsource work for all sorts of reasons, some of which aren't really about cost minimization at all but are about bureaucratic constraints or need for speed and agility.

Contract work in that vein can be part of a remunerative and enjoyable career, if you have the right personality, skills, and ambition for it.

- You need to be tolerant of risk and able work proactively to keep abreast of the latest technologies and ways of operating in your field.

- You need to derive your self-worth and identity from something besides having a recognizable, name-brand employer.

- You need to be gregarious enough to be able to interact directly with customers, yet comfortable working in isolation most of the time rather than with the trappings of an office culture.

- You need to be comfortable not having any obvious path into managing a large team or becoming a senior executive.

- You need to be organized and disciplined enough to get the accounting right, properly counting the trade-offs involved in having to pay for benefits, work equipment, and the like.

Chapter 10:
A Quarter-Million Hours

The ideas in this book are meant to help you achieve career success. But really, it's worth thinking of success more broadly.

Typical adults have about 250,000 waking hours between the time they finish their schooling and retirement age. The real goal is to optimize across the different areas of life—career, family, hobbies—in ways that will be satisfying.

The idea of Pareto optimality applies to these broader trade-offs, not just to the acquisition of skills in different functional areas that can make for a successful career.

Acknowledgments

This book has its origins in many years of conversations, sometimes over morning coffees and other times late-night drinks, with hundreds of friends, acquaintances, colleagues, classmates, bosses, and sources. The common topic has been how to navigate work in the modern economy, as we all seek a career that is fulfilling, lucrative, and durable. Sometimes I have been the advice seeker, sometimes the advice giver, and other times we were both just trying to feel our way toward answers. All of those conversations informed this book.

I am deeply grateful to the people whose stories are contained in these pages. In a narrow sense, they told me the stories of their careers, but in effect that meant telling me the stories of their adult lives. I hope I have done justice to them, both in terms of factual accuracy and capturing the truth of their stories.

The idea to take on this topic as a book came from one of the aforementioned late-night conversations with my agent, Howard Yoon, with the Ross-Yoon Agency, who noticed that I was more energized by discussing this intersection of career management and the changing economics of my own industry than by any of the other ideas we discussed as potential book topics. Tim Bartlett at St. Martin's Press has proved the perfect editor to turn that raw idea into the book you hold in your hands. Dara Kaye and Jay Venables at Ross-Yoon and Alice Pfeifer at St. Martin's played crucial roles guiding it into form.

The graphics in this book were created by the insanely talented Alicia Parlapiano. Andy Parsons contributed an essential, sharp-eyed round of editing as the project made its way toward a final manuscript.

I owe thanks to many people whose names do not appear in this book but who made the interviews and case studies that form this narrative possible. In particular, thanks to Vanessa Gray and David Gougé of Weta Digital; Jennifer Friedman, formerly of General Electric; Johan Larsson of Volvo; Clarkson Hine of Beam Suntory; Andrew Williams of Goldman Sachs; Blake Jackson of Walmart; Stacy Elliott of Microsoft; Helen Goodman of Union Square Hospitality Group; Hannah Brown of LinkedIn; Caroline Cammarano of LaunchSquad; and Jane Park of the OutCast Agency.

A number of people proved essential sounding boards for ideas contained in this book. They include Paul McDonald and Maureen Carrig of Robert Half International; Lyles Carr and Stephen Nelson at the McCormick Group, and their colleagues, Chris Schroeder, Lester P. Bonos, Katherine Boyle, and Anna Soellner.

The New York Times has been my professional home during the gestation and execution of this book, and I couldn't have asked for a better professional setting for this step in my own efforts to become a Pareto-optimal journalist.

Helping build The Upshot, the *Times*'s site for analytical journalism, has been the joy of my professional life. David Leonhardt recruited me as a founding staff member before our launch in 2014, and Amanda Cox has led our team with a blend of rigor and compassion since the start of 2016. A recurring theme of this book is that it behooves all of us to find a workplace where our colleagues make us better, and that is very much the case with our team at The Upshot—Emily Badger, Quoctrung Bui, Laura Chang, Nate Cohn, Kathleen Flynn, Josh Katz, Claire Cain Miller, Toni Monkovic, Kevin Quealy, and Margot Sanger-Katz.

Beyond our team, I've benefited at the *Times* from colleagues across this sprawling organization. In Washington, where I am based, bureau chief Elisabeth Bumiller has been a remarkable leader in a time of nonstop Washington news, while also being supportive of us interlopers from the data journalism world who occupy space in her bureau. Colleagues including Binyamin Appelbaum, Jeremy Bowers, Annie

Daniel, Lisa Friedman, Brad Plumer, Nadja Popovich, Alan Rappeport, Rachel Shorey, Deborah Solomon, Ana Swanson, and Jim Tankersley make it an energizing place to come to work every day. Colleagues across the *Times* including Adrienne Carter, Ben Casselman, Patti Cohen, Conor Dougherty, Jack Ewing, Max Fisher, Natalie Kitroeff, Kevin McKenna, Ellen Pollock, Eduardo Porter, Nelson Schwartz, Nick Summers, Amanda Taub, and Jia Lynn Yang have sharpened my work in countless ways. The *Times*'s senior leadership, including A. G. Sulzberger, Dean Baquet, Joe Kahn, and Rebecca Blumenstein, create an environment that encourages journalists like me to do our best possible work, for which I am grateful every day.

Friends who have offered great ideas and encouragement during this process include Daniel Drum, Steve and Tara Goldenberg, Nick and Erin Johnston, Bill McQuillen and Amy Argetsinger, and Aaron and Ellen Rosenthal.

I owe a great deal to my family, for their support as I pursued this project and in so many other ways, including Co and Nancy Irwin; Nick, Ellerbe, Lilia, and Charlie May; Molly Irwin; Greg and Mary Halzack; and Eric Naison-Phillips and Laura Halzack.

Sarah Halzack, who watched this project evolve from its earliest kernel of an idea to its final execution (and married me somewhere in the middle of that), is my greatest source of inspiration and joy.

Notes

Chapter 1

1 Details of the production techniques used in the 1933 and 1976 versions of *King Kong* are drawn from Ray Morton's book *King Kong: The History of a Movie Icon from Fay Wray to Peter Jackson* (Applause Theatre and Cinema Books, 2005).

2 The numbers for "crew" in this chapter are drawn from IMDB's "cast and crew" lists for each movie, with all cast members as well as stunt performers excluded from the count to try to arrive at the total number of off-camera workers involved in the production of each film. For the 1933 film, the visual effects count of 21 includes both special effects and visual effects teams.

3 Movie box office statistics are drawn from the author's analysis of data published by the website BoxOfficeMojo.com. This includes only movies distributed in the United States, and therefore excludes many films made in other markets that were never shown in the United States. But it seems a reasonable assumption that films made outside the United States that achieve mass box office success in their home market will receive some showing—if only in a single theater in a single market—in the United States; this amounts to a reasonable proxy for the overall global movie market. For example, the 2017 listing includes the Chinese film *Wolf Warrior 2,* which notched only $2.7 million in ticket sales in the United States but was a blockbuster with $854 million in box office revenue in China.

4 This winner-take-all dynamic helps explain what might seem like a paradox: the cost of producing a film *for any given level of complexity* is lower than ever, yet the budgets for the biggest releases are higher than ever. The barriers to entry are low—with digital cameras and widely available editing software, almost anyone can create a film, and more movies are made worldwide than ever. But that makes it all the more important for the films with the strongest financial and artistic backing to distinguish themselves by featuring the most stunning visual effects, the most charismatic actors, the most entertaining scripts.

5 Revelant and the team who built Barbershop won a technical achievement award from the Academy of Motion Picture Arts and Sciences for their efforts. Those awards don't come with quite the red carpet glamour of the regular Oscars, but actress Margot Robbie did present the award to them.

6 Morieux said this in an interview, but if you would like to further understand

his thinking, and how to rectify it, see his book *Six Simple Rules,* written with Peter Tollman (Harvard Business Review Press, 2014).

7   Chris McCann, "Scaling Google with Eric Schmidt," https://medium.com /cs183c-blitzscaling-class-collection/class-8-notes-essay-reid-hoffman-john -lilly-chris-yeh-and-allen-blue-s-cs183c-technology-84ebbbaf6fa7.

8   Morten T. Hansen, "IDEO CEO Tim Brown: T-Shaped Stars: The Backbone of IDEO's Collaborative Culture," *Chief Executive,* January 21, 2010.

Chapter 2

1   As one small piece of evidence for the shift, in the entire year 2000 the phrase "data scientist" appeared in only 129 English-language articles in the Nexis database. In 2017, it appeared in 500 or more per week, often with headlines like "Data Scientist of 2020: Sexiest Career of the 21st Century," as ITWeb Online put it in December 2017.

2   Burning Glass does publish research on hybrid jobs and related topics on its website, www.burning-glass.com, which should be updated with more recent information.

3   Niklas Pollard and Heather Somerville, "Volvo Cars to Supply Uber with up to 24,000 Self-Driving Cars," Reuters, November 20, 2017.

4   Andreessen's archived *pmarca* blog posts are available at https://a16z.com /2015/01/09/pmarca-blog-ebook/.

5   Cláudia Custódio, Miguel A. Ferreira, and Pedro Matos, "Generalists versus Specialists: Lifetime Work Experience and Chief Executive Officer Pay," *Journal of Financial Economics* 108, no. 2 (May 2013): 471–92.

6   The falloff in the benefit of an MBA between top-tier and middle-tier programs was striking. An MBA from a program ranked in the top five was equivalent to an extra thirteen years of work experience in helping a person's odds of reaching a top job, whereas a non-top-ranked program offered a boost of five years. Still, considering that full-time MBA programs are only two years and some can be done part-time while still working, there seems to be a decent payoff even from graduate degrees in business from midlevel programs, though, of course, much depends on the details of tuition costs and opportunity cost of lost wages.

7   The Americans and Irish spell it "whiskey," the Scots, Canadians, and Japanese "whisky." You can spell it however you like.

8   Mike Esterl, "CEO Bulks Up Beam, Aiming to Keep It Single," *Wall Street Journal,* October 9, 2012.

9   Amy Hopkins, "Matt Shattock on the 'East-Meets-West Phenomenon' of Beam Suntory," *Spirits Business,* April 12, 2018.

Chapter 3

1   Jennifer Merluzzi and Damon J. Phillips, "The Specialist Discount: Negative Returns for MBAs with Focused Profiles in Investment Banking," *Administrative Science Quarterly* 61, no. 1 (March 2016): 87–124.

2   For an overview, see Neeru Jayanthi et al., "Sports Specialization in Young Athletes: Evidence-Based Recommendations," *Sports Health* 5, no. 3 (May 2013): 251–57.

3   Adjusted for inflation, the 1999 Goldman balance sheet of $231 billion is the equivalent of $339 billion at the end of 2016, meaning it grew 153 percent in seventeen years.

4   Of the major investment banks, Lehman Brothers went bankrupt (many of its assets were acquired by the British firm Barclays), Merrill Lynch was acquired by Bank of America, and Bear Stearns was bought by JPMorgan Chase. The difference between investment banking and commercial banking has become significantly more muddled; JPMorgan, Bank of America, and Citigroup in particular are major players in deal-making, and since the crisis Goldman Sachs and Morgan Stanley have been organized as bank holding companies. But however you slice it, a range of data points to the US banking sector being more concentrated among big firms than it was in 2007 or 1997.

5   For some professionals at Goldman, the title "executive director" is used in place of "vice president," especially outside the United States. Goldman partners are also managing directors (though not all managing directors are partners).

6   It's hard to overstate what an odd state of affairs it is when a journalist shows up to interview a banker at Goldman Sachs and the journalist is the one wearing a gray suit.

7   Mike Ozanian, "Murdoch Buys Control of New York Yankees Channel for $3.9 Billion," *Forbes,* January 24, 2014.

8   The (admittedly obscure) 1966 reference to a "career lattice," the earliest in this context in Google's Ngram data set, is from a monograph published by the California Personnel and Guidance Association, reading, "A career lattice should be available that will enable those who do not wish to remain in the entry level jobs to move either horizontally or vertically when qualifications have been met."

9   I am particularly partial to *The Corporate Lattice: Achieving High Performance in the Changing World of Work,* by Cathy Benko and Molly Anderson (Harvard Business Review Press, 2010). See also *The Career Lattice* by Joanne Cleaver (McGraw-Hill, 2012).

10 In her book *Lean In* (Knopf, 2013), Sandberg attributes the career jungle gym metaphor to Pattie Sellers, the longtime writer and editor at *Fortune.* Sandberg notes that "the ability to forge a unique path with occasional dips, detours, and even dead ends presents a better chance for fulfillment."

11 One other reason I like the career lattice metaphor is this: as if you were climbing a lattice in real life, lateral moves are much less perilous the lower you are in the hierarchy. The higher up you are, the more risk of falling when taking one of these sideways steps. It is much riskier, for example, for a chief information officer to try to jump over toward being a chief financial officer—a greater risk of falling on one's face—than it is for an entry-level technology worker to spend some time working in financial planning.

12 For a summary of this argument, see Reid Hoffman, Ben Casnocha, and Chris Yeh, "Tours of Duty: The New Employer-Employee Compact," *Harvard Business Review,* June 2013; for a longer and more detailed exposition of these and related ideas, see their book *The Alliance: Managing Talent in the Networked Age* (Harvard Business Review Press, 2014).

13 Case articulated his case for this next generation of important companies in *The Third Wave: An Entrepreneur's Vision of the Future* (New York: Simon & Schuster, 2016).

14 Saudi Aramco, the Saudi state-owned oil company, narrowly edged out Walmart for highest-revenue company in the world in 2017, $510 billion to $481 billion.

Chapter 4

1 Dieter Bohn, "Microsoft Surface Laptop Review: Worth the Wait," *The Verge,* June 13, 2017.

2 Nick Pino, "Xbox One S review," *TechRadar,* November 17, 2017.

3 This number actually implied that Hunter was overpaid. The Yankees had signed him to a five-year contract that included a total of $4.75 million in compensation, so his $950,000 in annualized pay was higher than Gennaro's $680,000 estimate of Hunter's marginal revenue product.

4 Stan Isle, "New Rating System Puts $ on Player's Value," *Sporting News,* March 24, 1979.

5 Cumulative historical data are from Baseball-Reference.com, based on Major League Baseball statistics dating to 1876. There is some dispute as to whether to include data from a predecessor league, and there may be some missing data.

6 See his book *Diamond Dollars: The Economics of Winning in Baseball* (CreateSpace Independent Publishing, 2013).

7 L. Jon Wertheim, "All the Right Moves," *Sports Illustrated,* August 30, 2010.

8 There are other ways of getting on base that are both rarer and less under the control of the hitter, including benefiting from a defensive player's error and being hit by a pitch.

9 Technically, the contract included only $225 million in additional money, but combined with compensation to which the Reds had already committed, this was the value over the life of the contract.

10 Paul Daugherty, "Joey Votto at Center of Scouts vs. Stats Debate," *Sports Illustrated,* May 24, 2013.

11 Video of the interview is on YouTube: "Keith Hernandez Interviews Joey Votto on SNY—9/24/13," posted September 25, 2013, by SNY.

12 Paul Daugherty, "Votto Makes No Apologies," *Cincinnati Enquirer,* October 1, 2013.

13 Jessica Leber, "The Immortal Life of the Enron E-mails," *MIT Technology Review,* July 2, 2013.

Chapter 5

1 Danny Meyer, *Setting the Table: The Transforming Power of Hospitality in Business* (HarperCollins, 2006), 61.

2 The article that cover was promoting, by Peter Kaminsky, was titled "Why Ask for the Moon When He Already Has Three Stars" and tells the saga of Meyer and Colicchio negotiating their lease deal for the Gramercy Tavern space, hiring employees, and so on. It is the bold promise of the cover that most people remembered and, in Meyer's telling, resulted in some disappointed customers in those early months.

3 In 2009, they even launched a business, underneath the Union Square Hospitality Group umbrella, offering consulting services to other companies seeking to improve their customer service; Salgado was managing partner. In 2017, she and Meyer went their separate ways, and she began offering consulting services on organizational behavior independently.

4 Alfred D. Chandler Jr., "The Emergence of Managerial Capitalism," *Business History Review* 58, no. 4 (Winter 1984): 473–503.

5 Alfred D. Chandler Jr., *The Visible Hand: The Managerial Revolution in American Business* (Belknap Press, 1977), 87.

6 Charles D. Wrege and Amedeo G. Perroni, "Taylor's Pig-Tale: A Historical Analysis of Frederick W. Taylor's Pig-Iron Experiments," *Academy of Management Journal* 17, no. 1 (March 1, 1974): 6–27.

7 Peter F. Drucker, "The Manager and the Moron," *McKinsey Quarterly,* December 1967.

8 Peter F. Drucker, *Management Challenges for the 21st Century* (HarperBusiness, 2001), 20.

9 Donald Trump's presidential campaign was considerably smaller, with only about 130 direct employees. Data are from Alex Seitz-Wald, Didi Martinez, and Carrie Dann, "Ground Game: Democrats Started Fall with 5-to-1 Paid Staff Advantage," NBC News, October 7, 2016.

10 Swift, the lieutenant governor, had been serving as acting governor since Governor Paul Cellucci's appointment to an ambassadorship.

11   I acknowledge here the irony that this is a mass-market book that you may well have purchased at an airport bookstore, and thank you for your indulgence that it does not meet the peer-reviewed standards of the professorate.

12   The full list of eighteen management practices and scoring criteria is described in Bloom and Van Reenen's "Measuring and Explaining Management Practices Across Firms and Countries," *Quarterly Journal of Economics* 122, no. 4 (November 2007): 1351–408.

13   For a full exploration of these findings, see Nicholas Bloom, Raffaella Sadun, and John Van Reenen, "Management as a Technology?" Harvard Business School Strategy Unit Working Paper 16–133, October 8, 2017.

14   In 2008, Bill Bishop wrote a book titled *The Big Sort* that focused on how the US citizenry was becoming more divided by geography, economics, and politics in ways that he argued were deleterious for the nation. Bloom is using the term focused only on the economic dimension of this self-sorting, but Bishop makes a compelling case that the employment-and-careers dimension of the sort is only a small piece of a bigger shift, which of course has only become more intense since publication of his book.

Chapter 6

1   This estimate is from the *Forbes* article "The World's Highest Paid Musicians of 2016," by Zack O'Malley Greenburg (November 30, 2016). The ranking is volatile from year to year (Sean "Diddy" Combs took the top spot in 2017, with Swift estimated to have earned a mere $44 million that year) and not completely reliable, based as it is on estimates of concert earnings and the value of licensing and merchandising deals. Directionally, of course, it is accurate: there is a handful of wildly successful performers who make many tens of millions of dollars in a year.

2   These data are for the job classification "musicians and singers" from the May 2016 National Occupational Employment and Wage Estimates published by the US Bureau of Labor Statistics.

3   Two early, ahead-of-their time works that captured the emergence of these winner-take-all dynamics were *The Winner-Take-All Society: Why the Few at the Top Get So Much More Than the Rest of Us,* by Robert H. Frank and Philip J. Cook (Penguin, 1995), and Steven Pearlstein's series "Winner Take All," in *The Washington Post,* which began November 12, 1995, with the article "Reshaped Economy Exacts Tough Toll."

4   For a particularly persuasive articulation of the issues around antitrust and market power, see Barry C. Lynn's *Cornered: The New Monopoly Capitalism and the Economics of Destruction* (Wiley, 2010). For more on network effects, see *Platform Revolution: How Networked Markets Are Transforming the Economy and How to Make Them Work for You,* by Geoffrey G. Parker, Marshall W. Van Alstyne, and

Sangeet Paul Choudary (Norton, 2017). As mentioned, for more on the rise in the relative importance of information over physical capital, see Jonathan Haskel and Stian Westlake's *Capitalism Without Capital: The Rise of the Intangible Economy* (Princeton University Press, 2018). Similarly, Thomas H. Davenport and Jeanne G. Harris's *Competing on Analytics: The New Science of Winning* dives into the importance of data analysis as a competitive advantage in modern business (Harvard Business Review Press, 2017).

5   For an overview of this research, see "Labor Market Monopsony: Trends, Consequences, and Policy Reponses," an issue brief published by the Obama administration's Council of Economic Advisers in October 2016 and available at https://obamawhitehouse.archives.gov/sites/default/files/page/files /20161025_monopsony_labor_mrkt_cea.pdf.

6   To be clear, these companies operate many brands: Marriott includes the likes of Sheraton, Westin, Residence Inn, Ritz-Carlton, and dozens more. Hilton includes Hampton Inn and Waldorf-Astoria. Choice International includes Comfort Inn, Econo Lodge, and other mostly lower-end brands. And these companies encompass many different precise arrangements, including franchises, management contracts, and in some cases direct ownership.

7   See, for example, Deirdre Bosa, "Airbnb Lashes Out at Marriott as Clash Between Silicon Valley and the Hotel Industry Intensifies," CNBC.com, November 20, 2017.

8   Jeremy Siegel identified this long-term outperformance by Philip Morris/Altria in *The Future for Investors: Why the Tried and True Triumph over the Bold and New* (Crown Business, 2005).

9   In Centers for Disease Control survey data, 42.4 percent of American adults smoked in 1965 and 37.4 percent in 1970; https://www.cdc.gov/tobacco/data _statistics/tables/trends/cig_smoking/index.htm.

10   There is an interesting lesson about intergenerational inequality here. If Caldwell had come from a more affluent upbringing, with no school debt and a parental backstop if things went wrong, he might have been more willing to take a chance working at a pre-IPO Google or an even smaller, riskier startup. It seems notable that the two most famous college dropouts turned tech founders, Bill Gates and Mark Zuckerberg, both came from more upper-middle-class backgrounds. Caldwell has had a great career and no one should feel sorry for him, but coming from wealth sure makes career risk-taking easier to stomach.

11   This chapter was written in Microsoft Word, so Caldwell's work on grammar-checking and proofreading tools helped prevent errors within the chapter. Any grammatical errors that remain are solely the fault of the author.

12   Rachel Witkowski, "How an IPO Recap Pulled HomeStreet from the Brink," *American Banker,* March 8, 2012.

Chapter 7

1   Guy Trebay, "Brooks Brothers Celebrates 200 Years with a Party—in Florence," *New York Times,* January 11, 2018.

2   Marc Andreessen, "Why Software Is Eating the World," *Wall Street Journal,* August 20, 2011.

3   Sarah Kent and Christopher M. Matthews, "Big Oil's New Favorite Toy: Supercomputers," *Wall Street Journal,* April 10, 2018.

4   Attracta Mooney, "BlackRock Bets on Aladdin as Genie of Growth," *Financial Times,* May 18, 2017.

5   Janice Eberly and Nicolas Crouzet, "Biggest Companies Get Bigger by Investing in Intangibles," *The Hill,* August 31, 2018.

Chapter 8

1   Among the alumni of early 1990s Sun Microsystems were people who would go on to be chief executive of Google (Eric Schmidt), Motorola (Edward Zander), and Yahoo (Carol Bartz).

2   John Koblin, "Netflix Says It Will Spend up to $8 Billion on Content Next Year," *New York Times,* October 16, 2017.

3   Blockbuster's failure to see the competitive threat from Netflix is an episode for the business history books. Reed Hastings reportedly offered to sell Netflix to Blockbuster for a mere $50 million during its cash-strapped 2000. See Mark Graser, "Epic Fail: How Blockbuster Could Have Owned Netflix," *Variety,* November 12, 2013. That said, John Antioco, the chief executive of Blockbuster at the time, argues that he was hamstrung from more aggressively competing with Netflix by activist investors. He tells his story in "How I Did It: Blockbuster's Former CEO on Sparring with an Activist Investor," *Harvard Business Review,* April 2011.

4   This dialogue is from McCord's recollection nearly a decade later, which Hastings did not dispute.

5   Michael Corkery and Amie Tsang, "Kimberly-Clark Cutting 5,000 Jobs amid Pressure on Prices," *New York Times,* January 23, 2018.

6   "Kimberly-Clark Announces First Quarter 2018 Results," press release issued by the company, April 23, 2018. The company's net income did fall substantially; however, that was mostly due to a $577 million charge tied to the restructuring program—that is, the severance paid to all those laid-off employees.

7   To use the two companies mentioned in this paragraph, General Motors (and other US automakers) made terrible cars in the 1970s and 1980s even as Japanese manufacturers were making rapid strides toward more reliable vehicles. And while Eastman Kodak was responsible for key innovations that would

become part of digital photography, it was making so much money from traditional film technologies in the 1990s that it was largely left behind as digital photography became more widespread.

8   For an excellent history of this shift, see *The End of Loyalty: The Rise and Fall of Good Jobs in Ameirca,* by Rick Wartzman (PublicAffairs, 2017).

9   Data on union membership in advanced countries from chapter 4 of *OECD Employment Outlook 2017,* published by the Organisation for Economic Co-operation and Development, June 13, 2017.

10 One common but frustrating salary strategy some major employers have adopted is to have no standard, across-the-board raises, even to match inflation. That means the default option is, in inflation-adjusted terms, a pay cut, and so rather than fire underperformers—an expensive and unpleasant task—the employer can just whittle away at their pay year by year until they depart voluntarily.

11 Ben Casanocha, Chris Yeh, and Reid Hoffman, *The Alliance: Managing Talent in the Networked Age* (Harvard Business Review Press, 2014).

12 Data on Citigroup's employment levels from the company's 2009 annual report, reflecting worldwide, full-time employment at year-end 2008 and year-end 2009.

13 McCord's book is worth reading: *Powerful: Building a Culture of Freedom and Responsibility* (Silicon Guild, 2018).

Chapter 9

1   Neil Irwin, "To Understand Rising Inequality, Consider the Janitors at Two Top Companies, Then and Now," *New York Times,* September 3, 2017.

2   See, for example, "Growing Apart: The Changing Firm-Size Wage Premium and Its Inequality Consequences," by J. Adam Cobb and Ken-Hou Lin (*Organization Science,* May 2017), which finds that large companies shifting away from offering premium pay for people on the low and middle parts of the pay spectrum is responsible for 20 percent of the rise in wage inequality in the United States from 1989 to 2014.

3   Arguably, "gig economy" platforms like Uber accomplish a version of this as well. Uber drivers decide when they wish to work based on demand and their own preferences, with no central authority directing them on this or on exactly how to do their job.

4   Williamson's ideas are spelled out in many papers over many years. For an overview, see "The Theory of the Firm as Governance Structure: From Choice to Contract," *Journal of Economic Perspectives* 16, no. 3 (Summer 2002): 171–95.

5   Arindrajit Dube and Ethan Kaplan, "Does Outsourcing Reduce Wages in the Low-Wage Service Occupations? Evidence from Janitors and Guards," *ILR Review* 63, no. 2 (January 2010): 287–306.

6   Deborah Goldschmidt and Johannes F. Schmieder, "The Rise of Domestic Outsourcing and Evolution of the German Wage Structure," *Quarterly Journal of Economics* 132, no. 3 (April 2017): 1165–217.

7   Matthew Bidwell, "What Do Firm Boundaries Do? Understanding the Role of Governance and Employment Relationships in Shaping Internal and Outsourced IT Projects," PhD diss., MIT Sloan School of Management, 2004.

8   Or, as Bidwell writes in dissertation-ese, "The most striking finding is the similarity with which managers view and treat consultants and regular employees. This suggests that the importance of employment relationships may have been greatly overstated in theorizing on human resource management." Page 80.

9   Stephanie Overby, "Offshore Outsourcing Pioneer GE to Hire 1,000 American IT Workers," *CIO,* August 22, 2011.

10 Elizabeth Stinson, "How GE Plans to Act Like a Startup and Crowdsource Breakthrough Ideas," *Wired,* April 11, 2014.

11 That restaurant is called Kathmandu Grill, if you're curious.

12 Salvador Rodriguez, "Will.i.am's Startup Raises $117 Million, Enters Enterprise Market," Reuters, November 6, 2017.

Chapter 10

1   While the goals of empire-building and maximizing income may seem aligned, they are really more orthogonal. Sure, the chief executive of a large company is likely to get rich in the process. But there are also people who run large organizations with more modest pay—in the nonprofit sector or government, for example. And there are people who are highly compensated while not really managing many people, such as elite hedge fund traders or top engineers.

2   Nick Lovegrove, *The Mosaic Principle* (PublicAffairs, 2016).

Index